The Incredible
PARALLEL

To: Kelsey Maye Jr.
May the Holy Spirit
grant you divine favor
to unlock the solutions
to life's greatest treasures.

07/30/2024

The Incredible PARALLEL

Identifying Ten Animals of Growth
or Predators in My Life

Marlon A. Reid

Library of Congress Control Number: 2021909233
ISBN: Hardcover   978-1-6641-7309-5
                 Softcover   978-1-6641-7308-8
                 eBook   978-1-6641-7307-1

Scripture quotations marked NIV are taken from the Holy Bible, New International Version®. NIV®. Copyright © 1973, 1978, 1984 by International Bible Society. Used by permission of Zondervan. All rights reserved. [Biblica]

Scripture quotations marked NKJV are taken from the New King James Version. Copyright © 1982 by Thomas Nelson, Inc. Used by permission. All rights reserved.

Scripture quotations are from the ESV® Bible (The Holy Bible, English Standard Version®), copyright © 2001 by Crossway, a publishing ministry of Good News Publishers. Used by permission. All rights reserved.

Scripture quotations marked NLT are taken from the Holy Bible, New Living Translation, copyright © 1996, 2004, 2007. Used by permission of Tyndale House Publishers, Inc. Carol Stream, Illinois 60188. All rights reserved. Website

Scripture taken from the King James Version of the Bible.

Scripture taken from the New Heart English Bible Version of the Bible

Print information available on the last page.

www.marlonreidministries.com
Follow us on Instagram: @MarlonReidMinistries

Rev. date: 05/13/2021

To order additional copies of this book, contact:
Xlibris
844-714-8691
www.Xlibris.com
Orders@Xlibris.com
808933

CONTENTS

DEDICATION

This book is dedicated to several categories of individuals. To my wife, Althea; son, Seth; and daughter, Gabriella, this has been an inseparable journey interweaved with joy, pain, perseverance, and commitment that has strengthened the core of a healthy family foundation. This book acts as a window to provide my children with an outward view of the potential within that nothing is impossible.

To my grandmother, Myrtle who passed away at the age of ninety-four while this book was being written. My spiritual life and walk with God is indebted to you, as I recall your resonating voice that says, "Whatever you do, don't let me reach church before you."

To my mother, Monica and Tyndale family members who have stood together over the decades and pushed each other to heightened success so that the next generation can always surpass the current. I can recall not having enough to eat, yet my mother would ensure that I carry two parcels of lunch to school to give to someone less fortunate. "No matter how hard life becomes, someone has it worse than you," she would probe into my mind.

To my brothers and sisters in the kingdom, and the wonderful people of this world seeking answers to the common and inescapable challenges of life, this book is guaranteed to make a significant impact and difference in your life.

FOREWORD

Marlon Reid is an inspired thought-provoking writer of uncommon intellect. Since I met him, I have found him to be a student of great knowledge, always venturing into various avenues of higher learning with a quest to conquer the unknown. He is a well-spoken gentleman of renowned character, worthy of emulation. It is of great gratitude to watch his progress in the various aspects of his sojourn, whether in the sacred or secular vocations. His humble disposition and stature could easily deceive you until he begins to speak with such commanding voice like that of a military general, then you will have a taste of the real deal.

When Marlon began his journey to become an author, you could feel his passion to bring new ideas to the readers. No doubt such passion and enthusiastic determination is illustrated in this very interesting book on relationships that will serve as a capstone for all peoples. This in-depth writing of extraordinary talent and skills is a gift to the human society and will certainly be of tremendous help to all those who read it. The author's thoughtful insights and inquisitive investigations into the deep immensity of human interactions are highlighted on the pages of this penned volume of brilliant oratory that are well needed in a modern anthropological age.

Marlon's book, *The Incredible Parallel*, gives uplifting insights into the human behavior and their relationship with the animal kingdom. This brilliant work of art will mesmerize your minds as you venture upon such rare parallelism of various species of God's creation. His psychological and theological training, coupled with the discipline of his various professions of law enforcement occupations, allows him to develop a wide perspective of experiences in the understanding of the human thoughts and attitudes as it relates to the lower class of animals. Subsequently this book emerged from such perspective and will no doubt serve as an important tool for people of all colors, creeds, and social strata of society.

Consequently, I deem it an honor to be given the great privilege to glean into the scope of this fascinating work of a genius. Marlon's approach to this book epitomizes a man with deep understanding of the human interactions and their connectivity with the animal domain and ultimately the creator of the universe. The most profound part of his life is his ability to relate with the sovereign deity. Therefore, this helps to culminate his vision in the penning of this well-needed educational instruction and informative guide to a more lofty relationship among humanity. His dedication and consistency and unparalleled quest in enhancing a better dialogue among men is without question and is set forth in this incredible epitome.

Aubrey C. H. Brown Jr., Th.D.

*****

In his book, Marlon Reid chooses the allegories of animals to portray characteristics of humans in the spiritual sense. He makes excellent comparisons and provides material for thought and application on a personal level.

A popular children's song from years ago contained the lines "If I could walk with the animals, talk to the animals . . . And they could talk to me . . . What a lovely place the world would be." The animals in Reid's book will hopefully speak to you and give you guidance in your walk with God.

Andrew Binda, Field Director Asia/Pacific
Church of God World Missions

PREFACE

Why do I think and function in the manner in which I do? Every action committed is preceded by a thought process, whether you are sleeping, in a coma, or even insane. The mind is one of the most powerful tools to possess. We are products of our environment, a compilation of exposure, experiences, information, social interaction, observation of symbols, monuments, historical data, intake of truth, lies, whether through a platform of Hollywood production or influence insinuated by the mainstream media. Our perception of life has been intruded and infiltrated and inevitably becomes and plays out as our reality. We are fashioned and conditioned to a particular way of thinking that stimulates our emotions and influences our choices in life, often causing us to encounter unbearable consequences and live in regrets.

This book will flush out the contaminants in your thought process and help you to avoid the common irreversible errors found among humanity, by breaking unhealthy conditions. Regardless of age, ethnicity, or racial background, this book will confront you and provide self-growth; prepare you for successful living; help you understand and overcome fear; bring reconciliation to marriages; influence you to live a life of integrity; restore you from emotional pain and challenges of single parenthood, abandonment, and abortion; and impart knowledge necessary to transition from your parents to a fully committed marital relationship and become the leader that you were created to be.

ACKNOWLEDGMENTS

The Incredible Parallel is a culmination of quality information and teachings that have been birthed out of professional development and personal growth that has transformed countless lives, and like a tidal wave, these invaluable lessons and principles will move you into greater measures of momentum toward successful living. It is of poignant interest that I express special gratitude to the many people who have contributed and made this journey possible.

To my immediate and extended family members whose unconditional love and selfless acts have propelled me in avenues that the mind and natural sight could not comprehend (Tyndale family: Myrtle, Jennefer, Channis, Olivean, Joan, Wanson, Monica, Sonia, Tanishia, Rohan, Kerry, Renee, Shaunelle, Omar, Shavonnie, Fitz Reid, and Viris McLemmon). Thanks to Duran Fontaine who attended and expressed gratitude with reassurance of a unique and powerful encounter.

I am truly grateful to family members who have played an integral part in the life of my wife and children, such as my wife's grandmother Rubie Fagon; her mother, Eula Palmer; and her aunt Sonia Codner. Your support, kind words, and warfare prayers have been the driving force and pillar of strength in many accomplishments. Thank you.

My mental fortitude and spiritual formation were fashioned through the constant molding by my brothers and sisters of the faith and in particular Brooklyn Cathedral of Praise who have encouraged, prayed, challenged, and kept accountability measures on this spiritual walk. Special thanks to Wayne Reid and members of Wesley Methodist, as well as Pastors Dean Brown and Selwin Gutzmer who challenged and rerouted me on a path to salvation in Christ as I surrendered at a revival that was meant to be for a few days that "exploded" to over a year at Faith Assembly Ministries.

Special thanks to Bishop James A. Nelson who recognized my potential beyond my awareness as a young man and provided mentorship, spiritual guidance, and discipline. Special thanks to Dr. Aubrey C. H. Brown Jr. who recommended the publisher and encouraged me of the possibility to archive these teachings like he has done in his books.

While teaching at a three-day youth and men's retreat, I was approached by Peter Goding, who was the men's president at his local church in Brooklyn, New York, who invited me to come and teach at an upcoming convention. In your hand, you are holding an expounded version of the life-changing message. Special thanks to Bishop Urlin Grey, Bishop Joseph Grey, Alicia Lewis, and members of Classon Avenue COG who facilitated with great hospitality.

Over the three-year period in writing this book, I can recall on my days off from work, I would set my alarm and sit at my desk at home to write for the same duration as my work shift. If I could invest in my job, I will invest in myself. However, there were days when I thought to myself of aborting this project, but my friends and coworkers (inclusive of Tony Marshall, Aston Ferro, Barrington Morris, Garnett Salmon, Odayne Rhoden, Velda Thompson, Mekeisha Moxey, Gay Moncrieffe, Elizabeth King, Tina Turner, and Warrington Walters) who knew about my writing constantly checked on the progress of the book and expressed great anticipation in holding a copy in their hands. Thank you.

Special thanks to Tackees Bruen in the front cover design as she captures in her mind my expressed idea in the manner that I envisioned.

I cannot conclude without expressing gratitude to the teachers and leadership of Mandeville All-Age School and DeCarteret College High School who have pioneered and instilled values that have led to many successful individuals over the years, especially the class of 1998 whose friendship today is truly adored as we excel across the globe.

I am extremely grateful to the men and women of Xlibris Publishing who have done such an amazing job in the editing of this book, especially Joy Daniels, Greg Griffin, Emman Villaran, Dez Suarez, Sheila Legaspi, Elaine Ochada and others who have contributed to this great work of art. Thank you.

INTRODUCTION

This book was initiated by a statement made by one of the wisest men to ever walk the face of the earth when he said,

> There are four things which are little on the earth, But they are exceedingly wise: The ants are a people not strong, Yet they prepare their food in the summer; The rock badgers are a feeble folk, Yet they make their homes in the crags; The locusts have no king, Yet they all advance in ranks; The spider skillfully grasps with its hands, And it is in kings' palaces. (Proverbs 30:24–28 NKJV)

The wise man later challenged us to free ourselves from poverty and binding contracts of agreement that constantly enslave us, by studying the lifestyle of the ants.

> Go to the ant, thou sluggard; consider her ways, and be wise: Which having no guide, overseer, or ruler, Provideth her meat in the summer, and gathereth her food in the harvest. (Proverbs 6:6–8 KJV).

The Incredible Parallel highlights the ten animals of growth or predators in your life and reveals the in-depth animal nature and how it parallels our lives. We all have a story to tell and know someone who is overwhelmed by the inescapable web of life's misfortune. This book, filled with real-life experiences, events, demonstrated integrity, counseling sessions, resiliency, and expressed faith, will be one of your life's greatest teachers by exposing the potential hazards that we can become susceptible if we fail to establish boundaries. Each chapter was written with several days of fasting, earnest prayers, and constantly seeking divine revelation. There is a baboon that was tied up and fed salt by a hunter and left without water throughout the night in order to intensify its thirst. The baboon was released in the morning and ran toward the source of water, leading the hunter to discover a large pond underneath a cleft of rocks. Let us expose some of the ways in which we can be manipulated and yet remain unaware. Today there is someone with a teenage daughter who has been sexually exploited and on the verge of committing abortion and fearful of disclosing to her parents, or a teenage son struggling with sexual promiscuity. Unless we master certain techniques and discipline, we will continue to eat of the salt that we are being fed and become thirsty with no other option but to drink from the fountain of manipulation.

Male (father) porcupines often play a minimal role or no involvement at all in the raising of their offspring. The porcupine is very fearful and highly defensive. Are you tempted to trigger reasons to create a relationship separation? Are you filled with fear of being divorced, being insecure, or encountering feelings of a failed relationship? Do you undergo a major panic attack before you even attempt to accomplish your goals? A man's car will have issues, he fixes it! A man's house will have issues, he fixes it! He recognizes the growing value, he fixes it, and he invests in it. He does not walk away from it. A man instead oftentimes walks away from his family, his wife, his marriage. He becomes reluctant to fix his problems. He listens to the sound of his car, but not the pain of his family, friends, and loved ones. Is it possible that as a husband, wife, father, mother, or guardian you are living with someone drowning in the lack of attention and affection yet you are oblivious and desensitized? Let us discover tools in overcoming emotional disconnect and abuse that cannot be substituted with gifts.

It's incumbent upon us to prepare our children, friends, and loved ones for a quality and successful life. Many challenges are underestimated because they come in very sophisticated form. The frog will adjust its body like a thermostat so that its temperature can withstand and survive the different seasons and climatic conditions. A frog will be dying on the vine in an abusive relationship; the man hits her upside her head and she manages with a frog mentality to adjust and convinces herself that she is at fault.

"For *fear* of the young male's life, she will psychologically train him to be *mentally weak* and *dependent*, but *physically strong*." This is the principle used for breaking a horse from a wild state to being tamed. Many of us are exposed to a lucrative system that constantly stimulates our desire to want more, and yet never satisfied. We are then exploited and encounter many compromises and accumulate liabilities because of the lack of contentment within our soul, by risking the precious commodities that we already possess. Many individuals are afraid of change, simply because they have been conditioned to remain comfortable in their environment. Unless we understand the process of breaking our condition and discover how to unbecome a horse, we will continue to walk around in the circle of wilderness while being exploited and equate motion for progress.

Usually if someone should call you a snake, it may not be a compliment. The boa snake feels the heartbeat of its prey and is sensitive to their pulse. You cannot apply logic, cover up, or pretend to be dead in an attempt to deceive the serpent. But snakes seem to know the depths of your hearts and the language of your emotions. They can steal your breath away and seemingly understand and connect with your inner thoughts. This is why in life, so many individuals wonder why a woman with so much brilliance and potential would underwrite her self-value and sit on a clearance shelf of damaged goods.

How do you avoid dating or committing to a wolf? Encountering some form of interaction or associating with a fox or wolf is almost inevitable. No man or woman wants to commit his/her life to a relationship, only to discover that it was disrupted or built on the foundation of deception. A wolf in sheep's clothing speaks of entrusting your life in the hands of someone for protection and spiritual guidance yet his/her true nature is inwardly a ferocious wolf! Why does he come or choose such outfit? Apparently, he knows the attributes of his prey and qualities of association that attract the victim into vulnerable conditions.

Young elephants upon reaching sexual maturity either initiate to leave the herd or are forced out by the older male elephants. There is a cultural epidemic in the lives of many male figures when they have reached the age of adulthood. Many men reach a point of turbulence. They have reached a stage of awakening and realize that in order to start his family, he will have to take on a wife and detach himself from his current family or home. The man can physically leave his current geographical location but will soon encounter an emotional shock and trauma, because he has never been taught or prepared to depart from his mother. Are you in a relationship and encounter feelings of inadequacy as though you are still on a quest to transition from boyhood into adulthood, or a wife who fails to understand the temperament of your husband, or a parent who needs to understand the principles of preparing your child for leadership and independence? This chapter will give you major insights.

The sight and range of visibility by insects and other animal predators may be impeded upon by the camouflage effects of the zebras' stripes. How beautiful is it when you can defeat your enemies by just being your natural self! The battle is not yours, but it is the Lord's.

How about the size of the brain of an ant? How does it function with such intuition, creativity, and excellence? There is no monitored system of supervision or leadership to ensure that each ant does what is expected. There is a natural state of initiative and compliance to exercise diligence. The ant is not discouraged by the absence of validation. Validation for productivity is simply awaiting an antidote, like an addict searching for a dose of motivation.

Humanity is oftentimes compared and contrasted with the eagle. The eagle usually has one partner for a lifetime. Eagles make the nest uncomfortable and eventually push the eaglet out in order to make it learn how to fly and maneuver in preparation for life and survival. Our success is usually one more step or application of self after a failure or discouragement. Eagles do not associate with other birds. Our circle of association will have a direct impact on our progress in life. During times of severe storms, ordinary birds fly away south to dry areas. Some people will run away from relationship storms, flee educational goals, refute self-development, negate health and physical conditions, and abuse friendships and trust. They have never been taught to embrace the tornado circumstances as fire drill preparation for life.

This book belongs in your library and is suitable as a priceless gift for any occasion, whether birthday, anniversary, holiday, or simply a token of appreciation.

CHAPTER 1
WAY OF THE BABOON
(Power of Self-Understanding)

Sometimes the things that are meant to break you are sent to build
you before you rest comfortably on a faulty foundation.

—M. Reid

Open your hands! I repeat, open your hands! Could refusal to open your hands and release what you possess accumulate more liability than walking away empty handed?

Let us meet the person who can tell you all about the day when he almost lost his life! Baboons are sociable and protective and can be comically charming. The baboon is a creature that is curious in nature; it is very observant yet inquisitive. The baboon cannot help itself but to always seek to get to the center of the situation at hand.

There is a well-known documentary that shows a trap created by a hunter who wanted to find water in the midst of the dry Kalahari Desert. The hunter, knowing that the baboon is very inquisitive and loves to eat salt, created a hole in the dirt bank just large enough for the baboon to insert its hand. The hunter, being well aware that the baboon was staring, placed wild melon seeds in the hole and walked away. The baboon then went to the hole, inserted its hand, and grabbed the melon seeds. The baboon grasped the seeds, causing a clenching of its fist, which made it impossible to pull its bulky hand out of the hole.

As the hunter approached the baboon, the baboon started to scream and panic, entrapped by its own fist stuck in the hole. The baboon did not exercise wisdom to release the melon seeds to slide its hand out in order for a grand escape. The hunter caught the baboon and tied it up underneath a tree. The baboon was then fed salt and left without water throughout the night in order to intensify its thirst. The baboon was released in the morning and ran toward the source of water. As the baboon ran to find water, the hunter jogged behind the baboon and discovered a large pond underneath a cleft of rocks. The baboon knew that the hunter was jogging behind, but due to desperation of thirst, the baboon did not detour nor become evasive. The hunter then engulfed in his satisfaction and celebrated his discovery of fresh water!

Life of the Party

What formulated such mindset of the baboon? What are the sources of influences and learned behavior that developed such condition and pattern of thoughts? Does the baboon observe everyone and think that they are crazy, until it discovers otherwise? Are there people in your life who know your weaknesses and how inquisitive you are, to the point in which you have been victimized and lived a lifestyle under constant manipulation? Is it so common that people no longer need much effort to utilize your service? Have people forgotten that they have conditioned you to eat of their salt, because you have been registered in their subconscious and considered a loyal friend? Do people treat you with contempt, because it's uncommon the moment you develop the strength to refuse their request?

There are so many teenagers who are lured into their curiosity, not realizing that they will be fed salt in the process. A female may enter a party or a room thinking that she will just verify what was being placed in the hole. Sometimes she is plotted against by her own circle of friendship who wants to tarnish her reputation because of her state of purity that outshines their glossiness. This innocent female becomes the center of a vicious joke under peer pressure not knowing that she will be entrapped when a stimulant is placed in her drink. Like the baboon sticking its hands into curiosity, the female either takes a drink or enters a lonely room. She is being touched and seduced only to realize that her state of resistance is being minimized. The baboon within her didn't realize that when her mind and body become excited, adrenaline causes more blood flow to gravitate toward the heart. This causes less blood flow to the brain, and in the process oxygen is reduced, resulting in the same effect as someone who is intoxicated. When the baboon wakes up in the morning in her sober mind filled with the right amount of oxygen, like Eve in the garden, she wonders what happened and who to blame. She misses her menstrual cycle and wonders if the evidence of a child will expose her secrecy. At the feeling of every itch, she wonders if she contracted the acronym STD. Make no mistake; that meant sexually transmitted disease. The path of the baboon is usually driven and also disrupted by the same element, which is the state of curiosity. This is why it becomes extremely difficult to blame others for their motives or the part that they played. You can bring a horse to the water, but you cannot force it to drink. You can lure a baboon to the hole, but you cannot force him to put his hand in it. Even though your actions may be influenced, you are totally accountable especially when you act alone.

The Making or Breaking of a Baboon

If someone calls you a baboon, this real-life illustration conveys why it is not rendering the implication of being very smart. Throughout the years and stages of development, we are more prone to cherish individuals based on their ability and what they can bring to the table and contribute to our lifestyle and agenda. But what if perceiving someone as a baboon is more frequently an internal mirror into my soul and mental concept of self-reflection? Failure to recognize the potential or identify the value in others is a reflection of self rather than the other. Can anyone blame the hunter for exploiting your lack, to benefit his gain?

Do I therefore treat another according to the way that I perceive him/her? Or do I treat this person as an asset, assignment for investment, and a purpose for change?

How many people remember the life story of the United States of America presidential candidate, the neurosurgeon Benjamin Solomon Carson, who was at the bottom of his class? During his childhood, many classmates and teachers labeled him as a failure. His mother, recognizing this challenge, instructed him to go to the library on a weekly basis and to provide a book report. The moment of opportunity arose when an instructor asked the class a question, and Ben Carson articulated his response so well from the book he had read that the class who initially laughed at him became amazed at his brilliance in response. This was the turning point of his life. The instructor walked into his life and became his mentor. What are the odds in life that one moment, one question, one encounter, can become the path and ultimate change agent in preparation for life's journey?

Ben Carson now realized that the "baboon" that he saw in the mirror was a mere reflection of his perception that others have asserted, influenced, and pinned to his fundamental belief system. The baboon is acting out what he believes of himself.

It's being said that many people in life do not live according to what they believe of self, or what others believe of them, but what they perceive others think of them.

In the United States and Western culture, medical doctors, politicians, and certain professions are viewed with prestige. The significance and definition of the person becomes the label asserted by his/her career. In certain other countries, the medical profession is more of a humanitarian calling and is not sought after based on monetary gain. The lives of individuals are therefore cherished equally on a level field, as opposed to pedestal or pyramid levels of importance.

Do you have any friends in your life, as you begin to evolve and change, who treat you with malice and contempt and tell you that you have changed? This art of manipulation is appealing to your subconscious by executing guilt feelings in an attempt to have you return and be recycled and reused like disposable materials. Will the baboon in you appeal to their hurts like a healing balm, yet you become sick in the process from their contagious madness? Will you allow such individuals to make a baboon out of you by making you the oppressor who has inflicted pain upon the victim?

Will you eat of the salt that you are being fed and left thirsty with no other option but to drink from their fountain of manipulation?

If these are true friends who mean you well, they would release you to freedom whether or not you bring them to their water source of satisfactory results. Don't be deceived in the process of their happiness as they drink with you from the same source of water underneath the rock.

The happy facial expression is internal satisfaction and should not be misinterpreted as appreciation.

You are no longer needed; they have just eliminated the liaison in you and have gone directly to the contracting table. Don't be deceived by the gifts and tokens of gratitude after the fact. You are just being established for future endeavors!

Inability to Refrain

A baboon likes to be on demand. His contact is on speed dial. He shows up in the most recent call list. He perceives himself to be loyal, while others define him as naive. In times of crises, the baboon is there; in times of war, the baboon is there. If you have any baboons in your life, you may be led to think that they are very loyal toward you but may feel betrayed when you see them around other people whom you may have previously deserted or gossiped about. But don't be alarmed or heartbroken! It's just the nature of the baboon; it has low resistance in overcoming its curiosity. The baboon is what the Bible would constitute as having an itchy ear, can't help itself but to find out "spicy" information. These are the friends who will tell you, "Try it. It's good." Before long, you are addicted and find yourself in the grasp of a stronghold, unable to find obvious solutions. These are the friends who will tell you, "How long have you been dating? Did you kiss him yet? Did you give it [sex] to him?" It's just the way of the baboon. It cannot help itself; it is very curious! Don't blame the baboon when you get caught up into a situation. The baboon does not know how to let go and will always throw your past story in your face. There is a uniquely captured story in Genesis 19:26. Lot's wife found it very difficult to let go. She looked back and became a pillar of salt. Individuals who struggle with letting go oftentimes find it rather challenging to overcome deep-rooted unforgiveness of the past. Moving forward is comprehended to be very difficult for many individuals. It's like walking against the sea waves toward the shore. They would rather turn around and go in the direction the waves are flowing, even when plunging into the deep.

Uber vs. Medallion Drivers

During the time of Uber's (a taxi service with an online mobile application for booking) evolving process expansion, many "yellow cabdrivers" ("Yellow Taxi" – medallion), who signed contracts, spent a major fortune in investment with the hope, expectation, and projection to earn a profit over a period. These taxi drivers were now at the heart of a fierce competition against Uber that is equipped with online capabilities, swift booking, and tracking operation system. Many consumers were now enjoying the leverage of booking a cab with their cell phone or mobile device and a tracking system to monitor the estimated time of arrival, travel time duration, group and individual travel booking, online calculated payment, mapped-out distance, and other amenities. This became and created a recession for medallion taxi operation. The medallions were now faced with challenges with what once had many promising factors for hardworking men as the sole provider and protector for their families. This economic collapse with high debt-to-income ratio led many to an alarming rate and state of suicide.

In this journey of life, circumstances can shatter one's sense of hope and can reveal the deep underlying depth in which our hearts can become connected to our possessions. It then becomes relatively difficult to reach a state of acceptance where resiliency is naturally activated. The grief cycle is oftentimes associated with death. But not many individuals realize that they are in a constant state of grief and bereavement due to an ongoing cycle of emotional crisis that perpetuates and revolves in an intensified motion. If help or intervention does not disrupt this pattern of behavior, one's life can become utterly detrimental and conformed in a pattern of habits and behavior that interweave into our normal routine, which presents itself and masquerades as part of our personality. Many individuals who have never experienced this type of hardship may consider themselves immune, or invincible, and be an objective critic. But within the scope of human limitation, anyone can be pushed to the edge of doing the unthinkable.

For where your treasure is, there will your heart be also. (Matthew 6:21 KJV)

Jesus spoke profoundly about the dangers of sentimental attachment to the temporal things of this world:

> In that day, he who is on the housetop, and his goods *are*
> in the house, let him not come down to take them away.
> And likewise the one who is in the field, let him not turn
> back. Remember Lot's wife. Whoever seeks to save his
> life will lose it, and whoever loses his life will preserve
> it. (Luke 17:31–33 NKJV)

Could this be the type of preparation that Jesus tried to impart with three particular statements? First, to the man who wanted to follow Jesus: foxes have holes and birds have nests, but He has no place to lay His head. Following Jesus is very costly and sacrificial. Second, to the man who wanted to go and bury his father: Jesus said let the dead (spiritual) bury their own dead (physical) because the kingdom must be preached now. Third, to the man who wanted to bid farewell: Jesus said if you put your hand to the plow and look back, you are not fit for the kingdom (Luke 9:57–62). The rich young ruler referred to Jesus as the good teacher and told him that he has obeyed all the laws and wants to know what it takes to inherit eternal life. Jesus told him to go sell all his possessions then follow Him. The young man became sad and chose to hold on to his riches rather than to sell his possessions and follow Jesus. Jesus said how difficult it will be for the rich to enter the kingdom; it is easier for a camel to walk through the eye of a needle (Synoptic Gospel of Matthew 19:16–30; Mark 10:17–31; Luke 18:18–30). This should not be misconstrued for having humility while dwelling in a constant state of poverty. Special emphasis shows that we cannot serve two masters. A man has to closely assess his attachments to the temporal things of life and carefully examine himself, ensuring he is detached. The baboon within should not risk losing its life over possessions that he chooses to simply hold on to.

A person who likes to hold on reciprocates the truth of the difficulty to give. The character trait exhibited by the baboon shows he doesn't like to give or pay tithes. The baboon justifies not giving by rationalizing the usage of the funds. The baboon, however, is usually the first to grab and dictates how to spend and allocate.

Hope for the Baboon

The baboon has a great hope. The way of the baboon does not have to define the baboon. The question then becomes why does the baboon act the way that it does? Is the baboon always exposed to individuals who think lowly and possess the inclination to exploit on all different measures? Is the baboon's attitude formed within based on the distrust experienced by a partner who used you for sexual gratification? The baboon enjoys salt!

As a woman, were you deceived in the process into believing the man was giving you "salt" in the form of a wedding ring? The man may have catered to your need knowing the baboon within can be ignited with intensified desires by using salt as a stimulant. But you later discovered he ignited your desires to gratify his needs. What happens when the one who is giving the salt has undisclosed motive?

You became shocked to realize that he was not chasing after you; he was simply running in your direction.

You became disappointed when he bypassed you and went to the source of his desire and intention to drink water.

Can you blame the baboon for not being able to trust the person who comes along after such experience of distrust, even if the person genuinely wants to offer a gift? Can you try to analyze the baboon's level of curiosity and the constant inquisitiveness to acquire full details, and quest for reassurance and resolution? If the baboon seems skeptical and questions every move in a relationship, whether it be male or female, one has to check the baboon's history, experiences, parental relationships, father figure, missing role models, abuse, manipulation, constant bullying, and lack of knowledge due to stress and distractions. Can we truly label the baboon and define that individual as a baboon? Or do I need to detox, uproot, and destroy that destructive nature and rehabilitate self by genuinely loving, mentoring, and planting in a field of positive perception and growth opportunities?

During a sermon taught by T. D. Jakes, he explained that as a child of destiny, you are likely to interact with three basic types of people. The first group is "Confidants" that are like David and Jonathan, individuals who genuinely love unconditionally. T. D. Jakes further explained that one of the challenges is that many individuals have confidants that are below their level, forever feeding them and unable to be fed in the process. As a result, you may become drained in constantly helping others. Confidants are few and remain with you for a lifetime and help you to reach your destiny. Without a confidant, you may not be able to fully accomplish what God has called you to do for the kingdom. T. D.

Jakes called the second group "Constituents" and explained that they are never with you. Constituents are only into what you are for, and if they meet someone else who can further their agenda, they will leave you. T. D. Jakes warned that if you are in a broken state, you run the risk of confusing your Constituents for your Confidants. T. D. Jakes mentioned the third group as "Comrades" to be individuals who are not for you, but they are simply into what you are against. Comrades will team up with you and fight a greater enemy. Comrades are like scaffoldings that come into your life to fulfill a purpose, but once the task is complete, they are removed. T. D. Jakes expressed that Comrades and Constituents will leave, so be very careful who you share your dreams with; otherwise, you will be disappointed.

Improvement and Reflection

I believe if we better understand the principles of this chapter and apply them to our daily life, we can self-actualize and save ourselves from a lot of hurt.

Genogram

It is highly recommended to have a genogram counseling session, by understanding your family tree and generational history, in order to break the cycle of major dysfunction!

The fact of the matter is that we all have the nature of a baboon. If it takes one to know one, then identifying, perceiving, and understanding inevitably possesses the trait. Adam and Eve had the knowledge of good and evil. This activated the potential for the thought of awareness or hidden curiosity. Some individuals have different temperaments, support systems, accountability measures, resiliency based on circumstances presented in life, or thoughts invested toward or against these entities.

During the time of "Black Wall Street," many individuals who were freed from slavery were employed because of their skilled labor. These workers soon discovered that their significance wasn't recognized in the process due to racial discrimination. Because of their racial background, they were not allowed to use the restrooms or the restaurants of the owners. Instead of becoming a baboon in the process, these workers went back to their hometown and developed infrastructures inclusive of hospitals, restaurants, banks, grocery stores, movie theaters, schools, churches, libraries, law offices, transportation systems, etc. Instead of remaining in a continuum of dysfunction, they evolved to independence rather than returning to a source that keeps them athirst. Our past and current situation does not have to define or determine our future outcome.

> And he answering said, Thou shalt love the Lord thy
> God with all thy heart, and with all thy soul, and with all
> thy strength, and with all thy mind; and thy neighbour
> as thyself. (Luke 10:27 KJV)

What does the Scripture tell us about forgiveness?

Make it your point of duty to call your loved ones whom you have not spoken with for a while.

Be deliberate and work on the areas of the relationship that need improvement.

Pursue your healing beyond your ego and self-resistance.

Loving God gives us the wisdom and strength to understand self and value the eternal things of life.

CHAPTER 2
THE PORCUPINE SYNDROME
(Power of Self-Confidence)

A man who does not have a vision to navigate his future path will find himself replaying his history and memories for a source of direction.

— M. Reid

One of the greatest obstacles of humanity is not having a vision of the future. A mind that does not have a vision to navigate its future path will find itself replaying the history and memories for a source of direction. Having no goals is like a navigational system left with no focal point. You will be like a man caught in a heavy downpour of rainfall without covering. One of the main culprits that will sabotage, debilitate, and derail a man from making progress or pursue his endeavors is fear.

Porcupines and hedgehogs have great similarities in their characteristics and personality traits. Hedgehogs rely greatly on their sense of sound and smell because of poor eyesight. They have unique hair, which are spines that are like a shaft. They constantly huff and are oftentimes nervous and duck their head in defense, which is reflected in their constant raising of their spines. Any type of unfamiliar sounds and loud noises can cause hedgehogs to react in a defensive manner. Upon experiencing or perceiving threats or discomfort, hedgehogs roll up as a ball and utilize their sharp spines to pierce their prey or any entities of opposition. Hedgehogs remain in their confined space alone, and the males are said to constantly fight. Hedgehogs have large ears and have an excellent sense of hearing.

Porcupines have quills that lie flat like feathers that can also be erected like spikes. Male (father) porcupines often play a minimal role or no involvement at all in the raising of their offspring. According to National Geographic, the mother porcupine will care for its young, usually one to four babies at a time, over a duration of twelve to twenty-four months. Let us embark on this journey, exempt by no man, known as the porcupine syndrome!

A Man's Wife vs. His Car

A man's car will have issues, he fixes it! A man's house will have issues, he fixes it! He recognizes the growing value, he fixes it, and he invests in it. He does not walk away from it.

Why am I willing to spend excessive money to repair my car to carry me on a long journey but fail to invest in the quality and longevity in the journey of my relationship? Why do we declare negative words, like "I am only with you because of the children"? Why do I absorb the negative forces of energy that say, "You are not attractive like when we first met"? Does such a man wish he could trade the love of his life like he would in the showroom for a new car?

A man instead oftentimes walks away from his family, his wife, his marriage. He becomes reluctant to fix his problems.

He listens to the sound of his car, but not the pain of his family, friends, and loved ones.

He will stand at the scene of an accident to ensure his car makes it to the mechanic shop, but not few minutes to pray with a friend on the job. His time is too precious and important. He finds himself rushing in the circle of his wilderness, confusing his motion for progress. How many young girls and boys are crying internally for their fathers, not recognizing the origin or understand the depth of their pain? Like a porcupine, the father is nowhere to be found. Sometimes we can become disconnected even while living under the same roof. The mother is left attempting to play a dual role and facing major rebellion, unable to fulfill the task of a masculine figure.

If I am in such category, this is approaching a danger zone like taxiing an airplane to the runway, plotting my escape, and getting ready to flee. The mind naturally searches for the path of least resistance. But facing the greatest opposition in life oftentimes leads to greater benefits. For emphasis, one of the greatest obstacles of humanity is not having a vision of the future; with no goals, there is no focal point. A man who does not have a vision to navigate his future path will find himself replaying his history and memories for a source of direction.

We have to break the cycles of destructive thoughts and responses. We have to carefully analyze and deliberately address and fix them. We may not be able to become perfect and correct everything at the same time, but initiating and fixing the situation can be far rewarding. Fixing the leak on the house is addressing one challenge that prevents a whole lot of other headaches and preserve the life and values of other possessions. In a similar sense, addressing certain simple issues in a relationship that may seem like a simple crack or leak in a house will break certain bad attitudes or the potential cycle in other areas. This also declares and sets the standard of expectation. Other people who understand and are aware of our expectation can also hold each other accountable in our absence and presence. We have heard individuals say that your word is your bond. When someone verbally states and agrees, it is embedded in his/her consciousness and conviction. His/her attitude, integrity, and ego will execute self-accountability. Let us not play the blame game. Let us equally assess ourselves and be inclined for self-propelled change.

Why are the males and father figures missing? Why is it that the same porcupine/hedgehog that produces male and female offspring has one gender that is willing to stay and face its obligation, while the other, namely, the male gender, just keeps on searching for fulfillment? Is this a cultural norm? Are the males not fully trained or equipped to handle the pressure and responsibilities that come after the sexual pleasure? Do the male figures fail to recognize the value that they possess, or do they feel inadequate, leading to a failure to recognize or perceive how paramount their duties and roles of responsibilities are?

Porcupines raise their offspring without the father. In our society, this would mean single mothers left with the responsibility to raise children without fatherly influence. These single mothers are individuals who will oftentimes say that "this is just the way that I am." These individuals can oftentimes feel independent and like doing things the way that they think it should be, not open to suggestions or other points of view.

Are the females partially responsible for always being physically available for the pleasure and in the process enabling the negative cycle of absentee fatherhood? Why would a female porcupine deny the presence of a protector and one who could help find food for survival? Is this more of a cultural epidemic that formed over the years? Does this have a direct correlation to the fear factor and defense response of this creature?

Family life could be dysfunctional, but sense of independence and intuition to survive will create a continuum of the same absentee operation. If you have these friends, or if you confess to be a porcupine, you may conduct a self-assessment and discover that you feel insecure and quick to roll up in your ball, resorting to self-defense then self-justification. You have not mastered conflict resolution. You are likely to discover that the battle still exists within. You may find yourself being overly aggressive with your offspring who are defenseless.

Do you know anyone in life who gets defensive very easily? Usually such individuals have had experiences that have caused or resulted in hypersensitivity defense mode. Could it be that you are a loner, because letting people in your space will reveal your flaws and cause you to feel vulnerable and nakedness exposed? As oftentimes mentioned throughout this book, Adam and Eve hid from God in the Garden of Eden when they heard His voice in an attempt to cover up their flaws (Genesis 3:8).

Fear, irrespective of humanity or animals, is a mental perception, whether realistic, impending, imagined, instilled, learned, or experienced. Why did this creature develop such level of fear to the point in which sounds become a trigger mechanism to react and hide? A child will hug a teddy bear as much as a dog if perceived to be safe. There is no creation throughout history that was designed with a spirit or attitude of fear. In fact, genuine love given and received will eradicate fear, danger, hatred, and hurt.

Forming Cohesiveness in Marriage

As a wife or husband, do I become fearful and uneasy when my spouse opens the door? Do I feel unappreciative, some sense of devalue, fear, or rejection? Am I nervous or uneasy and fearful to respond to his/her request and expectations? Do I have to neglect everything that I would like to accomplish for myself and cater to his/her demands, or else there will be no peace? Otherwise, the relationship may result in singleness and separation. When differences arise, do I threaten to separate or divorce or envision myself moving out, moving to parents or other relationships, or assessing ownership of property, house, possessions, and child support? Why do I think the way that I think? Why do I constantly cultivate these negative thoughts and behavior? Have I not overcome self and singleness to sacrifice and embrace the compatibility of the other?

There were times in my relationship when my day was stressful coming from work. When I reached home late from work, my wife and children would be sleeping. I have recognized that my wife did an excellent job; she assisted with homework, gave the children a shower, cooked a wonderful meal, then put them to sleep safely and lovingly in a comfortable bed. I recognized this, but lurking in my subconscious, I pondered where did I fit in? I am home; I am stressed, same environment tomorrow at work. I wanted my wife. I wanted someone to speak with, understand my pulse, what's making me tick, sexual gratification. Where do I fit?

We have spoken about taking the initiative, anticipate my arrival home, give me some effort that comes without being so drained and tired. My frustration would intensify. I felt rejected. My emotions were tampered and tested severely. Thoughts of anger and justification would challenge my interest and present all sorts of justification. The devil was speaking!

I quickly realized that my state of anger toward my wife would not create a genuine and spontaneous response. She was now responding with a level of fear or compromising herself to prevent my hurts. I didn't want a love relationship produced out of duress or hostage negotiation. I wanted a relationship fostered through the building of a healthy, loving, and desirable relationship. I started writing and making a list of issues and challenges that I have observed. I then made a list of possible solutions. My wife and I would genuinely talk through the issues and how to resolve them. I would ask her questions like "What are few things that you would like for me to change about myself?" When she gave me a long list, I knew there were many more; I was hurt and wanted to explode and wanted to highlight how long her list was. I could have asked her if she thought she was perfect. I quickly caught myself! I said thank you and told her I will try my endeavor best to become better because it is making me a better person and contributing to the health of our relationship. I would start to see my mistakes as I made them. She would sometimes smile. I could have said, "What in the world is so funny? What are you laughing at?" And of course sometimes I did. But more importantly, what I found myself doing was apologizing when I offended or dropped the ball. I also quickly discovered that she was now trying to become better at pleasing and fulfilling my desires. Our communication and kindness toward each other improved significantly. When she yelled, I responded as though it was a genuine conversation. I also reassured her that I am not patronizing her. But I have recognized that she is venting. I would assure her that I am willingly listening so that she could have an outlet and platform for her anger, but I am choosing not to respond with the same intensity. However, you have my undivided attention, and I would also rather you not shout. She looked at me as though she was defeated, but the look in her eyes admitted that wisdom has prevailed. Throwing pots and pans and spoons could have been an alternative route for many. But a physical war does not, should not, and can never solve emotional, mental, and spiritual battles!

Let us take a look at the blame game, justification, and consequences.

> The man said, "The woman you put here with me—she gave me some fruit from the tree, and I ate it." Then the LORD God said to the woman, "What is this you have done?" The woman said, "The serpent deceived me, and I ate." (Genesis 3:12–13 NIV)

According to verse 8, Adam and Eve went to hide when they heard the sound of God. An accumulation of faults, guilt, and fear can permeate our thought process and trigger constant flight response.

What internal conflicts or compromise did Adam rationalize, knowing the instructions that God had given him? Eve seemingly asserted her influence unto Adam, persuading him to accept the fruit. What was Adam thinking? What were his thoughts? Adam subsequently blamed Eve after God reminded and repeated the prior instructions. Adam knew better while he was accepting the fruit. Eve also knew better because she rebutted the serpent's initial approach by saying, "Well, God did say otherwise" (Genesis 3:3). Was Adam trying his best not to displease the woman that he loves? Did Adam succumb to a vulnerable state because of the way that Eve might react to his possible rejection of her offer?

One thing for sure is that the assertion of Eve could not justify the disobedience of Adam.

Both parties are equally responsible for their actions. The fault of one individual does not justify the reaction, choice, or path taken by the other. Each individual has to stand independently accountable. The decisions that we make in life will impact others around us. The consequences are not always seen in the visible or physical realm but undoubtedly do exist (Genesis 3:17).

Adam and Eve hid from God as an attempt to cover up their flaws. One of the highest forms of betrayal is covering up the track marks of deceptions in an attempt to prevent the discovery by the other party. If the tree falls in the forest and no one hears when it falls, does it make a noise? I will ask this question differently by stating if the action committed is never discovered by the other party, does that mean there is no consequence, or is the action justified? Will there be any effect? How many relationships of infidelity continue simply because the other party is unaware? Do you feel guilty after being caught or perhaps discovered you have sexually transmitted disease? Do you admit the guilt of your actions when your teenage daughter starts to date someone with your similar character traits or exhibits the same potential and symptoms? Do you get a self-awakening when your young child asks if you have ever cheated? Surveys have shown that women who are victims of infidelity get the appeasing result of revenge by cheating on their spouses, even though they never confess or reveal to their spouses that the action was done. Women confess that it is the thought, feeling, and inner satisfaction in getting even and revenge! Individuals are hiding facts in their own secret garden of Eden, not knowing that the Omniscient (All-knowing) God will ask you, "Where are you?"

We have to reach that place of vulnerability, trust, and integrity in which we share our hurts, pain, and discomforts before issues escalate. We also have to seek resolution from healthy sources to an acceptable standard and quality of life. We should not allow the vulnerability of exposing our weak areas prevent us from disclosing it to the ones we love and trust. On the other hand, we should develop the maturity in not exploiting and ensure we protect and cover each other.

We have heard these words before, after we respond to the question "Do you _____ take this man/woman to be your lawful wedded husband/wife?":

Vows: I, _____, take you, _____, to be my *lawfully* wedded (husband/wife), to have and to hold, from this day forward, for better, for worse, for richer, for poorer, in sickness and in health, until death *do* us part.

Everyone who gets married has a unique personality that will have to be embraced, conform, complement, and synchronize with the other to create a successful journey of marriage and relationship. Individuals are constantly learning about themselves and adjusting to the rapid pace of changes in this demanding world. It is even more complex in trying to assess, understand, and function with someone who has his/her unique personality. No one should therefore try to change another person into his/her own liking. In life, individuals try to influence change in others due to fear or past hurt and experiences. What may have initially been with good intention may have then resulted in control and abuse. Life should be treated delicately with love and compassion, exercising the patience that will foster and enable functional and healthy growth. Forgetting about personal needs and self-desire and focusing on the other can guarantee fulfillment for both parties. We can try to outdo fulfilling the needs of each other with healthy competition.

In recognizing the symptoms of a personality that is closely associated with the operation of a porcupine, one has to readily admit his/her current status and be realistic to the possibilities and room for adjustment. One should be very cautious in understanding oneself and be flexible and adaptable to compromise to please and unselfishly satisfy each other. One should also be very cautious in not trying to change the other individual or influence such change according to preference or the way one sees fit. Let's admit it, how many times have we tried to change ourselves or formulate new disciplines that never materialize or come to fruition?

We live in a world of media influences that portray relationships in a negative manner. The media portrays relationships, romance, and fidelity with grave distortion. Nonmarital or out-of-wedlock relationships are the epic of media production. Teen sex, contraceptives, and advocate groups seem to promote this dysfunctional attitude as though it is an impossible feat to bring under control or in subjection to righteous living. There are many politicians who are parents, who speak highly and have great expectations for their children; yet they pass bills and laws that are contrary to fundamental beliefs, as though they are qualified and everyone else lacks the potential to attain such status.

The person with a porcupine personality oftentimes functions on a level of hurt that depletes inner fulfillment. This individual will have the capacity to fulfill the needs of others but will be defeated and also transmit to her spouse a feeling of defeat, and impossible task, to accomplish the given satisfaction to the spouse. When in conflict, a wife could use her body as a weapon by denying sexual access or being inactive and disengaged emotionally. There are many trigger mechanisms that will incite the sexual urge and nature. If disconnected from the spouse, the sexual urge and desire can be misunderstood as attraction to or for another individual. This is due to the search for satisfaction while turning away from the spouse, the source of fulfillment. Trust, loyalty, and walking according to the precepts of our vows are crucial and fundamental. Many spouses who have cheated will try to justify but will be the first to tell you that they would never remain in a relationship if the same action or fraud was to be committed against him/her. This action and attitude of double standards is sending the message that I am qualified to commit such act, but it is illegal for the other who should be executed or sentenced to death penalty.

On the contrary, an individual who shares this kind of hurt or feelings to the point of severe withdrawal usually does not like the feeling of being responsible for hurting another person. If the relationship seems like it is getting too close to the point of indifference or possible conflicts, withdrawal or stopping short at the edge usually takes place. Some individuals resort to silent mode rather than using hurtful words. Though silence can be wiser than negative verbal expression, utilizing self-control and articulating self can be far more beneficial. There is an unwillingness to take chances or even venture into unknown territories. Stigmas will be the highlight and flashing billboards in the mental faculty of such individuals, declaring, "All men/women are the same," "I will never get married again," or "I will forgive but never forget."

The porcupine mentality knows how to make "self" become a victim and feels someone is always attacking or about to get him/her. If I walk into a room and individuals are whispering or laughing, do I immediately become sensitive and subjected to hurt believing that the conversation is negatively directed toward me? How many street fights, deaths, or brawling have been the result of such mindset? People have responded to a stare by asking, "What are you looking at?" It could be as simple and innocent as the person not looking or being mindful of you. Perhaps the individuals thought you looked familiar or you reminded them of someone special. Maybe something that you were wearing created or presented a pleasant memory. The bottom line is that the way we feel or envision ourselves creates our perception and self-reaction whether internally by emotional flares, anger, or explosive outbursts. The opposite extreme may not be healthy, on the other hand, in which an individual believes he/she is of greater superiority and reduces the value of others.

A highly defensive person can be very easily angered. Such victimized mindset has a great propensity to give the other person, namely, the perceived perpetrator, reasons to act negatively in order to justify my actions and liberate me as victim to leave. This action is usually executed out of fear, and with the occurrence of a breakup, the victim maintains or gains a positive reputation against the statistic of another person walking out of his/her life. A porcupine mindset constantly probes and internally ponders, "What's wrong with me?" instead of waiting patiently in perseverance to acquire a change. If you ever get married into a porcupine relationship, the Scripture reminds us the following:

> Better to dwell in a corner of a housetop,
> Than in a house shared with a contentious woman.
> (Proverbs 21:9 NKJV)

> A continual dripping on a very rainy day

> And a contentious woman are alike;
> Whoever restrains her restrains the wind,
> And grasps oil with his right hand.
> *As* iron sharpens iron,
> So a man sharpens the countenance of his friend.
> (Proverbs 27:15–17 NKJV)

If your life is going well, you can't judge these individuals. These individuals may be victims of sexual abuse or father wound due to absenteeism, parental divorce, constantly moving from foster homes, lack of validation and affirmation, and verbal abuse while experiencing lack of approval. Such individuals can possess a shattered self-esteem, creating a distorted lens and outlook of life, causing a constant series of questions to your motives. There will be a life lived with a lot of stigma and unhealthy perspectives, like I will never date this particular race, nationality, etc.

> A good man out of the good treasure of his heart brings
> forth good; and an evil man out of the evil treasure of
> his heart brings forth evil. For out of the abundance of
> the heart his mouth speaks. (Luke 6:45 NKJV)

> So then, my beloved brethren, let every man be swift to
> hear, slow to speak, slow to wrath; for the wrath of man
> does not produce the righteousness of God. Therefore lay
> aside all filthiness and overflow of wickedness, and receive
> with meekness the implanted word, which is able to save
> your souls. But be doers of the word, and not hearers only,
> deceiving yourselves. (James 1:19–22 NKJV)

There is a great book that I have read at a pivotal point in my life that created a massive growth and change. *Who Moved My Cheese?* I consider to be a book with a significant impact. This book speaks of change and being able to move from your comfort zone in order to maximize your full potential.

I strongly believe that my willingness to change is a vital role and momentum that will be far rewarding than remaining stagnant in my current self. (If my spouse, friends, associates, strangers, anyone, anything, or entity that I encounter may challenge myself to make a change, it's incumbent upon me to extract the positive from the offense and use the positive as my greatest asset to springboard and propel into a greater self. It is and will be worth it!)

Boiling Point: The Porcupine Kills the Lion

Predators such as lions usually underestimate the potential and capability of the hedgehog, until they are defeated by sharp piercing spikes to their mouth.

During one of the prayer and fasting segments at my local church, many individuals were being transparent and spoke about past relationship problems. One woman in particular stated how she had endured an abusive relationship. This particular woman would be physically abused by her husband practically every day. She felt hopeless and lived in fear. Each day the husband entered the house, she would enter into a frantic state of fright. The woman then became transparent during the discussion and said, "Pastor, I got tired of the abuse; and when I heard him enter the house, I said to myself, *This is the last day he is going to put his hand on me.* Pastor, I took the frying pan and hid it behind my back; and as he placed his hand on me, Pastor, I gave him one hit across his head. He was knocked out cold. Pastor, from that day on, he never put his hand on me again."

I will never condone abusive relationships in any form. I also strongly implore anyone experiencing abuse to seek immediate help. How many of us today are afraid to express ourselves and confront troubling issues? How many times in the media women of sexual abuse are coming forward decades later to confront their predators? How many individuals are comfortable within to address conditions that are in the early stage, before these conditions get worse and spiral out of control? Do we take the same approach with our health, finance, relationship, education, etc.? Do we procrastinate or try to wait for the "perfect" time? Do we seek justifiable measures by telling ourselves that if the person already knows, why should I bring up the issue?

If my temperament is more of an introvert, I may need to utilize sources, network with individuals, or get involved in groups and support systems.

A constant system of attitude or operation, left unchanged, will become a new habit or discipline.

Let us bring changes to the negative and model and improve the positive. As we make the necessary self-assessment in search of improvements, we may find ourselves becoming angered by the mental confrontation of truth. Let us not dismiss these self-actualizing thoughts but embrace them for the teacher of positive change!

Psychotherapy Declared in a State of Emergency

Self is equipped with what is known as adrenaline. This is the hormone that becomes secreted by the adrenal glands in frantic, stressful, and fearful moments. When the blood flow increases, you breathe faster, and muscles receive strength. Many people refer to adrenaline as the emergency hormone. The porcupine is very sensitive to sounds, which are a main entry point that stimulates fear, especially of the unknown. As a boy who grew up in the Caribbean, I have been chased by cows; I have been chased by vicious dogs and other animals. I have jumped fences and climbed trees like Spider-Man in order to escape. I felt incredible and invincible. But let's put self into proper perspective. If I perceive with a lens of fear or have anxiety, my body naturally responds as though I am going through the real attack. My body simply responds like I am in a state of emergency. My body cannot tell real from the state of imagination. My body simply responds to the dictates of the mind. When my house was going through major repairs, I almost pleaded the blood of Jesus one late night when I saw someone moving in the dark.

But then I started quarreling with myself when I realized I had left the big glass mirror in the hallway. I was responding to my own reflection in the glass in a state of fear. My heart was beating harder. I was out of breath. The body responds to imminent or perceived danger just like the real encounter.

Whatever the mind perceives, the physical body will naturally respond. The body does not know how to differentiate reality from imagination. If the mind becomes fearful, the body reacts, causing even dogs to smell his fear! That toxic odor from adrenaline rush. If we rest our mind, we rest our body!

If I should dislike someone, or be in constant conflict with my family, or dislike his/her very presence, the mind sends a signal to the body, initiates anger and resentment, and secretes toxic chemical reactions into the bloodstream.

Sickness will inhabit and find a nesting place in the body accordingly, because whatever the mind beholds, it simply dictates to the body.

If I am sick in the body, psychologists assess the mind to find anger and unforgiveness. The body willingly follows whatever commands that the mind executes. That's why the power of forgiveness is so important. Forgiveness is releasing self from a hostage situation and in no way implies that I am defeated. If Jesus is the head, our lifestyle and body have to come into subjection and total submission, responding according to the precepts of God. It forces the mind to let go of all toxic commands it is about to transcend throughout the temple, this bodily tabernacle.

Self also likes to launch attacks on others. It's called character assassination. We perceive or call others dumb, instead of saying the choice or decision that you made was of poor judgment. We make comments like "I am not that dumb. I wouldn't have done that," instead of saying, "Do you mind if I assist or offer you some help?" We tell our kids that they are wasting our money and cannot graduate kindergarten much less high school. In the military, we tell people to quit the army and go join the Salvation Army. There is a story about one guy in the military who tried to commit suicide, but he was unsuccessful; the supervisor told him, "You are so dumb you don't even know how to properly kill yourself." It's one thing for people to inject me with their negative philosophy, but it's another when I constantly dialogue negatively with myself!

If my body could translate into a mathematical formula, I would realize how many years that I am allowing to be deducted and reducing from my life span with constant negativity. I would also realize the shock waves, bar graphs, and financial pie charts of activities of great injustice occurring throughout the body even when I should be sleeping. In order to get to work, my mind has to execute a command, and my body willingly follows. That's why when being late, angry, and frustrated, I have to check the temperament of my mind. As a man thinketh in his heart, that's exactly who he will become. My body did not get up in the middle of the night to steal, kill, or find a sweetheart in the dark. No, somebody has to check and constantly assess the mind. How many men have claimed that adultery was a mistake as though it is a trip and fall situation! I did not get up and secretly despise my fellow brothers and sisters who are created in the image of God, then try to justify my disgust. Absolutely not. I have to do a diagnostic test on my mind. If we ever monitor the sickness and pain that is directly attached to our thought process, we would begin to feed upon the love of God every step of the way. We would hug and smile with others until they wonder if something is wrong with us.

Moment of Reflection and Meditation

> Husbands, likewise, dwell with *them* with understanding, giving honor to the wife, as to the weaker vessel, and as *being* heirs together of the grace of life, that your prayers may not be hindered. (1 Peter 3:7 NKJV)

Fathers, do not provoke your children to anger, but bring them up in the discipline and instruction of the Lord. (Ephesians 6:4 ESV)

Fathers, do not provoke your children, lest they become discouraged. (Colossians 3:21 ESV)

Hear, my son, your father's instruction, and forsake not your mother's teaching, for they are a graceful garland for your head and pendants for your neck. (Proverbs 1:8–9 ESV)

But if anyone does not provide for his relatives, and especially for members of his household, he has denied the faith and is worse than an unbeliever. (1 Timothy 5:8 ESV)

Above all, keep loving one another earnestly, since love covers a multitude of sins. (1 Peter 4:8 ESV)

CHAPTER 3
THE EGOTISTICAL FROG
(Power of Influence)

A man that walks around with a title on his chest instead of his heart will feel disrespected when approached by the blind.

—M. Reid

What if it was possible for you to adjust your breathing, heart rate, body coloration to environment, or body temperature to the different seasons and climatic conditions wherever you should travel? How successful or detrimental would we become against the odds of life? Well, let's investigate this creature with such phenomenal character.

Quite interestingly, studies reveal that the frog's body contains high levels and concentrations of glucose, which protects the frog from freezing to death during hibernation in frigid winter conditions. The heart of the frog will stop beating, and its breathing discontinues. As the temperature rises above freezing level, the frog goes through a defrosting state, and body organs such as heart and lungs begin to function as normal. As the frog adjusts its body like a thermostat to the different temperaments of life, does it truly know its limit or have something to prove? Unfortunately, during extreme and extenuating circumstances, the frog meets its demise before it is able to recover.

Is my environment or condition slowly killing me without realizing it? Have I been relying on my natural ability or perhaps a failed system? Have I become so toxic that I am blinded in my stench?

Is my success at a heightened position causing me to drown in my own desensitized state of arrogance?

Am I being challenged by the temporal things of life that will eventually die? I have forsaken the most essential and eternal!

Frogs are able to adjust their body temperature according to the temperament of the environment, and they hibernate during the winter season. Frogs do not need to drink water; they absorb water through their skin. Frogs have a very distinct sound that is recognized by its specie. Frogs can be heard from very far distances, concluded to range up to a mile in distance. Frogs will blend and try to fit in for survival and acceptance. They adjust themselves to a system that does not guarantee a specific timeline. A frog will confess and tell you, "I am my greatest enemy." Can a person be too smart for his own good?

Have you ever met some classmates who could just show up on the day of an exam and receive an excellent passing score with little effort? You can't help but to wonder if something is wrong with you. The teacher begins to lecture, and you start to wonder if you came to the right classroom or perhaps brought the wrong textbook to class. If the teacher calls on you, you begin to sweat profusely and panic like you have forgotten your own name.

There are many leaders who rely on their natural gifts and wisdom and refuse to be thoroughly prepared. Many homes and families are facing hardships because of miscalculations and total self-reliance that equate to failure of preparation. Some preachers will show up and articulate eloquently without seeking diligently the simple details from God. Many leaders evolve on the basis and foundation of charisma, rather than formulating character with integrity and for longevity. Some doctors administer medical attention while failing to do due diligence in studying the charts of the patient. Some lawyers party all week and then try to go through the motion of the case for those they pledge to defend.

Frogs are said to be very persistent, bold, and exploration driven; enjoy activities; and are symbolic of abundance, wealth, prosperity, creativity, awakening, health, and friendship. Obviously they are the life of the party and attract progress. Samson will tell you to be very careful how you get comfortable in your strength and lay your head to rest in Delilah's lap of major deception and misjudgment. He was rocked to sleep and woke up searching for his strength and solution, only to face utter disappointment.

Upon closely examining the personality of a frog, one can conclude that the frog is the perfect achiever and can be perceived as the visionary who should be on every leadership team to produce growth and revolutionary results. Others who are introvert may not necessarily feel comfortable around a frog-like personality and may feel disrespected, overlooked, or incompetent in the company of a frog. A frog-like personality may not like to be challenged but appreciate the exposure of blind spots and weak areas. This is because the frog will quickly adjust to exploit and maximize in order to satisfy his flamboyant ego, to excel in any environment or temperature. A frog is usually confident, because it is granted the spotlight opportunity to prove itself. Unlike the frog, others may be in self-doubt because of lack of opportunity, exploration, or confidence gained through self-discovery and exposure.

There is a very well known statement that says the road to hell is paved with good intentions. The frog did not wake up one day and decided, "I am going to risk it all today." The frog did not analyze his circumstances and have an ultimate epiphany or assessment, which concludes that "today I will definitely meet all my demise." The frog simply relies on its ingenuity to ascend to the plight of conquering the odds. Luke 12:18–21 tells us of the man who brags and decides to tear down his barns and build bigger ones for a greater surplus. He stored up many supplies to last him for many years and planned to eat, drink, and have a festive time. But God then shook up his consciousness and said, "You fool, this night your life will be required from you." God then implores us to live in the riches of His blessings, rather than the temporal things of this world. The danger zone for the frog is that his swift thinking, flexibility and adaptability, among many other notable attributes, can create a lot of blind spots, misjudgments, and miscalculations that can be extremely detrimental to the lives of those involved or dependent on his judgment.

A Lesson for Leaders

The great leader Moses was responsible for overseeing six hundred thousand men with women and children (Exodus 12:37). Moses would take a seat on a daily basis to administer his duties and settle disputes as the conflicts were presented to him. People would wait from early morning to late afternoon hoping to have their cases being heard. You can almost imagine the tension and anxiety developed while expecting a favorable outcome, especially without an appeal process. Jethro, the father-in-law of Moses, visited and observed the stressful system and warned Moses that he will eventually become worn out, and the people will be discouraged. Moses responded that he is just doing the work of God. Jethro suggested to Moses that he should instead get capable, honest men who do not like bribes and set them over the people in small groups while Moses oversees the more challenging cases. Moses took his advice, and it became an instant effective solution to the current and foreseeable challenges (Exodus 18:13–27). Our passion to lead and to serve oftentimes impedes upon the proper judgment of our capabilities. This does not necessitate the negating of our obligation but calls for the exercising of wisdom, in delegation, multiplication, and exponential growth.

The workload became very tedious, and like many individuals, Moses's passion and drive to achieve his goals impeded upon his judgment. Moses had good intentions, but he was on the verge of wrecking his life and a major corporation. Moses failed to delegate the workload and to develop new leaders. Moses tried to accomplish the task by himself and found it hard to trust others to lead. Moses was a perfectionist and needed to exercise patience to allow others to grow and mature in their role. Moses initially failed to mentor the next generation ahead of the demand in tasks. Moses only recognized the need when circumstances warranted, and his blind side exposed the immediate need for new leaders. Desperation should never be the reason to recognize the true value, quality, and potential in others. With a receptive heart and openness, a frog personality can become a very impactful leader.

A leader in any capacity who lacks vision or fails to help others to discover their potential is like putting a lid on a pressure cooker and trying to entrap the growth potential of a man forever.

We then breed dysfunction and run the risk of reacting when not being able to contain the explosion. If you destroy a man's potential, you erase the future of an entire generation that he was sent to impact. A frog has to admit that the task is beyond his reputation, is greater than his image, rises above his ability, and stretches beyond his life span. The insecure frog is like a man who fails to look beyond his biases and will plot to destroy your life and potential. His insecurities and desires will become like a constant focus in the mirror. He sees himself while driving and runs others off the expressway by forgetting that their potential also exists as a integral part of the journey. Such a man will plot your demise while lending the appearance to care even if he suffers in the process like Pharaoh. Exodus 7:25–8:15 tells that a plague of frogs had to come upon Egypt and die after swarming the palace of Pharaoh, entering his bedroom, kitchen, oven, and personal space before his heart was sensitized to the stench.

In their own eyes they flatter themselves too much to detect or hate their sin. (Psalm 36:2 NIV)

The life of leaders in a variety of capacities, whether a father in the home, a teacher in the classroom, or a CEO of a company, inclusive of Moses over the civil and spiritual affairs of humanity, can become like driving a vehicle with a lot of passengers. Your core responsibility is to get people safely to their destination. According to Exodus 18 verse 21, find men who love God and hate bribes. Choosing the right people is as important as equipping and placing them in the appropriate position. Verse 22 encourages finding men who are available to solve disputes. It is very important to highlight that this intrinsically implies that there were many individuals who were accustomed to compromise by yielding to dishonest practices and briberies. However, as a leader, the job of Moses was never to throw them off the bus but assist in a safe arrival by exercising wisdom. This does not mean to condone the negative act, but also not a destroyer in the process while admonishing judgment. A second point to note is that as a driver directing the affairs of the company, you cannot constantly pull over to the side of the road to solve disputes among rowdy passengers and family members in the vehicle. You have to trust the process and those chosen to grow and accomplish the task. Otherwise, you will be burned out, waste precious time, or be replaced by another driver possibly without the necessary qualifications or vocation, who might be reckless in abiding by the protocols of a higher calling.

Leaders, especially those who are goal-oriented, get satisfaction through their accomplishments. This can be whether negatively or positively channeled and challenged. The passion of an individual oftentimes leads to a lot of fights in schools, peer pressure, and drug abuse. Individuals seek to satisfy the desire of ego and validation, with actions that prove against public scrutiny. The choices made by us as individuals can be determined frequently by the expectations, needs, and desires projected unto us by others. This type of submission to any act of demand can be translated into a similar fashion like infidelity in the scope of a relationship. We trade our desires and fulfillment to engage in the task. We have to leave room for the Holy Spirit and not yield to our own vulnerability and constant empathy. The need or desires projected unto someone can be interpreted as love and affection. If this attention is not transcended by the other party, it can be misconstrued as the absence of love and affection or registered as rejection. One then develops the propensity to yield or be pulled into the direction of passion to give and to satisfy in a reciprocal manner. On the other hand, there is a repelling action and attitude toward the party that is perceived to lack giving of self or attention. Moses found himself compromising in an attempt to appease everyone. This is like constantly aiming at moving targets!

The frog allows circumstances or others to set or insinuate its temperament. The frog uses its ego to challenge its odds or adversities or to excel to a new platform or elevation of accomplishments, even if it means at the expense of others.

The one who controls and influences your thought process will ultimately determine your actions and reactions. This influential effect is the thermostat of your life that constantly gauges your temperature, source, level of your anger, and peace of mind.

How many times did Moses become angry and ask God, "Why did you give me these stiff-necked people to carry, like they are my babies!" God then sent others to assist Moses. A manipulative or innocent individual can easily predetermine your self-disposition or result, the intended outcome. The innocent, pure, and sincere individuals in your life can be misunderstood based on your state of blindness, becoming a trigger mechanism to your misconception and distorted views. A leader has to be very keen to his limits and stress factors and not put them to the test. Abuse will become inevitable.

Leadership and friendships that put their trust and invest priceless resources in frog operation can easily suffer and become victims of the twisted mindset. Though frogs may have good intentions, absence of practicality can result in catastrophic predicaments, and they can be labeled as perpetrators. The frog can be perceived as a go-getter, one who adjusts to the height and plight of any challenges. The results can be attractive and accomplished as expected but can be built on a faulty foundation of mixed motives on the grounds of absence of true self-actualization, the wisdom of self-understanding and discovery.

Deciding to walk or strive with a frog can be very painful. If you are analytical and specialize in the full details of the journey, the frog may be focused on the bigger picture and leave you behind on a lonely road. You may find yourself being hurt and feeling abandoned and rejected in bitterness. The frog, on the other hand, seems either oblivious or nonchalant; and you cannot understand its apparent insensitivity. It can seem like a person who walked away from a relationship and left you heartbroken, only to return and want to pick up from where he/she left off. You are trying to comprehend if he/she thinks this is a movie that was paused or a college paper you decide just to continue writing from where you stopped. If you have friends who are successful with a frog mentality, they can party and drink and quickly adjust to the work environment, while you suffer after trying once. My family members usually warn me by telling me that cats and dogs have two different lucks (fortunes)—what one escapes may be the demise of the other.

Infiltration Elimination

A study was done in the aviation industry revealing twelve preconditions that lead to errors or unsafe acts, referred to as "the Dirty Dozen." Every leader should constantly take this litmus test in order to eradicate the acidic contents in his/her life.

These twelve preconditions are lack of communication, distraction, lack of resources, stress, complacency, lack of teamwork, pressure, lack of awareness, lack of knowledge, fatigue, lack of assertiveness, and norms.

This list should be a constant reminder to every person in a home or a leader of an organization. If easily offended when someone points out the truth, this list can be a great voice without a person to attack. A frog should recognize the values in others before it is too late and be willing to grow together even if the other is not at the starting point or destination of his/her journey. Too many leaders aspire to arrive and outrun others in order to lead from a distance. Such individual fears his/her equal potential in others and would rather hide his/her vulnerability by creating measures of demarcation. Moses wanted to go to the Promised Land, but because he reacted to the rebellious attitude of the people, he stood back and watched while the new generation subsequently and joyfully inherited the blessing of the land. When you develop positive leaders and share the journey equally, we lessen the propensity of obstacles and unnecessary stress. James 1:8 reminds us that a man who is double-minded essentially is unstable. Verses 22–25 of the said chapter warn us that if a man listens to the Word and doesn't obey, he is like a person who looks in a mirror and after walking away forgets his image. It is therefore vital to obey the words of truth and receive our blessings as God honors our obedience. If we recognize negative traits within, let us not be inclined to reject change but wrestle self into positive transformation. Jacob said, "I will not let go until you bless me!"

Relinquishing Your Authority

I know your deeds, that you are neither cold nor hot. I wish you were either one or the other! So, because you are lukewarm—neither hot nor cold—I am about to spit you out of my mouth. You say, "I am rich; I have acquired wealth and do not need a thing." But you do not realize that you are wretched, pitiful, poor, blind and naked. (Revelation 3:15–17 NIV)

A person with a frog mentality that becomes infiltrated is one that is lukewarm and arrogant and can die with extreme intelligence or extreme ignorance, because he/she lacks godly wisdom. He/she oftentimes reacts to extreme heat or cold by jumping out in an evasive manner but then gets quite comfortable in the lukewarmness of his situation. This is not bearing disrespect or directing the notion as to define the person as being dumb. Everyone has the capability and potential to acquire knowledge, wisdom, and understanding to aid in the eradication of nonsensical habits. We are therefore implored, if we identify any of these symptoms or conditions within ourselves, not to offensively reject the challenge to change.

> Instead, God chose things the world considers foolish in order to shame those who think they are wise. And he chose things that are powerless to shame those who are powerful. (1 Corinthians 1:27 NLT)

Many copilots who are in training are oftentimes afraid to challenge the bad habits of the pilots. The copilots are usually very sensitive and alert to critical issues because they are still in training and have not yet developed complacency or ulterior measures to circumvent the operation. However, copilots oftentimes dismiss their inputs out of fear or counteract their thoughts as of lesser importance due to the expertise of the trainer or veteran pilot.

There is a story of a pilot who oftentimes does stunts during regular missions. The veteran (expert) pilot is usually challenged by the amateur copilot about his uncalled practice and unnecessary risk factors in doing maneuvers. The veteran pilot disregards the concern of the copilot and continues to do his stunts as though he was invincible. Until one day, the pilot did a maneuver that he was unable to recover from. Moments before their deaths, the black box recorded the copilot in the cockpit stating, "Thank you . . . You have just killed us both."

Frogs are difficult to counsel. They are very disobedient to leadership, rules, and regulations; they travel in big groups and believe that the majority must be right. Their flamboyant personality attracts a lot of individuals, which will in turn grant a major support even in the midst of their grave madness and destructive tendencies. Frogs can be self-destructive and can be looked upon as having a personality with a swinelike trampling effect. Sometimes people are placed in our lives, homes, workplaces, and social groups that we take for granted. We fail to recognize their significance and constantly treat them with a spirit of ingratitude. We should therefore stand faithful in the relationship of self, embracing the process of change, and not conspire against self-transformation. The greater self that we have become, the greater self-help we will be for others.

Relationships and Frog Mentality

A frog will be dying on the vine in an abusive relationship; the man hits her upside her head, and she manages with a frog mentality to adjust and convince herself that she is at fault. She adjusts her mindset and concludes that she must have done something to trigger the behavior. A frog has a great tolerant level and will adjust to great quality, which is equally applicable to the nonsensical aspects of life. Many individuals believe that being a recipient of such abusive attention must constitute true love and care. A frog thinks tomorrow will always get better, while the temperature of the water is increasing to the point of destruction.

A frog functions with a nostalgic mind frame that reflects on the good old days and does not embrace change very easily. A frog runs up its credit card and finds it difficult to pay debts while experiencing no change in lifestyle or without any job promotions. A frog mentality still goes holiday shopping while drowning in further financial debt for people who do not like you any differently, because a frog's optimistic attitude believes the debt will be paid off soon. Gifts should never be used as an attempt to substitute the quality and essential needs of life. A frog contributes the basic minimum in offering and charity for several years and saves very little and believes that the curse of debt will be broken. Giving is a reflection of attitude and discipline to either save or invest in others, which in return will attract investment to self. People are more inclined to give or support those who are generous. Mark 12:41–44 tells us that Jesus sat near the collection box at the temple of worship and observed many rich dignitaries giving a large sum of money. But there came a widow who gave two small coins, which were all that she had. Jesus made mention that she gave more than the others. Your entity of giving or any kind of contribution, regardless of the source, is a reflection of the heart's attitude. An uncommon type of giving results in a greater harvest and circumstantial breakthrough.

A frog will fail to understand that it is slowly submerging underwater in the ignorance of its fatal decisions.

When a frog is put in a high position, its level of basic discipline and poor habits is then magnified on a different platform, which often tramples and abuses in usurping of authority. The one who is impacted or becomes surprised by the frog is the one who will be utterly disappointed and live in despair for putting his/her full trust into a broken system.

> Pride goes before destruction and a haughty spirit before a fall. (Proverbs 16:18 NKJV)

One has to develop wisdom and grow in a deep understanding of self. Otherwise, you become prone to the devastating manipulation and selfishness of others. In Matthew 12:8–14, Jesus went to the synagogue where He observed a man with a deformed hand. The Pharisees inquired if it is lawful for a person to work by healing someone on the Sabbath day. Their motive for the question was to entrap Jesus in breaking the law by giving an inappropriate response. Jesus responded with a rhetorical question, by asking, "How many of you would walk away from your sheep if it should fall into a ditch on the Sabbath day? And how much more is an individual more precious than a sheep? Therefore, it's vital to always do good on the Sabbath." Jesus then healed and restored the hand of the man. The Pharisees then left and plotted to kill Jesus. How ironic is life when we attempt to please others, and they never seem to be satisfied. We need not become disgruntled but stand in the full confidence of self. How wretched and wicked our hearts can become when we get offended and start to develop resentment against others who have addressed us by presenting the truth. Do we plot against them with internal hatred, mockery, and gossip? Do we fail to realize that our temperament and reaction is far more outrageous than the point that we are trying to dictate into controlling the attitude of others?

The Black Swallow of Death

We live in a fast-evolving world, which relies on growth and technological advancements to not fall victim as endangered species as a nation, especially in the hands of our adversaries. We tell our children, this generation, "You can be anything you want to become. Nothing can stop you." We then create certain criteria as the only path of qualification, which can pose or become a major stumbling block. Across the globe, there is an epidemic that declares unless you are authorized and endorsed by certain entities, you cannot be a pilot or sailor, utilize weaponry, or save someone's life. Such was the case with Moses, as all matters had to go through his leadership and approval. But how about in modern-day world war and the status quo of society?

Let us analyze this scenario at hand of a true historical event:

Eugene Jacques (James) Bullard was born on October 9, 1895, and died on October 12, 1961. Mr. Bullard was the first African-American military combat pilot who flew for France. Another renowned combat pilot during World War I was William Robinson Clarke, from Jamaica, West Indies, who was the first black pilot to fly for Britain in the Royal Flying Corps.

Mr. Bullard was born in Georgia in an area known as Columbus. His father was from Martinique with Haitian ancestors. While Bullard was in his teens, he fled on a German ship in order to escape racial discrimination. Bullard explains an instance in which he had observed his father escaping death from a lynching incident. Bullard later visited Paris and resided in France. Bullard served in the French military (170th Infantry), subsequently volunteered in October 2, 1916, accepted, and eventually enlisted in the French Air Service as an air gunner. He was trained and received his pilot's license May 5, 1917, and later joined the Lafayette Flying Corps, in which there was greater feasibility in selection from a list of designated pilots instead of the limited challenge in joining a unit. The American volunteers would then fly with the pilots in the French military. Due to his skills and ability to destroy multiple enemy planes in each mission in World War I, Bullard was nicknamed the Black Swallow of Death.

With his training and expertise, he applied for a position in the United States military and was rejected. Bullard then later rejoined the French military and served in World War II that began September 1939. Bullard understood and spoke German and was assigned by the French government to spy on the Germans who would visit Bullard's nightclub. Bullard later returned to New York in 1940 and settled in Harlem after the German invasion of France.

Mr. Bullard was invited in 1954 to light the flame at the Arc de Triomphe in France. Mr. Bullard was acknowledged and declared a hero in France in 1959. Mr. Bullard passed away October 12, 1961. The United States Air Force recognized and commissioned Mr. Bullard in 1994 to the rank of lieutenant—thirty-three years after his death!

I can remember vividly being at a retiree ceremony and happened to observe a gentleman walking around. I knew nothing about this individual. He was just another person. While everyone was assisting the elderly who were the main focus of the day, he stood out based on his sporadic behavior while promoting his personal agenda. Then I saw his name tag that said "Council Member." In his mind, he equated his level of importance according to his title. In his mind, he believed that we have perceived him to be on the pedestal because of his position as a council member. Such is the danger found in society, when we set up a dynasty according to certain criteria. We promote the position of self, undermine servitude, and in the process devalue those we are meant to serve. Our body language, social behavior, and accolades can be interpreted as unless a person has your level of achievements, he becomes irrelevant and subservient.

Sadly, we have become a force that sets up a wall of demarcation to maintain a status quo, as opposed to the mission at hand. There are many high-ranking law enforcement officials who have not mastered the art of transitioning from a work environment to a home or social conduct. Law enforcement officials are accustomed to both executing and following commands without resistance. Though this is a great model, a person has to be able to transition and deal flexibly with opposition from a child, a spouse, or civilians who do not analyze and interpret their mode of conduct and significance like computer-coded entries. Otherwise, anger, frustration, and abuse will take effect for resistance against perceived attacks.

During the war on Pearl Harbor, when the main gunner on the ship died, one brave man stepped up, who was disqualified from shooting and restricted to the kitchen as a cook. He took a hold of the weaponry and destroyed the opponents like he was born to kill.

A leader should not wait to recognize or admit his shortcoming at the point of death, when he is left without options. We congratulate a lot of individuals at funerals and after death while neglecting or conveying love and appreciation in life. Worse is the element against us if we fail to recognize the values, potential, talents, and giftedness in those around while we are alive. Everyone is expendable. Mr. Bullard was recognized when he returned to the United States and went back to France. He subsequently and eventually returned to the United States where he worked menial jobs. He was an icon in a foreign country that was recognized by the government with high regard but, on the other hand, rejected in his hometown in New York, not only by a physical door with no blacks allowed but all levels of racial discrimination. A man has to be strong in his sense of purpose to survive against the odds of life. Otherwise, he is on a quest to self-destruct. Too many funerals have become the venue for expression of love and appreciation. Jeremiah 1:4–10 tells us that the Lord knows us and sets us apart with a purpose, even before we were formed in the womb of our mother. The Lord then reassures us never to feel insignificant; neither believe that you are too young. The Lord commands us to be obedient and go wherever He sends us, because He has equipped and will always be there to protect us.

A leader ought to look beyond the horizon and see in the future of self and the next generation and pave a path of preparation. Moses did not make it to the Promised Land, but he ensured selflessly that the next generation did.

Martin Luther King Jr. had this great vision and conviction as professed in his "I Have a Dream" speech and realized that he may not live to see it manifest, but he implemented measures to mobilize with momentum.

Harboring hatred, anger, animosity, resentment, bitterness, and all the various vices in our hearts that hinder our love from family members, and from making others around us productive, is like rejection of the application process to become an asset to utilize our gifts and walk in purpose.

The average suicide is a result of lost of purpose and a sense of not belonging. We oftentimes encourage others to pursue their dreams with confidence. We also reassure them that they are unstoppable, but we release them to fight against Goliath with only a slingshot they have not been trained to use.

Let us look at the qualities that a frog should quest to possess.

A frog has to be confident in its purpose, be willing to change, and not deviate according to the temperament of the crowd.

In John 6:60–71, after Jesus had done a lot of miracles and multiplied fish and loaves to feed several thousand people, He was continuously followed. But after recognizing the content of the people's heart, Jesus exposed their hypocrisy and told them that they are only there for the physical and temporal food. Unless they accept that Jesus is the Bread of Life, they cannot enter the eternal kingdom through the narrow gate. The crowd grumbled, and what looked like a megachurch quickly decreased to the twelve disciples.

Jesus also knew that one of the twelve would betray Him, and one would also deny Him. Jesus was sure and confident of His purpose and had no need to destroy others for their shortcoming. Every experience in life is a profitable lesson. Jesus asked the remaining disciples why they were not also leaving with the crowd. They acknowledged that there was no other place of life to go!

Too oftentimes leaders rely on numerical growth to assess their level of success. In 1 Chronicles 21, King David relied on military power, wealth, and number by taking a census in an attempt to gain victory over his enemies. David trusted in his strength and did not exhibit faith in God. David then repented because of the wrath of God against him. It behooves us to refrain from fighting in our own strengths and motives, as though we can survive flawlessly on our own. When we are true to our purpose, conviction, and getting direction from the Holy Spirit through prayer and discernment, even a frog personality will experience an internal wrestling to change for the better. A man/woman will wrestle to remain faithful in all his/her affairs, whether relational or financial. Such individual will not justify his/her actions based on retaliation or desires or conclude that he/she has a weakness that his/her strength cannot handle. A man/woman who conquers self is a masterpiece with positive attributes and adaptability as a frog.

A frog ought to model what he ought to be and without fear execute an exemplary attitude to develop others to emulate his path!

In 1 Corinthians 9:27, the apostle Paul said, "I have to make sure after I preach, I also make it in." When a person leads, preaches, or conducts an affair, it has to be free from double-standard traits and contains exemplary contents for self and others. Frogs' ability to endure will have to monitor and filter complacency and stagnant elements for resiliency. When you have a positive attitude of self and a great understanding of your purpose, you will be able to develop others around you to accomplish the higher calling of the kingdom. Every loving parent has the best endeavor and desires to develop their children.

> So if you sinful people know how to give good gifts
> to your children, how much more will your heavenly
> Father give good gifts to those who ask him. (Matthew
> 7:11 NLT)

There were ten lepers who received healing, but one returned to say thank you. Jesus was not offended by the gratitude failed to express by the nine, because a grateful and thankful heart that expresses gratitude is a vertical worship to God and not unto self. The earthly man who desires praise is a man with the intention of robbing God. If your glory is given to you now, you forsake your eternal appreciation. We therefore should not function or execute due diligence on the virtue of satisfying our egos, even if it means forsaking fame or entitled recognition. *The 48 Laws of Power* reminds us never to outshine your master. A leader who fails to walk in his authentic self is like a genetically engineered plant that is contaminated within. It's not edible, and it has been compromised with a replicating effect.

A man in his sense of purpose at first has to willingly confess and acknowledge that the world owes him nothing. A man has to recognize himself as a steward and a conduit sent to forsake himself and to benefit others. To the mind that objectively rejects is failure to understand the benefits that are equally reciprocated.

There is a major indifference between standing to give with the motive of self-recognition and making a difference while standing and giving selflessly. Such a man will be utterly destroyed by the one who lacks awareness or the means to grant you approval and affirmation.

A man who walks around with a title on his chest instead of his heart will feel disrespected when approached by the blind.

CHAPTER 4

UNBECOMING A HORSE
(Power of Change)

*You will continue to walk around in the circle of wilderness
while being exploited and equate motion for progress.*

— M. Reid

Do not make a horse of yourself! This is a very common phrase and expression. But what if you would discover that you have been conditioned to think like a horse, but you do not know the process of unbecoming a horse? Unbecoming a horse is very vital! How many people in life would consider themselves to be warmhearted, enthusiastic, energetic, upright, positive, passionate, sociable, challenging, or fearful? Well, studies conducted on horses have concluded and attributed these character and personality traits to the horse.

There is no surprise when horses are being used in hospitals for therapeutic purposes or civil duties within the community. To befriend and condition a wild horse to socialize harmoniously with the human population, the same steps are implemented with mankind.

Are you taking my kindness for weakness? Why does everyone else seem to get away with it? Why does the one who comply get the end of the stick? If you are often faced with or identify with these questions, I suggest you read this chapter attentively and read the scenario exercises at the end.

Have you ever heard of victimology? Can I blame a victim of rape because of the way he/she was dressed? Some stigma and accusations would render your attire as provocative. Can I blame a child for being bullied because of his/her perceived naivety preyed upon by others? Can I blame you for the circumstances of occurrences in your life? Will you rejoice and attribute the success stories to your natural ability yet blame nature for the odds against you?

Why does my life get rerouted like a ship shifting course in the midst of a storm? Was the storm meant to direct me when the calm meant to pacify me? Do I curse the process of the pain but celebrate the victory after the discovery?

I am so glad that your mind is engaged! This may be one of the greatest counseling sessions you may ever live to receive, right here in this session and chapter of this book. In every man is found a horse. Taming a bird with restrictions from flying is like conditioning a wild horse to human submission for zoo entertainment. Many animals that were tamed then released to the wild have proven to have low survivability rate. Can my state of resistance be my kingship, while my submission and compliance be enslavement?

There are several circumstances in which a horse is tied to a simple plastic chair or movable object, yet the horse just stands still and refuses to move.

The horse is strapped to an obstacle that even a child or strong wind could move. Yet the horse's perception is its major dysfunction. The horse has been conditioned to be loyal and to believe that it is confined to its environment. The horse is at a disadvantage and blames its circumstances of life. Depending on the period the horse decides to remain immobilized, stand still, and refuse to apply its thoughts and break its condition, then that's the amount of time the horse will blame someone for its failure for being unproductive. Why do I think the way that I do? Why do I attract certain measures and patterns of thoughts? Do I feel overwhelmed and argue about the simple circumstances of life? If I should encounter this horse as my mentor, friend, close associate, sympathizer, empathizer, adviser, parent, teacher, social media, news broadcaster, genre of music, book, attraction, spouse, icon, main influencer, source of help, or role model, very soon I will realize that I, am also standing still without even being attached to a leash.

Many individuals who enter a relationship during challenging times may have found themselves encountering a standstill stage of reality, whether a financial, educational, or housing leash of limitation. As time progresses, one individual may come to a state of awakening and decide that it's time to unleash from the mental holds of limitation. Whether relationship or business activities, if one party now decides to break forth out of an enclosed box, relocate, expand, and explore a new horizon, it is important to communicate and prepare the other spouse for the change that is about to occur. If the other party or spouse is still crippled and blinded by a high measure of foolishness to change, it will make the relationship stagnant and filled with increased frustration. You will now have a highly educated or motivated wife and a disparity with the husband who thinks and relies on working harder to accomplish more. Very soon, divorce is at a high probability, and abuse becomes inevitable, which could have been easily managed and reconciled by various methods of intervention.

When a man is mentally enslaved, his mind could be rather cloudy, and his analytical processing may have distortion. A person or an associate has to recognize that timing, healthy communication, and intervention are needed. Otherwise, the man will spend most of his time buried in work as a means of escape and tactical approach, due to fear of confronting his reality and uncertainties. He will also attempt excessive sleep to dilute his feelings of hopelessness.

> Where there is no vision, the people perish: but he that
> keepeth the law, happy is he. (Proverbs 29:18 KJV)

> If the ax is dull and its edge unsharpened, more strength
> is needed, but skill will bring success. (Ecclesiastes
> 10:10 NIV)

Humanity, nature, and animals are codependent. Humanity, animals, and plant life coexist and function in a system of reciprocity. Men and women inhale oxygen and exhale carbon dioxide. Vice versa, plants intake carbon dioxide and excrete oxygen. This harmonious system of survival is an automatic cycle and system of exchange, with a very vital commodity and essential entity. When a person recognizes the importance of certain things in life and its arrangement and sequential priority, he/she will learn to love, cherish, appreciate, and treat the other with value.

> Do not give dogs what is sacred; do not throw your
> pearls to pigs. If you do, they may trample them under
> their feet, and turn and tear you to pieces. (Matthew
> 7:6 NIV)

The major imbalance comes when one of the parties fails to recognize his/her value, and then it is discovered by the exploiter, who is in need of what the other has to offer. If you find yourself at the disadvantageous end of the stick, you will be at the mercy and exploitation of the one who has a selfish motive. Ironically, oftentimes the abuser or oppressor is focused on his/her gain and does not recognize the dehumanizing act of his/her behavior. We have seen many talented individuals in the sports and recreation industry being used to generate billions in revenue yet being paid a small portion. The exploiter feels as if he/she has created you and only recognize your value when you go through the process of "unbecoming" a horse and decide to walk away. The exploiter can be compared to the motive of an individual who is dying of starvation and decides to take food without consent in order to survive. Life and the instinct of survival are at a higher calling or priority than the consequences, which will cause justification to evolve or surface. In our everyday conversation, we can hear and recognize how it is filled with justifiable statements for our toxic actions.

Instead of helping a person who is willing to learn, a selfish individual will condition the one who is ignorant (fails to recognize / is blinded) to his/her gifts and stabilize him/her to function at his/her minimum, while reaping the maximum output.

The Russian psychologist known as Ivan Pavlov is known for his study on classical conditioning. Ivan Pavlov conducted this study by presenting food to a dog while ringing a bell. The sight of food associated with the bell would cause the dog to salivate. Very soon, the bell, which is one of the stimuli, would sound without presenting any food. The dog would begin to salivate every time it hears the sound of a bell. Ivan Pavlov conducted this study in the late nineteenth century and won a Nobel Prize in 1904.

Many of us are exposed to a lucrative system that constantly stimulates our desire to want more, and yet we are never satisfied. We are then exploited and encounter many compromises and accumulate liabilities because of the lack of contentment within our soul, by risking the precious commodities that we already possess. As a child growing up, I have seen two pieces of bones being thrown to multiple dogs in the front yard. The dog that is in possession of a bone drops its bone to chase after the other dog that also has a bone. Not being able to catch its prey, the dog decides to return to retrieve the bone that was dropped, only to realize that it was claimed by another dog. The concept of the greedy dog losing its bone finally made sense like a live film. Something triggered the greed in that animal. Some individuals may praise you for taking risks but will also blame you for making unwise decisions. Let us exercise wisdom in all that we do!

The man who buries his talents and gold in ignorance will lose it to the one who recognizes its value (Matthew 25:29).

Not that I was ever in need, for I have learned how to be content with whatever I have. I know how to live on almost nothing or with everything. I have learned the secret of living in every situation, whether it is with a full stomach or empty, with plenty or little. For I can do everything through Christ, who gives me strength. (Philippians 4:11–13 NLT)

Many trigger mechanisms originate in the realm and concept of our thought pattern. I know several individuals who have confessed to develop and be triggered with hatred for others, simply because they are reminded of negative encounters of the past just by the mere presence of such individual who has nothing to do with the circumstance. How is my heart's condition? Who are the people, what are the circumstances that trigger painful memories? What are the movies, music, conversations that trigger emotional changes or thoughts to execute good or counterproductive behaviors?

How many people have been conditioned and misled by people who appear to be genuine yet in the process have conditioned you to function below standard? Every master feels threatened by a servant who is about to sit on his throne, especially when in a position to prematurely relinquish. How many people have been conditioned to produce the results and expectations of another person than pursuing their own dreams, passion, giftedness, and talents? Are you pursuing a career, job, or school because of someone else? Are you afraid to ask for pay raise or initiate a conversation? Have the fear of disappointing others, false notion of expectations, and lack of self-understanding conditioned you to operate in a dysfunctional way?

As you begin to self-actualize and develop a greater understanding of yourself, your awareness of self-worth and value will likely increase. Don't become disappointed and crippled as you now begin to experience resentment, when you expect celebration. Do not be surprised if instead of receiving an increased measure in pay, you are being told you are overqualified, you are no longer a fit, or there are other greater opportunities. Your measure of growth and self-discovery will be a great threat to those who are specialists in exploitation and operate with fear.

Don't try to settle or pursue less by downgrading your significance; keep soaring instead.

How many of us can willingly take a self-assessment and be transparent in the mirror of integrity? When was the last time we have challenged ourselves, to weed out, uproot, and destroy the roots that have set standards and foundations of failure and low expectations in our lives? Let us start by asking some very intuitive and hard-core face-to-face questions:

What are the bad habits in my life that I have failed to address, confront, or adjust?

What are the habits or practices that I have accepted to be the norm yet unproductive to my goals in life?

What are the hidden secrets in life, heart, and thought process that I am tempted to actualize yet if executed or discovered, could be quite detrimental to myself and others?

What are the thoughts that mostly consume my mind and analytical process?

What are my desires, and what path do I take to pursue or channel these passions?

What are my goals for the next five, ten, fifteen years?

What is my associate or circle of influence?

Have I written out my goals to make them realistic and make plans to execute them?

What are my mental, emotional, physical, spiritual, social, and financial obstacles?

Do I share the same drive, interest, and compatibility with others?

Am I crippled by fear of my history, experiences, or others who may be more advanced?

If the time spent with excessive play, work, and social fun was used to apply concentrated energy and time in my quality self-investment, what would have been the results, success, and condition of my life?

On the other hand, if you are an individual who knows that you have been conditioned, either by uncontrollable circumstances or lack of discipline, unless you change the way you think, you will voluntarily place yourself on a leash in acceptance of your present circumstance.

You will continue to walk around in the circle of wilderness while being exploited and equate motion for progress.

The man who has recognized his value and knows what he wants will condition others to conform to the direction and orientation of his goals. This person, who is the exploiter, will define and explain his vision, goals, and the purpose and role that the horse will play.

The exploiter will make promises and entice you to accept his offer, as though he is doing you a favor. If you willingly accept the role based on lack of knowledge, failure to conduct thorough research, or an unfortunate circumstance, it will be a challenge to blame others for the outcome. The exploiter, irrespective of his motive, will show you the signatures that you signed and will remind you that you were made aware of the agreement at the initial contract.

How many people today know that one of the main psychological methods of leadership and control was conducted through conditioning wild horses?

To highlight with an in-depth sense of approach, below is a caption of a few highlights from the letter in *The Making of a Slave* by Willie Lynch. There is a system of discipline that is being acquired simply by experiments being done on horses. Be patient enough to read and absorb and digest this content.

The Breaking of the Horse Principle

The breaking of the horse principle is a method used to condition a horse from its natural wild state to being tamed and friendly. It has been reasonably believed and concluded that the Willie Lynch letter was delivered as a speech in 1712 on the bank of James River in Virginia. Willie Lynch was a British slave owner living in the West Indies who responded to an invitation to teach slave owners methods of control to keep their rebellious slaves in check and obedient. Lynch started out by explaining his blueprint and emphasized that if used successfully, it will naturally control the slaves for at least three hundred years. The methods implemented included highlighting differences such as size, color, race, age, intelligence, status, attitude, hair texture, gender, and skin tone then magnifying the differences to trigger dysfunction and ongoing conflicts.

The next step would be to use the differences to create fear, distrust, and envy. The slave masters would then distrust the slaves but create an atmosphere for the slaves to trust and depend on the master. The same methods of beating the horse then feeding the horse will create a dependency syndrome.

> Train the female horse whereby she will eat out of your hand, and she will in turn train the infant horse to eat out of your hand, also. When it comes to breaking the uncivilized nigger, use the same process, but vary the degree and step up the pressure, so as to do a complete reversal of the mind. Take the meanest and most restless nigger, strip him of his clothes in front of the remaining male niggers, the female, and the nigger infant, tar and feather him, tie each leg to a different horse faced in opposite directions, set him afire and beat both horses to pull him apart in front of the remaining niggers. The next step is to take a bullwhip and beat the remaining nigger males to the point of death, in front of the female and the infant. Don't kill him, but PUT THE FEAR

OF GOD IN HIM, for he can be useful for future breeding.

By her being left alone, unprotected, with the MALE IMAGE DESTROYED, the ordeal caused her to move from her psychologically dependent state to a frozen, independent state. In this frozen, psychological state of independence, she will raise her MALE and female offspring in reversed roles. For FEAR of the young male's life, she will psychologically train him to be MENTALLY WEAK and DEPENDENT, but PHYSICALLY STRONG. Because she has become psychologically independent, she will train her FEMALE offspring to be psychologically independent. What have you got? You've got the nigger WOMAN OUT FRONT AND THE nigger MAN BEHIND AND SCARED.

Experts also advised that knowledge has the power and possibility to correct this dysfunctional phenomenon, so it's important to shave away the mental history and multiply a state of illusion.

A powerful visionary who can see and make goals beyond your life span can control you for a lifetime. Why does a child sit and doesn't move after being instructed and reprimanded by the parent? How do few slave masters control hundreds of slaves on a plantation? The consequences weighed and instilled perception can either protect or warp the fashion of thinking. Many relationships are filled with dysfunctions and constant warfare because of mental illusions and no scope of solutions. The mind therefore has to be challenged to dream and manifest the authentic revolutionary measures instead of going in search of constant movable, altering, and evasive solutions. This letter, along with knowledge, awareness, and the changes of life, should be able to illuminate our minds, turn on the mental light, and see a greater clarity of the true nature of self—the man in the mirror. (A powerful book to read is *The Mis-Education of the Negro* by Carter G. Woodson.)

We should be able to see possibilities beyond our measure of imperfection. Many individuals are afraid of change, simply because they have been conditioned to remain comfortable in their environment and develop the fear to venture into other areas or avenues that may present opposition. We have never developed the skills and tenacity to overcome adversities. We therefore creep back into our crevices and hideout spots to prevent disappointments or any entities that appear to be of rejection in nature. Companies that have high growth and set new levels of expectations will function out of sync due to this pattern of mindset by the employees. Before long, expenses and liabilities will increase if visionaries fail to identify and understand the strengths and weaknesses of its members.

If you desire to gain better understanding of your gifts and strengths, another highly recommended book is *StrengthsFinder 2.0* by Tom Rath.

Can I look myself in the mirror to conduct a self-assessment with integrity, to let character and honesty prevail? Self-transparency will be able to assess the way that I predominantly function amid challenges. Do I sabotage the quality of the work? Do I develop anger and prolonged hatred for others and authority? Or do I have enough love, respect, and wisdom to recognize that the issues faced are oftentimes misplaced anger and the circumstances are external? Do I recognize that I become less productive if I should absorb and negatively process information to the extent of developing the inclination for revenge?

Whether I function at this maturity level in my relationship or association with others, it is important that I become very honest and admit my internal faults and shortcomings. Otherwise, needed changes become a prolonged or delayed process!

Leadership and Horse Mentality

A horse mentality can evolve when self or someone in leadership has a powerful vision that needs to be developed and executed, yet the operation is stagnant and unable to move forward or give birth because we lack clarity and can't figure out the direction of the vision. There then erupts internal warfare; and followers either scatter, stand still, or team up in opposition. Leadership then finds creative ways to break the followers, while the followers find tactical ways to become evasive. How many relationships fail to lift off the ground, or marriages in turmoil, simply because of constant competition and elevated distrust instead of a unified force?

Habits displayed can become very contagious to others, especially when the tone of leadership is set by such individual. A leader will condition others to develop his temperament. It is therefore necessary to embrace creativity and foster an environment in which people are valued and gifts are provided an outlet with implementation. A leader should not become complacent in his own home. Otherwise, the children will become confused by the double standard of expectations. The children will feel dejected, bearing the burdens of unauthentic productivity, at a level that has never been demonstrated by those they emulate for guidance. Fierce opposition can break and influence individuals to a desensitized state of acceptance. This can cause one to become conformed to traditions and cultural norms and not be able to move past the lens of limitations. A leader or a person who brings about revolutionary changes to a complacent environment is then perceived as a troublemaker who comes to cause major disruptions. Let us establish boundaries and discipline for growth and attainable greatness for the entire body and not operate by chance.

The famous book known as Exodus gives a historical account of the Israelites who were released and freed from slavery out of Egypt. Over one million people inclusive of children, animals, gold, and prized possessions on a journey for redemption and greatness. The story ended with a separation of the adults who all died out in the wilderness, from the young children who inherited the land that was promised! The adults having a toxic mindset would have infiltrated the new generation and affect the cultivation and productivity of a newly established infrastructure. According to Exodus 16 and also Numbers 11, when the Israelites had faced challenges, they then revolted against their leader and said it was better in Egypt. The food was available with different options to choose. God blessed them with manna and instructed them not to store up too many but recommended they should have enough on the sixth day so that they can devote the Sabbath wholeheartedly. Not only did they store up excess, but they also went in search for more on the Sabbath day and complained that they are tired of this filthy food. They even requested seafood and different meat kinds from God. Their ingratitude and lack of trust triggered the anger and rage of God. This is a very poignant time for us to assess the anger and hurts that we may constantly create and not realize that we are damaging the image of God like a child that carries our reputation wherever they go. One of the greatest forms of discouragement occurs with a lack of appreciation. An enslaved mindset will produce low expectations, which is an insult to the Creator of humanity. When we recognize our value and the power of our mind, we will discover that whatever the mind can perceive, we have the capacity and ability to bring it into reality. Our thoughts can extract things of the imaginary and invisible realm and orchestrate and produce it in the physical realm.

In Genesis 19, Lot's family knew that the land was going to be destroyed with explosives, and the wife of Lot was so attached to her history and sentimental values in the land of Sodom to the point where she would rather freeze in death and disobedience as a pillar of salt than to leave the land to go start and embrace a new future. A person who finds it hard to let go, forgive, or give away to others would have to check his/her mental attitude.

It is great wisdom to acquire knowledge and understanding of self by analyzing the content that impacts my mind to cause reluctance and resistance to progress.

Let us analyze the interaction between a person conditioned like a horse and his/her association with the ruler and exploiter.

Fear of Dating and Relationships

In the book of Ruth, Naomi had lost her two sons and decided to return to Bethlehem. Ruth, the widow and daughter-in-law, decided to return with Naomi regardless of differences in age, ethnicity, religion, and the prejudice that she will inevitably encounter. It wasn't long before Ruth met and married a highly reputable and wealthy gentleman. There were many ladies and people in the community who spoke about Ruth, before she fully established her own uniqueness. It is highly crucial and imperative that we reach a place of self-acceptance before we strive to accomplish acceptance by others.

> *Lacking self-understanding will always have an unquenchable desire to achieve fulfillment through the lens or actions of others, which can never guarantee or give success or fulfillment.*

If not properly dealt with by actualizing self, we will soon find ourselves blaming others for our own pain and miseries. We will also become blinded and hurt by the many different trigger mechanisms to our pain and make others the object of our problems. Others will be the issues, not because they contribute to the impacting factors, but because we have never learned the skills of freeing self from victimhood mentality and rising above the self-allowable and inflicting hurts.

> *Do not wait until you are sick, depressed, and highly dysfunctional before admitting that you are the only one who can set the temperament for your joy and happiness.*

There is a famous Jamaican hero and Baptist preacher known as Sam Sharpe (died May 23, 1832) who is well known for his statement "I would rather die upon yonders gallows than live my life in slavery."

Emancipate yourself from mental slavery

None but ourselves can free our minds. (Bob Marley)

We need to also assess ourselves by internally inquiring if the prolonged pain is due to the attention that I desire to achieve from others. Can this be an attracting bait to feed into my crave for comfort from others? Could this be an art of manipulation? Do I get into a state of anger, rage, resentment, and feelings of rejection when I cannot get the attention from others that I desire? Do I send signals of hurt so that others can feel guilty for not fulfilling and soothing my social and emotional pain? Do I show these signs by constantly replaying and talking about the issues that hurt instead of my plans to excel? Am I consumed with thoughts of failures, instead of working toward my short-term and long-term goals? The ultimate question should be, why do I desire and place so much demand on the support from others than to attain through self-independence?

Who is more guilty, the one who cannot give or the self who fails to produce?

The angel had to take Lot out of the land by force. The horse mentality will allow Ruth to come all the way from Moab to Bethlehem and marry Boaz, while you stand there waiting for the perfect moment then get upset and make comments like "They don't even know each other that well," "She just came in the church or community," or "She came just to find a husband."

Let us break forth from the horse-pattern mindset. The horse will tell you, "You can't make it. I have tried it before." The horse is conditioned and can't see past its environment of limitation. Do not be upset or feel discriminated against if the horse judges your capabilities by its limited views. The horse becomes dependent on the hands that feed it. You can't blame the horse. It is just the way of the horse; the horse is conditioned.

The Horse-Syndrome Scenarios

Scenario 1

You are married but jobless; your husband is the breadwinner. He might be physically and verbally abusive. You wish you could walk away but fear becoming homeless and in a worse predicament; you can't just walk away. You have to stand still. It's just the way of the horse! The horse recognizes the issues but left bewildered, left confused, and can't seem to find the solution. Don't be mad at the horse; it's just the way of the horse. You will need a long-term vision for your life. You will need to constantly network and not isolate.

Esther 4:14 shows that when the odds were against Mordecai, he reached out to his cousin Esther, whom he had taken care of like he was her uncle. Esther had made it to the king's palace and almost forgot that she was strategically placed to help others. Mordecai challenged her not to act like she was exempted from the pain and suffering that others are experiencing. It may be me today, but tomorrow the pendulum may just swing in your direction. Esther then became a beacon of hope and light. God will send people to rescue you. Don't give up! Seek help because closed mouths do not get fed!

Scenario 2

You want a promotion on the job. You are close to getting fired. The supervisor uses it against you; it's either you compromise your value or you become a jobless single mother with kids to feed and no way to pay your rent. Don't blame the horse. It's just the way of the horse. He is conditioned by uncontrollable circumstances. You conquer the horse syndrome by refusing to compromise your values and constantly growing and excelling with the rapid changes of life. You have to break the cycle by constant growth and remain relevant! Fight for what is right even when it seems like there is no other alternative. God is my ever-present help in times of trouble (Psalm 46).

In Luke 8:43–48, there was a woman who had been bleeding for twelve years; and society kept her bound because of stigmas, cultural laws, policies, and traditions. How many people know that slavery is also a law? But the woman said, "Enough is enough. If I could but touch the hem of His garment!" Don't blame her; she had a condition that doctors couldn't help. It's just the way of the horse. I have to break my condition; no one else will. It doesn't matter who know my story or publicly scrutinize me. My starting point and self-propelling change is the removal of stumbling blocks and a revolutionary breakthrough for others in the same line.

Scenario 3

Papa is a drunkard. Papa has a job, and he works very hard. Papa spends his money to feed his addiction. He oftentimes turns to his unemployed wife and asks for money. She gives him money, although she is not working. She is well aware that she enables his addiction and condition. She will get upset if you tell her the obvious. She recognizes that the only time peace will be around the young children and in the home is when Papa is not in his right mind. Don't be mad at the wife; it's just the way of the horse. She is conditioned and feels hopeless, helpless, and despondent. The same mouths and voices that blame the horse for the condition will be the same mouths that gossip and wonder why you walk away from someone in need and struggling with addiction. No one will fully understand your struggles of being held back, hindered progress after lifelong sacrifices, forfeited opportunities, prayers, tears, and intervention. You overcome this situation by recognizing early signs, confessing that you do not have the power to change someone, and seeking professional help from reliable sources.

In Luke 5:17–26, a crippled man was transported on his bed to a house in order to get healing from his condition. The house was filled with many individuals, which prevented him from gaining access. The man was then brought upon the rooftop and let down through a self-made hole while being on his bed in the midst of Jesus. He received his healing, and still many individuals were upset.

You may not be able to get help on your own. The needed help may not come the conventional way. But you have to come to grips with reality and say enough is enough. Whatever it takes, however long the process may be, today is the day of start and change. Unbecoming a horse may not be easy, but living in ignorance and limitation is more costly.

CHAPTER 5
A SERPENT'S INVITATION
(Power of Contentment)

Everyone thinks he/she is loyal until the devil invites him/
her (to the negotiation table) underneath the fruit tree.

—M. Reid

Usually if someone would call you a snake, it may not be a compliment. But snakes seem to know the depths of your hearts and the language of your emotions. They can steal your breath away and seemingly understand and connect with your inner thoughts. However, the motive of the human nature can be rather illusive and scary even to the one who has come to grips with his personality, motive, and capability. Our thoughts and imaginations will challenge and expose the double standards, hypocrisy, and dark alleyways of our mental faculty. Oftentimes, this detrimental trait can be like an inseparable cancer we have accepted as though it is a natural embedded part of our lives. We confess and profess things like "That's just the way I am," which can be interpreted as "I do not know how to change or overcome this condition." So let us take this journey of inner self and deep soul discovery rather slowly. This calls for a journey of change that will take consistency and formulating discipline to become the person that we ought to be.

There was a study conducted on the boa snake by using dead rats implanted with artificial hearts. Inside the chest of the rats were placed two small water-filled bladders used to monitor the squeeze of the boa snake. The heartbeat would be simulated with variation, which reveals that the snakes would squeeze the rats tighter according to feeling or sensing the pulse of the heartbeats. Whenever the pulse was switched to the off position, the snakes would release its grab or coil.

The boa snake feels your heartbeat and is sensitive to your pulse. You cannot apply logic, cover up, or pretend to be dead in an attempt to deceive the serpent. If you seem to understand, attempt to articulate, or act oblivious, the devil acts on your lack of faith and doubts like a dog that smells your fear. It doesn't matter how much you recite or declare, "I am not scared"; your heart and level of faith that is a potent weapon will determine the truth. The men who tried the work of an exorcist were beaten and attacked brutally after the evil spirit answered and said, "Jesus I know, and Paul I know; but who are ye?" (Acts 19:15).

The content in this chapter will be focused on three categories: relationship, leadership, and understanding of self. The principles and applied understanding can save and deliver us from a lot of heartaches, especially encountering the spirit or nature of a snake!

Let us discuss briefly the nature and character trait of a serpent and then delve into recognizing the snakes and major compromises in our lives.

> Now the serpent was more crafty than any of the wild animals the LORD God had made. He said to the woman, "Did God really say, 'You must not eat from any tree in the garden'?" (Genesis 3:1 NIV)

> Behold, I send you out as sheep in the midst of wolves. Therefore be wise as serpents and harmless as doves. (Matthew 10:16 NKJV)

Without a doubt, the serpent is one of the wisest creatures on the face of the earth. Like a parent would warn and implore a child to be very careful is the resounding warning given by God to His children. Matthew 10:16 gives a very interpersonal concept of the serpent by imploring us to take on its attribute of wisdom, yet ascribed being "harmless" to the doves. A simple implication will then convey to us that though the serpent is considered wise, you may not need to discover by experience that it is harmful!

Instead of exposing the whole family and different species of snakes, our main focus will be upon the python, boa, and paradise flying snakes.

Python snakes are constrictors, which actually mean that they will wrap their bodies around their prey and squeeze them until they are breathless to the point of death. Python snakes are hunters that ambush and do not produce venoms. A python therefore lacks the capability of poisoning its prey. A python will have to get *up close* and *personal* to entrap you. Once the heartbeat of the prey stops, the python then swallows that which it has just managed to suffocate. The python snake understands the *land* and heartbeat of its prey and knows when the opponent is fully subdued in ground battle. The python knows when your heart stops beating. The python knows when your pulse disappears. The python knows when you are powerless and no longer pose a threat against it.

Paradise flying snakes can glide airborne at distances up to 350 feet (106.68 meters). They stretch their body in a flattened strip, launch from trees, and glide across the *air* in a wavelike motion. Paradise flying snakes glide at speeds between 26 and 33 feet per second. Videos capturing this mystic operation reveal that the head of the serpent remains stable, which shows balance and control when in flight. The paradise flying snake also constricts its prey and is mildly venomous. It observes its prey then glides unpredictably and lands undetected, blending within the surroundings of its prey. The snake does not rely on sounds but senses your presence through vibration. You cannot hide behind barriers and think that you have outsmarted the snake. The snake will entrap you with illusion and thrill you with suspense if you stand long enough to become distracted by its ingenuity.

Boa snakes have the attribute of the pythons as constrictors. But the boa is also familiar with *water* and possesses swift and excellent swimming skills. The boa is keen to its surroundings and camouflages with the underwater background especially from predators such as crocodiles.

The Misrepresentation of Mankind/ Relationship Distortion

God has given mankind dominion over the fish of the sea, birds of the air, and every living thing that moves on the face of the earth. Humanity has been entrusted with such an awesome responsibility to take full control of these three domains (Genesis 1:26–28). There is a spiritual operation by the serpent in all three dimensions. The python has mastered the land, the boa has mastered the land and sea, and the paradise snake glides through the air.

The serpent is the master of distortion. It moves upon the *land* like the flow of water, it swims through the *water* creating waves of illusion, and it flows through the *air* in a slithering magical motion. You never want this dazzling movement like zebra stripes moving through your thought process. Not only will such a man become distorted in his mind and become self-distraught, but such a man will replicate the wave by destroying others.

Man has lost his ability to control his home and wants to be entrusted with the world. A man who is out of control with self will inevitably lead others to their ruin and demise. We should lead effectively by exemplary measures that others will emulate in a self-propelled manner. We have failed to subdue self, but we want to subdue others and control our spouses and children.

It was underneath the fruit tree, around the negotiation table, where the serpent twisted the mindset of Eve. Subsequently, Eve created a ripple effect and twisted the mindset of Adam. This is one of the first signs of infidelity against God, defying the vow and covenant. Humanity then justified his actions and blamed each other.

A man who has made a vow and married a woman then commits infidelity with another woman evidently has some form of rationale and justification to counteract his initial vow and commitment. The woman, on the other hand, who has joined as a cheater has encountered and walked in the web and tricks of the serpent. This woman believes that she has the power to transform his heart to a state of loyalty, not realizing that the same rationale that was used against his initial vow was defied to the lowest state. Just like Adam in the garden, when his back is against the wall, the man will turn against you like a swine and tell God, "It is that woman that you gave to me."

Never build a permanent bridge on a temporary column, on a property that was purchased by another.

When God destroys the serpent's head, and his magical wave ends, you will realize that you are at the same location, and the only thing that was in motion was your thoughts. Do not get angry; do not become stagnant. God has just saved you and mobilized you with the potential to make progress.

Ladies, listen up!

One of the most common mistakes to be made by women is to be pressured into a sexual encounter to prove your love. The woman in the process compromises her standards in an effort to guarantee a commitment. Don't use your body to pay for your future. Look closely— where there is curiosity and compromise, there is a snake! What you didn't realize is that you are obliging yourself into a contract based on your needed sense of security, but the man never disclosed his full intentions. He just told you to sign the dotted lines like a professional salesman. You are left feeling like another opportunity will never present itself. The first sign of distrust is to be put into a position where the man does not cherish your highest dignified status. The snake will cause you to touch or surrender that which is forbidden. The snake tells you what you want to hear ahead of your pattern of thoughts, causing you to rebut your own fundamental principles. The snake gets your attention with enticing information. The snake casts doubts on your confidence and applies pressure if you need time to think. It clouds your mind with distracting elements by suffocating you with ultimatums. Before you know it, you are wrapped in its distorted coils of maze and tricks. Now if you look at the fruit tree and remove your product from a high standard and lower it so that the man can have a bite and confirm that it is good to taste, don't run and hide when problems arrive. Didn't you know that if he marries you, he will be insured for life and guaranteed full coverage and access plan?

But this is what happens when the man doesn't want the fruit tree, but you bribe him with a bite of the fruit. Yes, he will taste it, but that's not the direction I am heading. The taster or recipient is like a man going grocery shopping. He will open the package, test the product, and put it back on the shelf like damaged goods. The same shopper then has the audacity to pick up a sealed unopened package and then walk to the cash register at the marriage altar. You are then left in a state of shock and wonder how he married someone else who is less presidential in status than you. Simple! Your body is not for food samplers or exotic wine tasters to determine if you belong on the market or should be returned to the shelf. Snake operation! He chose a sealed product not because of appearance. He was measuring if he could trust your stability and your likelihood of vulnerability. A man needs assurance against his own insecurities.

There are many distractions that insinuate and stimulate the sensory emotions of humanity. If the desires are not being met, it creates a conflict that parallels with justification. If there is lack of communication, anger, frustration, and lack of a strong foundation of self-control and integrity, there exists a recipe for disaster. In the waiting are explosive quarrels and a battle exchange of justifications, highlighting the limitations of each other.

Many individuals are familiar with the story of King David who got up from his bed and took a walk onto the roof of his palace. His eyes then became fixated on a beautiful woman who was bathing. David inquired by sending someone to fish for information, only to find out that she was Bathsheba, the wife of Uriah. David used his authority to send for her, and subsequently she revealed to David that she was pregnant (2 Samuel 11).

David was very familiar with Uriah who was one of his main military leaders. David sent Uriah home in an attempt to cover up the pregnancy. Uriah refused to go home to engage in intimacy with his wife because all the other soldiers were at war, and as a leader, he wanted to lead by example. David then sent him to the front line on the battlefield so that Uriah lost his life! Snake in the midst!

It's understandable that refusing the demands of a king can be detrimental. However, when a man is away at war fighting to take care of his family, he wants to know that he is safeguarded against other snakes who may call his spouse over to the fruit tree. He wants to know that curiosity or subtle speech will not lead to an opened container on the shelf. A person should not try to ascertain, assess, or discover her value after feelings of neglect and abuse by the hands of the enemy, like a shopper feeling up fruits on a market stand. Will you fall for a man of authority or with great influential pressure? A man knows that storms will come, and if you are afraid to get wet, you will run to the hissing sounds of the serpent calling you for comfort and shelter underneath the fruit tree. When you are feeling hurt and vulnerable, wait until the rain stops because the sun will begin to shine again. The snake does not use venom, so it appears nonthreatening. If you are feeling up close and personal, the serpent has started to warm you up in its coils. Danger zone, people! Snake!

According to Luke chapter 4, the devil tried the same old tricks on Jesus that he tried in the Garden of Eden. The devil tempted Jesus to turn stones into bread, like when Eve saw that the fruit was good (lust of the flesh), then tempted Jesus with the splendor of the world if Jesus worships him, like looking at the fruit (lust of the eyes), and challenged Jesus to jump off the pinnacle to prove himself, like Eve with the fruit that would make her wise (pride of life).

David fell for the same tricks when he *saw* Bathsheba, *desired* her, and used his *authority* with a sense of pride and deep arrogance. If you resist the enemy of temptation, eventually it will flee. There are so many leaders in authority who have executed this type of snake operation and victimized others with great deception of promises.

We are too comfortable sitting under the tree of life while trying to nurture and sustain it with a ground that is cursed. God blesses you from the fruit tree with a spouse. But then you want to get rid of her because you are tempted with a fruit from another tree called the secretary on your job. You have made the secretary several promises of prestige and promotions. But you can't seem to get past God, so frustration intensifies, and you treat your wife unkindly. On the other hand, some women are ashamed of their spouses because he is not like the supervisor on the job. You are ashamed to even invite your husband to a party sponsored by your company. The snake is whispering! God is warning us that these inner thoughts are subtle communication by the enemy in its camouflage.

When a man receives intimacy without hesitation, it's registered in the mental faculty as a high level of acceptance and appreciation. The man begins to think clearly. When confronted with challenges and struggles, the man now has no basis to blame or any recourse to take as a path of justification for future acts of temptation to be committed. The man is then forced to acknowledge and embrace accountability and change.

One of the main challenges faced during the early stages of a relationship is that a woman will overdose her husband with love to the point where he doesn't want to go to work. But as time progresses, she no longer overdoses him; instead, she gives him intimacy like seasonal cough drops. He feels sick and has no desires to rush home anymore.

If you should ever take a child to a candy store and he asks for the candy in the red wrapper, but you purchase a different-color candy, that child will have a temper tantrum. If a man asks for intimacy, and he is denied, he becomes like a child that you have betrayed by giving him a different-color candy. The temper tantrum boils within, even with a smile on his face. Everything that goes wrong, he will blame and justify on rejection. A man needs to be disciplined, and a woman needs to be understanding!

> Now for the matters you wrote about: "It is good for a man not to have sexual relations with a woman." But since sexual immorality is occurring, each man should have sexual relations with his own wife, and each woman with her own husband. The husband should fulfill his marital duty to his wife, and likewise the wife to her husband. The wife does not have authority over her own body but yields it to her husband. In the same way, the husband does not have authority over his own body but yields it to his wife. Do not deprive each other except perhaps by mutual consent and for a time, so that you may devote yourselves to prayer. Then come together again so that Satan will not tempt you because of your lack of self-control. I say this as a concession, not as a command. (1 Corinthians 7:1–6 NIV)

Well, did Jesus say! In any aspect of life, if an individual is not willing to abide by the precepts of God, such individual will undoubtedly, inevitably, absolutely not abide by the precepts of your beauty. Please do not negotiate and wonder if Jesus said by rationalizing if this man/woman will walk out of your life. That's the perfect time to let him/her go before he walks you down the aisle. He/she is on a glamorous road en route to the gates of perdition. Let that partner know that's the perfect time to travel alone.

As you look in the mirror, you will come to grips with the fact that your beauty that God gave you is not only changing, but also fading. If a man cannot love you for your heartbeat, he will squeeze and suffocate you not recognizing his inability to preserve it. The serpent has no ears; it relies on airwaves. The serpent doesn't listen! When you think the serpent has absorbed the content of your communication, the serpent was attentive to its next motive, which hopefully you did not misinterpret as his undivided attention toward you. Otherwise, you flatter yourself like a broken-winged butterfly, in deception believing the serpent was a good listener. The devil is a liar! The serpent wears a pleasant smile, which should not be mistaken for a charm. It's just the facial infrastructure of God's design, like a movie put on pause. If you think the snake is consistent, we must admit that it is conniving and wise, but let us not be the one to be consistent in stupidity. We will then move into the future with pain in our hearts and look back at the regrettable past and wonder, *How did I walk through that dark alleyway of life?*

One person once said that a relationship is like doing algebra; you look at your "X" and wonder "Y."

The Double-Standard Cheater (The Day the Devil Calls You Underneath the Fruit Tree)

The man who cheats on his spouse (and vice versa) with another woman can still uphold fundamental values, which could cause him to be biased against the one whom he is cheating and conspired with. When Nathan confronted David about his vicious act with Bathsheba and Uriah in a parable, David, unknowing that it was in reference to him, said, "That man deserves to die." This exposed his double standards.

The average man "cheater" will generally ask himself if he can truly trust a woman who has compromised herself to join with him in an affair, which brings to question her morals and standards of integrity.

A man will sleep with many prostitutes and desires none to be his wife.

In a similar fashion, though the man enjoys the pleasures of the affair, he still upholds his value in accepting a foundation built on trust. Obviously, the woman who has colluded in such conspiracy will likely not be on his long-term radar. Such a man will be plagued with the thought of being able to trust such a woman to participate in his future endeavors and being able to build a firm foundation on the basis of trust. Even if he chooses to separate from his wife, can the coconspirator be elevated from "Miss Runner-up" (second place) to the pedestal of the new queen in town sitting beside him on the throne?

When and if the clock does turn, and the man decides to execute his chances, the man will constantly replay at the forefront of his mind if he will be susceptible to become substituted. Though the man is more of the perpetrator, ironically a man will likely project unto others the way in which he views his suspicious self. The man will be plagued with the reality of being unable to maintain the financial and economic foundation of the bridge he has built. His fear will probe his mind to wonder if someone else enters the zone with higher glamour, will the woman yield to more opportunity with disloyalty like she did with him in secrecy? Will this woman return to the negotiation table and be pulled away by the dangling fruit on the tree? Will she empower herself to rise above his authority? The man has now become worried of his own scope of reality and high probability as he looks in the mirror to confront his self. Will the woman burn the bridge that was built on temporary columns of secrecy, with both parties having the blueprint of hidden details? Will she beat him at his own game by moving the chess pieces in the direction that he least expected with her pretentious trust? Will this man feel vulnerable when he realized that he does not control the temperament nor own her happiness? What desperate measures will he take when he realized that he initially departed from his vows when he attributed his state of happiness to the responsibility of his wife? Now, he has come to grips with reality, to openly and internally confess that his new elevated queen is in a state of despondence, and he lacks the capability to pour into her reservoir of void and emptiness. Will this woman flee and hold the man guilty and responsible for his incapability and inability to fulfill her in totality, like he did with his wife? What vengeance will erupt when he discovers that walking across the ocean filled with sharks or to the end of the world and back does not guarantee her satisfaction?

If such a man has low self-esteem issues or challenges that cause him to feel broken and unattractive, he will desperately seek other measures of control in order to maintain his boundaries of security and comfort. Will this man replay the constant plague of her voice in his head, like Delilah saying, "Samson, do you love me? If you truly love me, you would tell me your secret." Will this man, knowing that his secret has been told and used against him, react like Samson tying three hundred foxes by the tail together in pairs and attaching a bottle torch, setting them in the open field to destroy everything in their path (Judges 15:4)? If such a man lacks the financial capability to satisfy his ego of supply and greater demand of his love and need, such a man becomes even more dangerous. He will reduce the woman to lower significance and lessen her perception of self-value so that she develops the concept of being at a lower threshold of status quo.

This is why in life, so many individuals wonder why a woman with so much brilliance and potential would underwrite her self-value and sit on a clearance shelf of damaged goods.

If a dangerous man runs into a confident woman, he may resort to physical domestic violence, a territory and domain where he can explore his likelihood of greater strength and master with dominance. Snake!

The plan of the serpent is to suffocate and squeeze the value out of your life. The longer you stay, the more distorted your view and outward look on life. The serpent will squeeze your heartbeat to the point in which you are unable to decipher with wisdom. You will therefore self-negotiate and justify your every move as a source of survival and image protector, because you cannot see any possible way out of the grip of the serpent. People around you will warn you, and you will wonder about your inability to see what they perceive. You will begin to compromise your value by focusing on the positive perspective of the fruit from the forbidden tree, to convince yourself that the man is good, as a form of coping mechanism. The serpent will then use gossiping lips to distance you through your pain in order to cut off the life support of the wrestlers on the ringside whom you can touch to jump in the ring and join in your fight.

If you find yourself at this place today, suicide is never the solution. Distancing yourself from the ones who love and care is heading in the wrong direction. Convincing self that you are not loved is just an evasive tactic to flee from confronting the truth and reality of wrapping yourself in the arms of the enemy. At this point, you need to look deep into your soul and reach out for strength from above. You could be an infidel or atheist; you need to pray like you have never prayed before. The devil will bruise the heel of Jesus, but the Word declares that Jesus will crush his head. Your only solution is to reach out for help and wisdom from above. Help sometimes comes through the ones you desire the least to share your story. Oftentimes, individuals know your story, and it only appeared to be a secret due to your blind side. But those who were sounding the alarm in your oblivious and blinded state are the ones who could assist in the process of mending the broken pieces. Some women have taken drastic and extremely desperate measures like reaching out to the wife and apologizing for the interruption. This statement is in no way instigating this path. Guilt has forced people to acknowledge the damage done that they themselves would never appreciate having to experience. However, how much do your life and soul worth?

Will you become like a sheep walking to the slaughter and discovering the devil is the butcher?

Paradise Snake—Distortion

Man was created with faith to command and have authority and dominion over elements of the air. We have the authority to command the things that are not as though they are. Let the weak say I am strong. Let the sick say that I am healed. Let the poor say that I am rich. By faith, we have the ability to speak life into the atmosphere. This is why Jesus said, "Lazarus is not dead. He is just asleep." Lazarus came forth, and Lazarus was resurrected. To defeat the enemy of the air, we cannot dwell in the physical dimension only because this victory is claimed oftentimes through a realm that does not enter through the visibility of the eye gate. Natural perception or total reliance on your understanding will essentially lead to a field of deception.

The enemy does not rely on his natural vision to detect your vulnerability, so although we manage to deceive others that are on our team, the paradise serpent spots its prey several hundred feet away and will land on the tree branches undetected. Man is professional at hiding secrets from one another and has no fear for the Holy Spirit in his heart. That's why man will forget that the Holy Spirit dwells within; and man will travel to the prostitutes, bars, and drug houses and engage in forbidden activities. Man is more fearful of the animal in the sea than the Creator who places breath in his lungs. Man will refuse to praise God with the breath in his lungs but does not hesitate to curse out his neighbor or waste it in anger and exhaustion. There is no other way to defeat the enemy but to submit yourself in total obedience to the Word of God.

How can we survive this journey of life and never discover what God has ordained over our lives? We treat God in contempt and run away from Him more than we tame and wrap up with the snake. We are so convinced that we have the ability to tame the snake as a pet. We walk around with it on our shoulders and our necks. The devil, who is symbolic as a serpent, is not one to live a life with comfortability, and we should not attempt to tame it as though we can become friends.

Do not invite a serial killer to live in your house and expect him to protect you while you sleep.

The serpent spirit knows the pulse of your faith and the heartbeat of your belief. The serpent knows when it wraps you and suffocates you with doubts. The python will stifle you with frustration and depression, causing your spirit man to engage in constant carnal warfare.

The boa snake is familiar not only with land, but also with water. The boa snake knows how to disguise itself from predators by camouflaging with identical rocks or reefs. This shows a heightened awareness of self, the mindset of its predators, and what the predators may be thinking. The boa snake, just like any other living creature, will hide to protect itself or hide to launch an attack. This means that such creature is already measuring the capabilities of the opposing forces or threats. Man can hardly swim for a few minutes without lacking the ability to breathe underwater, much less control rebellious entities that do not need to fight to conquer the sea domain. Man will naturally be gripped and paralyzed with fear against any entity that sounds or appears to be abnormal. Man has forgotten his assignment and responsibility. Though pretending to be confident in his appearance, the enemies of his soul make him a laughingstock, because like a dog could smell fear, the serpent knows a man's faithless dysfunction. The serpent will possess man like it did with the swine and run them over the cliff to drown in the sea and ocean of his problems (see Matthew 8:28–34). Incredibly, the paradise snake has a combination of these capabilities! Not only does it attack by land and physical battle, but it inflicts constant fear with mere thoughts and possibilities like a hawk's sudden appearance in the sky.

Leadership Distortion

If I should lead on the basis of being liked, my foundation of leadership would be in trouble by the fluctuating love displayed by others. A leader ought to constantly wear at the front of his mind that I am here to lead, not to be liked! By no means is this advocating or rendering the inclination that anyone in leadership should govern himself or lead by displaying a negative attitude. There is absolutely no room for justification or condoning such act. Being loved is the essential nature of survival and the cohesiveness needed for a successful life. There comes a problem when the operation of leadership is impeded upon by the expectation of love anticipated from everyone. The crave or intense desire for love, affection, validation, and affirmation can damage the self-esteem and cripple the mental fortitude and function of a leader. The leader will then develop the propensity to engage in a battle of control and occasionally revenge. The leader will usurp his authority as a tool to receive the desired love or punish those who refuse to exhibit such love. If the opposing party or force would discover this void within the leader, they can manipulate and utilize it as a tool to sabotage or derail his concentrated force of focus and direction. A leader can definitely misinterpret an emotionally distressed individual, having misguided and misplaced anger, and perceive it as anger streamlined and directed as personal attack. A leader should develop the ability to suspend judgment and seek to understand and discover blind spots in self or others. A leader should never take ownership of individuals' problems, even if directed and launched against such leader. A leader should therefore be patient with self, be transparent to others, and accept the reality while growing earnestly and proactively in the role of his position. A leader will have to tactfully use wisdom and develop relationships while relying on the strength and expertise of others. Such leader will have to interview and assess himself and search for vulnerable areas and accept the reality as a starting point toward positive growth and change. A leader should never conclude in his heart that he should be better than others in every area of supervision. When faced with the hard-core reality of such contradictory assumption, the insecure leader will then search for ways to reduce the significance of others in order to elevate himself to a higher status.

Do nothing out of selfish ambition or vain conceit. Rather, in humility value others above yourselves. (Philippians 2:3 NIV)

A leader has to remind himself daily that he is there to serve in the best interest of the purpose and core values, not of himself. Jesus expressed this in the holy sacrament known as washing of the saints' feet, a job that was not for dignified individuals. A leader should always find ways to validate, affirm, support, and reassure, reinforcing in his memory his position of servitude. Otherwise, the unfulfilled self will derail the purpose by starving the process of others with streamlined distractions. A leader who instills positivity will reinforce confidence in others. Those who are being led will work willingly from the heart and not just use a lackadaisical approach to exist impatiently for the workday to be over. Such individuals (workers) will anxiously be in attendance with a sense of purpose and belonging. A leader should readily understand and accept that the emotional turmoil, frustration, and likes by others are likely to fluctuate. A leader therefore should not react and try to address every conflict with immediacy. Your silence can be most profound within a moment. It gives others time to self assess and not to justify their reaction or action by the leader's temperament. Self-initiated change can be a powerful growth factor influenced and imparted to those that you lead, especially when others independently recognize their error simply because of a positive display of attitude demonstrated by the leader. Your silence can be a better demand for a sincere motive and unquestionable apology.

Getting rid of jealousy and competition will foster a very healthy environment. Whatsoever things your hand findeth to do, do as worship unto the Lord. Keeping this at the forefront of your mind and applying in a practical way will keep the vessel of your heart clean and pure. A leader should occasionally step back and enjoy when others shine.

Every leader within his own right should recognize that whatever you do is bringing glory and adoration as true worship unto God. I do not have to be jealous or envious or sabotage the work of others. Such actions and attitude are therefore sabotaging and hijacking the blessings that belong and should be bestowed unto God. When Daniel was praying, the spirit of the air hijacked his prayer, and the principle of faith touching heaven was interrupted (Daniel 10:13).

Have you ever watched a wrestling match, and the person in the ring is trying to summon help from his partner outside the ring, but his partner cannot enter the ring until he is being touched? But once that connection is made, it gets really dangerous when your best fighter enters the ring and destroys the opponent. Even the spectators start to punch the air as though they are involved in the fight. So it is if I fail to recognize that we are partners on the same team engaged in a battle against the enemy. If I should hijack my brothers and sisters with jealousy, I sabotage their gifts and the request petitioned to God. I dishonor God, and doing so inevitably defeats myself and the purpose of the team. Desiring or demanding the glory is an attack launched against God.

As was previously mentioned, the serpent uses air and sound waves to detect the presence of other entities. You can't pretend like you are not there. You can't rely on empty spoken words without faith. The military across the world uses high-pitched vibration and frequency waves to distort the mind of the enemy to bring them into confession and submission. The paradise snake is very keen with this realm of communication and frequency waves.

Cain became jealous of his brother Abel. He hated his brother with a passion. Someone once asked, "How long did Cain hate his brother Abel?" Someone said as long as he was "able." According to the Scripture, we are desperately wicked; if we claim we love God and hate our brothers, we are murderers. This is how dangerous it is to keep malice and jealousy in our hearts. We have to admit that the seeds of jealousy and envy can enter through our emotional gates of hurts, pains, bitterness, and favoritism experienced against us, oftentimes deeply rooted from childhood. The hatred or love that is projected is based on the warping distortion in the mind. Let us reinforce this concept in our minds, take it to God daily, and admit and confess that we all have the inclination. We have to admit that it takes more than my natural love and limitation to overcome this force and stumbling block in my heart. While I am knocked down in the wrestling ring, and my opponent is sitting on me, I can stretch my hands to my source of help, validate others, love others, love self, forgive my enemies, set myself free, and more importantly know that God loves me, and endeavor to live by His commands.

> "Love the Lord your God with all your heart and with all your soul and with all your mind and with all your strength." The second is this: "Love your neighbor as yourself." There is no commandment greater than these. (Mark 12:30–31 NIV)

Procrastination through Distraction and Delayed Response

First Kings 13 gives a powerful illustration of a man of God who was sent on a mission and instructed by God not to stop for food or drink or travel the way that he came. But he was caught off guard by a man who told him that "I am a prophet too." The man of God decided to go with the prophet to feast. After departing from the home of the prophet, the man of God was killed by a lion. People passed by and observed his body, while the lion and the donkey stood beside him.

Indecisiveness and no decision can be as detrimental as a wrong decision. Our vision and conviction can be impeded upon when we relinquish and overturn our trust to those who are also in authority or close association. A leader should denounce and refuse to apply thoughts to distracted elements. There are times you may be traveling or driving, and time is of the essence. You are being caught off guard by congestion, but once the roadway opens up, you become focused and refuse to allow any distraction to further delay your pathway of travel.

In your mental faculty, you have important things lodged. Perhaps you may also be tired or stressed and cannot bear the burden of any additional stress factors. So you push and filter out all unnecessary and unproductive thoughts. Even if someone offended you, there is no time to stop and address the situation. But there is a voice that surfaces in your mind, which says, "Do not let that person escape your vengeance." Snake! A mature leader should recognize the voice of the enemy. To yield to the coil of the enemy is to drown out the voice that says, "Keep going and do not return." Do not deceive yourself into believing that God will take care of your compromising and disobedient situation.

A soft answer turns away wrath. Your positive attitude will be a teaching tool for transformation. But instead, oftentimes what do we do? We reschedule and delay our response. We place it on the calendar at the top of our to-do list. We prioritize and let God know that we got this one. We listen to our pride and ego; we tell God, "I don't want to hear it. I will handle it myself and in my way. I will call you in the wrestling ring to clean up the mess in the event that my ego allows me to confess that I am defeated or in need of help."

This is a major relationship and leadership error, in which we delay our negative responses based on the "importance" of our current agenda. But once our interest on the agenda is cleared up, we tend to abuse God's time in a revengeful manner to do what we want and however we feel. God tells us to keep going and to not return to that place to feast on bread of anger and drink water of wasting valuable and toxic time. But we take our chances, not realizing that we have escaped so many lions and the state of death by the mercies of God.

We ride our donkeys back to these old places of self-logic and think a patient ride will be a safe destination.

Another common error to be experienced by a leader is to feel unappreciated. A powerful illustration is the parable depicted in Matthew 25:14–30 entailing three servants who were given bags of silver to invest. The first was given five bags, the second two bags, and the third one bag. Each servant invested and doubled their return, except the third individual who buried the one bag. The master inquired of the servant why the bag was buried and not invested or simply placed in the bank. The servant responded by telling the master that he is usually harsh and reaps where he doesn't plant and that he was also fearful to lose the master's silver.

If a man has devoted himself to a task and felt as though he has not received his fair reward according to the value he has asserted unto himself, such a man will find ways to take by force and justify his actions by the victimized feelings of abuse. A selfish attitude will cause such man to bury his talent, because he feels as though his investment will give a major portion of returns that he himself will never gain any benefits. Such a man sees the task and those in authority as his enemy and that they do not deserve his excellence. Anything outside his basic and average standard of operation is doing the business a favor. Such a leader is inclined to listen to the voice of bribery and be inclined to join in forces of sabotage, even discreetly without disclosing motives to other entities, that he has secretly collaborated in his heart in joint force. Such leader will secretly execute the damage along with others who are rebellious in nature without disclosing his intentions in order to cover and protect his reputation. He just flabbergasts with outward expression yet enjoys seeing the demise and failures of others.

A man who reflects such attitude in the earthly dimension runs the risk of the spiritual entities. His attitude reveals blindness to servitude. Will such a man willingly volunteer to take care of sheep like David the Shepherd and reap the great unexpected rewards? Or will he seek payment in the temporal world and miss the eternal rewards? Will such a man be willing to love his enemies, sacrifice his life for his friends, and train his children to follow such selfless path? If such a man cannot demonstrate a positive and fruit-bearing attitude toward inanimate objects, how can God reveal to his heart the spiritual dimensions that require the forfeiture of oneself for the benefit of others you sometimes do not know?

Leadership: Believe in Yourself (Gideon)

A leader has to believe in himself and overcome his shortcomings by reassuring himself of God's attitude toward him. God called Gideon a mighty man of valor (Judges 6:12). Gideon challenged God by saying that he, Gideon, was of the weakest clan; and he was the weakest of his father's household. A man should not rely on his natural ability but rather climb in confidence through God's constant direction. In 2 Chronicles 16:7, Hanani, the seer, told Asa that because he relied on the king of Syria instead of God, there will be wars against him. Instead of listening to sound advice, Asa put Hanani, the messenger, in prison. A leader should deplete and eradicate the dangers of his ego and listen to words of wisdom even if it reduces his inflated state of significance. David tended to sheep before ascending to kingship. Nothing is too insignificant. Do not let your pride forfeit your blessings. Your blessing is wrapped in the simple yet profound things that appear insignificant. The direction of your future rests upon the simple thoughts in your head right now. You may not know the right decision or option to choose, but you will oftentimes know the wrong choices. Mark 4:35–41 shows that the disciples were in a boat that faced a raging storm. They started to panic and complained that Jesus was sleeping comfortably while everyone was about to drown. The self-confidence of a leader could be misinterpreted as a state of major insensitivity and lack of care and compassion. A good leader oftentimes rationalizes and factors the solution even when he asks questions, either to test the temperament or to seek the path of alternatives. Jesus woke up and commanded the fierce storm to be silent. Like the scene out of a movie, the disciples wondered what kind of man speaks to wind and waves, and they obey. Jesus was disappointed at their level of fear and lack of confidence toward believing that they also could have taken full command of the situation. The python spirit is a system of operation. The python is an external entity that impersonates and desensitizes you to a state of acceptance.

Self—Distortion (May 17, 1954, in the case of *Brown v. Board of Education*)

As I began to preach a message in one Sunday morning service, I can recall distinctively a moment as I did an introductory exercise. I asked the entire congregation to breathe in slowly and hold their breath for several seconds, then to slowly exhale. I then asked the congregation to breathe in one more time and hold their breath without releasing. Then I said, "*Without* releasing your breath, please look at your neighbor and say good morning." The congregation said good morning but began laughing hysterically, because it was virtually impossible to say good morning without utilizing the breath in your lungs.

We are intrinsically created in the image of God with designed intelligence. God has undeniably placed His breath in our lungs. Our God the Creator spoke this world and painted it into existence ("Let there be light, and there was light" [Genesis 1:3 KJV]). As we apply logic, we formulate our thoughts then articulate our words in sequential order as we audibly express and breathe them into the atmosphere. Your spoken words (life-giving breath) are then deposited into the ears of the recipients, echoing in the thought process; being translated, analyzed, and interpreted; deciphering the motives; sifting through the intentions of the sender; calculating the benefits; and becoming embedded, interweaved, and, like food for the soul, absorbed, registered, planted in our spirit man, and patterned in our identity. Who you are now is not a result of what you have heard today but information collectively nurtured over the past like learning a new language. The thought process is man's reality.

For as he thinketh in his heart, so is he. (Proverbs 23:7 KJV)

The body reacts to stress and manifests with the same waves and energy whether it is perceived or actually experienced.

> Death and life are in the power of the tongue: and they that love it shall eat the fruit thereof. (Proverbs 18:21 KJV)

Words like "I love you," "Will you marry me?" or "You are special" will renew the mindset of man. On the converse, words like "I can't stand you," "You are ugly," "Why are you wearing that?" or "You are no good" are very detrimental to the mental health of humanity. That's why a little child knows sarcasm and offense, which is naturally registered as contrary to the mind. Romans 12:2 reminds us not to become conformed to the pattern of this world, but we must be transformed through the renewing of the mind.

Men, fathers, and mothers need to validate and speak life into our children and this generation, empowering them radically against the beasts and serpents of the fields. In Acts 16, a particular practice is depicted in a town known as Delphi. There was a wide and common practice where the python snake, which was a mythical snake, would be worshipped. The people would allow the spirit to enter their bodies and speak through them as a medium, to the point where you would hear talking, but it's like your lips were not moving. Since individuals would speak involuntarily, the term *ventriloquist* was ascribed to them. Today we see this being used as comic and sense of humor. The story speaks of a slave girl, a fortune-teller, who was demon possessed; and the evil spirit would speak through her to make predictions. The master of the slave girl would make money and a lot of profit and gain based on this operation. But every time Paul and Silas would walk, she would yell, "I know who you are! You are men of God!" She did this day after day, provoking the spirit of Paul. The devil knows your potential and will hijack the destiny of your children. Paul turned around and said to the evil spirit, "Get out of here." She was set free instantly. The master of the slave girl went out of business, and Paul was incarcerated for messing up the fortune-teller industry. How about in Mark 5:1–20 when the demon-possessed man was chained up among tombs because he was out of his mind and very violent? Until he received a spiritual awakening and came back to a sober mind when Jesus cast out the demons and gave him back his identity (Leviticus 20:27; Deuteronomy 18:11, medium communicating with spirits).

Humanity is an ever-changing entity. Humanity is meant to grow, be fruitful, evolve, influence, and remain relevant. If a man ceases to adapt, grow, and improve with the rapid changes of the world, very soon his frustration intensifies; and he becomes at odds and in conflict with himself. A man who fails to produce will experience great inner turmoil.

The python waits for this opportunity to camouflage himself and wrap in the personality of mankind. The python impersonates the character of a person, leaving this individual in great bewilderment yet causing the person to accept this image of utter confusion as his true self and identity. If you should conduct a self-assessment and interview, how well do you understand the authenticity of your blueprint?

Brown v. Board of Education

In May 17, 1954, in the case of *Brown v. Board of Education*, the Supreme Court ruled it unconstitutional and a violation of the Fourteenth Amendment for the public schools to be segregated on the basis of race. This was done with a landmark victory according to the vote of 9−0. It was initially illegal for "black" and "white" children to integrate in the same school. Because of this condition, the lawsuit was filed to challenge the justice system, proving the psychological impact and adverse effects this bears on the self-esteem of young children.

This psychological doll test (doll experiment—white doll, black doll test) was used in the court system and was also broadcast by CNN. In this psychological test, many children were placed individually in a room to sit at a table that had one black doll and one white doll on the table. The black child would be asked to identify the black doll and the white doll. The child would then be asked to identify the ugly doll. These children would choose the black doll as the ugly doll. The child would then be asked why the doll is considered ugly. The child would respond, "Because it is black." The child would then be asked, "Which one is the pretty doll, and why is the doll pretty?" The child would then respond, "Because the doll is white." This child would then be asked, "Which one of the doll looks just like you?" Each child would have a stunning, shocking expression, followed by a pause. The child would then shamefully respond, "This one," while pointing or touching the black doll.

What do you believe about yourself? What is internally destroying and has become toxic and detrimental to your soul? How many people are you destroying because of your inner turmoil and pain? The doll test proves that the child has a very deep underlying false sense of self-acceptance and identification. The child exists in a body that he/she rejects. The child grows inseparably with an image of perception that is self-destructive and detrimental by means of character assassination.

A child that has truly rejected his/her sense and state of existence, living in constant deception, will inevitably grow as a continuum into adulthood. An adult, whether male or female who has not discovered his/her authentic self-value and lives in constant opposition and rejection to self, will never love himself/herself to the full potential and capacity. A man or woman who does not sincerely and genuinely love himself/herself can never truly be receptive of the love given by another. This also holds true to reciprocate this genuine love to his/her spouse. Your self-esteem will stand in the way and impede upon your perception and understanding to the greatness of God. Your subconscious thought process will be in constant motion of blaming God and falsely accuse God of not genuinely caring due to your distortion.

A child who looks at the doll and identifies himself/herself as that rejected child and becomes an adult that rejects himself/herself will definitely perceive his/her intimate lover as having the traits of that bad ugly doll. We need to protect the vulnerable from predatory conversations and poisonous words and languages.

Otherwise, this child will become conditioned and uniquely yield to his/her curiosity of the hissing sounds of the serpent under the fruit tree. A man who does not know himself is a prodigal son who will find comfort even in the pen with the pigs. A man who does not know himself constantly reacts with anger, not being aware of his trigger mechanisms. Such a man is vulnerable and should be very cautious when walking in the direction of the serpent. Such a man will be focused on the hypnotizing, mesmerizing beauty in the eyes of the serpent, while unaware that the tail of the serpent is wrapping him for a three-course meal.

Don't think the devil is about to surprise you with a nice gift because the table looks like it has been set for one person. Literally you are the meal!

It's no different than a young teenage girl being invited to a friend's house late at night, and upon arrival, she realized that the young boy is the only one home. It shouldn't take you long to discover that you are the meal, and the devil's tail made a rattling sound with the lock on the door. Will you respond to the hissing sound of the serpent by the invitation to the enclosed room, or will you remember the voice of God that says you shall surely die? Don't be fooled by emotional desire that says if pleasure is wrong, you'd rather not be right. There is a written blueprint and context that will safeguard your soul from the burning fire of death and destruction.

We ought to know ourselves! Too many times fear and uncertainties are lodged and conditioned in our minds. How many times have the police siren, ambulance, fire trucks, telephone ring sound, and the sounds of bullets become trigger mechanisms that cause parents to panic and wonder if their child is all right? How many times have wives wondered if their husbands are incarcerated? How many wives have the fundamental belief that their husbands ("doll on the table") could attain the skills or knowledge to gain a profession; become a doctor, lawyer, judge, or pilot; or obtain jobs with higher learning and long-term dedication? How many have the belief of success as opposed to perpetual failure? Why do parents encourage their children in an attempt not to disappoint them, while lacking the faith to believe in them? How many parents can see success for their children beyond where their natural resource and finance can facilitate? How many parents have conditioned their children to settle, simply because the parents could not see the possibilities beyond "the doll"? *Families need to show and communicate their love.*

Friendships and Association: Guilt—Forgive Yourself

There is a man known as Lazarus. The Bible declares that he was dead and buried for four days. A large crowd grew around him. The crowd cried and mourned at his death and burial. But when Jesus came and did a miracle, the crowd became angry at Jesus and didn't mind compromising the benefits of Lazarus coming back to life. The crowd was jealous and envious of the glory of another and was willing to sacrifice the life and friendship of Lazarus in the process (John 11:47–48).

The crowd began to disappear at his resurrection.

There are people present in our lives for our sinking, dying, and burial. In their hearts, there is great rejoicing and celebration, but they disappear at our resurrection and elevation.

When we are stuck at a junction point on our journey of life, we need to assess our association. We can get caught in the sabotage and cross fire process of the compromise and selfish motives of others. Don't be afraid to soar alone in your rough season. Not everyone wants to tolerate your misery; neither can they handle your glory. You are given the opportunity of a VIP ticket, and there is a limited first-class seating capacity.

Negative people will always come around when you are going down; but please remember, when you begin to soar, they will be nowhere to be found.

You feel most vulnerable to those who know your past and unpleasant history. But if you can defeat the power of your past, not by seeking an escape by fleeing, but by confronting your circumstance, you will be redeemed from self and hostage and constant negotiation from the influence and affirmation of others.

It's one thing when others hold you hostage, but what a major calamity and heightened catastrophe when we put shackles and restraints on ourselves. Even when your back is turned, or you share your story, there is someone in the crowd who is equally guilty but shows up to stone you to death as a camouflage in the process. Snake! The woman who was caught in the act of adultery, when vindicated, was asked by Jesus, "Where are all your accusers?" The people who hold you hostage are equally guilty with issues that are not exposed, so we should never be deceived by their camouflage of arrogance, neither should we wait until they walk away or are reduced in humility through exposure. We ought to stand in full confidence of the one who bore our guilt.

I have never seen a murderer holding a thief until the police arrives!

The state of hostage is first mental.

> Casting down imaginations, and every high thing that exalteth itself against the knowledge of God, and bringing into captivity every thought to the obedience of Christ. (2 Corinthians 10:5 KJV)

Let us not advance in anger against others for unkind treatment, when we are struggling and believing the lies against self. Let us examine our thought process and mental fortitude in order to conquer these elements that ultimately war against God's blueprint!

If someone tries to harm another who is in a relationship with God, you bring harm to yourself. We do not have to fear the one who can kill or harm the body but can't touch the soul/spirit. So many individuals commit heinous acts like spitting in people's food, physically hit, gossip, and inflict emotional hurt, not realizing they invite problems in their life. God punishes His own children, and those who act against His children should not expect preferential treatment, especially from a God who does not condone sinful acts.

The children of Israel complained about getting the same manna (bread from heaven) and dew to drink (Numbers 21:4–9). God released poisonous serpents upon the land that bit many of the Israelites who then died. When we complain against God and become unappreciative of His blessings, we release and create an opening for the serpent. Moses had to build a bronze serpent, and anyone who was bitten by the snake would have to run and look at the bronze serpent and by faith would survive (see also John 3:14). We should learn to conquer our battles through fasting. We have to deny ourselves the pleasures of this world. We have to live in total dependence on the manna, Bread of Heaven, Jesus Christ, and drink the heavenly dew by taking part in His shed blood. Exodus 12:13–28 depicts wiping blood on the doorpost in order to escape the plague of death, which foreshadows and is symbolic of escaping the death of the serpent's sting and being saved by hiding in the blood of Christ. When we repent and confess our sins to God, the accuser no longer has power. We are set free by His blood.

Prayer

We should cover our family in prayer. Our children on the playground are like chicken running around, being vulnerable to hawks flying and lurking. Prayer becomes like the mother hen that opens her wings to cover all her chickens from danger. The chicken that drifts away can cause division as the hen risks saving it from drowning at the expense of all the others.

Job covered his family in prayer, just in case they had sinned or blamed God in their hearts and subconscious state (Job 1:5). Prayer breaks down suffocating walls and enclosed barriers, giving you access to freedom that you oftentimes mistake as natural occurrence. In all things give thanks.

Abraham prayed for Lot, and he was saved from the calamity of destruction that came upon Sodom and Gomorrah. Lot could have believed that it was his own good who led him to victory and success. Sometimes our pride and ego cause us to believe that all we have accomplished in life were on the basis of our accolades and accomplishments. But the temple that was built over a span of seven years was destroyed in one day. Let us destroy pride, not considering it ignorance to attribute nothing of self, but give God thanks for all.

A major sign of searching for love and validation is becoming tearful at times when being told "I love you" and "I appreciate you." It's like the inner man receiving a drink of water after walking through the desert. When we call and speak with each other, it brings healing to the mind, body, and spirit.

The soul of man naturally needs God. In the book of 2 Samuel 13, after Absalom had killed his brother for raping his sister, he fled from his father, David. But three years later, his soul had a yearning to see his father, a void that could only be filled by returning to the presence of his father. He cried out and made petition then, when felt rejected, burned down the field of his father's attendant Joab that finally granted him a response from his father. There is a lot of misplaced anger and emotional spills that manifest in the attitude of our family members. We should approach with wisdom and caution, suspend all judgments, and refrain from unhealthy wars and reactions. People are searching for healing and find it hard to express the inner turmoil because of the complexity of a series of unresolved conditions.

How It All Began—The Genesis 3 Interview

Here we have a marriage with a couple that depicts the very essence of our relationship with God. Marriage is God's divine-created ordinance between one man and one woman. So as each individual devotes and directs his/her unselfish love to another in the midst of temptations, alternate choices, or ulterior motives, it's a direct representation of our faithfulness in our relationship with God in His kingdom.

The python spirit lured the woman into exploring her curiosity. The python then cast doubt in the mind of the woman. The python spirit asked a question with the power of suggestion, influence, and insinuation (Genesis 3:1). The boundaries were established, and the consequences were explained (v. 2). The serpent is attempting to gain trust and compliance in order to fulfill its agenda. The python stated that God just does not want you to become knowledgeable, successful, and established; rather, God wants you to remain stagnant and will become jealous if you start to increase and expand your territory. Be aware of individuals who present to you stories and information that alter the way you begin to perceive others. It's dangerous to shift your perspective of others on the basis and merits of association. Man has raged war against himself and turned against his brother. Matthew 12:22–28 is reflective of such when Jesus healed a man who was blind and couldn't speak. Many religious leaders said he was of the devil. But why would the devil work against its own kingdom, when any kingdom that is divided cannot stand? Joyce Meyers in her book *Battlefield of the Mind* tells us that we have to know the enemy and his strategies in order to defeat or win the war.

We should remain obedient to the Word of God, even when logic cannot comprehend or analyze. There are times when parents can see beyond the common understanding of their children (vv. 4–5). Adam and Eve were now covering themselves as though it will block their awareness, consciousness, and conviction. Adam and Eve sewed fig leaves together to cover their perception of shame toward their bodies. While they were covered, they attempted to hide from God. Their internal perspective dampened and created a self that became a perpetrator to the state of existence. This is indicative as was spoken previously in the doll experiment and lawsuit in *Brown v. Education*. In highlight and comparison, Adam and Eve have now recognized their nakedness and perceived it as negative like the children despising themselves through the lens of a black doll. So we have the same person, same body, same physical image, and same physiological makeup. But Adam and Eve both looked in the mirror and all of a sudden saw someone different. Adam saw himself as the ugly doll. He believed himself to be as the python has convinced him that he was. How is this possible? How do I love myself or someone else today, and all of a sudden within moments, I can't stand you or myself? How is it that I love my friends and spouse, and instantly I am ignited with rage, passion, anger, and hatred due to an altered perception? How is it that just by sitting down and thinking, life automatically becomes overwhelming, I just want to quit and give up on life?

How is it possible that I see you in a positive manner, and by the time the wind blows some negative thoughts, my mind begins to orchestrate and like a monster alter my emotional state to the point of self-disgust? How is that I can never come to grips with my natural self, I have to enhance my image or body with cosmetics; otherwise, I fear what others may think of me? Transparency builds healthy relationships regardless of shame (vv. 6–7). Is this why Adam and Eve hid from God, because they feared what God may think of them? Is this why even the person who does not worship God runs away from God's presence and blames God for his unfortunate circumstances and choices in life (vv. 8–11)?

No one wants to be accountable. When we refuse responsibility, we reject change and hinder transformation. According to Romans 12:2, we have to be transformed by the constant renewal of the mind. Maturity is coming to grips with our faults fully and responsibly. This will progressively propel us into a gradual advancement to experience positive change.

When a husband and wife war against each other, it's rebellion against God. When Moses struck the rock when God told him to speak to it in front of the nation, he misrepresented God's leadership by painting an angry God, when God is a God of compassion. We were made in the image of God, which means we must demonstrate His attributes (vv. 12–13).

Ephesians 6:10–12 reminds of our continuous spiritual warfare. We have to guard our soul and get the devil out of our mind. We cannot misrepresent God; otherwise, society develops a distorted view of God. We ought to wear the mindset of Christ. The power of sin has created a new rationale and distorts our perspective.

Hence, Adam and Eve viewed themselves according to how they think and feel, which is introduction of guilt and manipulation. I now project unto you how I feel about myself. So now let me cover with a facade of fig leaves and create a persona that I want you to perceive. That's why we oftentimes treat others according to our perception and analytical processing, oftentimes trying to turn people into a puppet that becomes obedient to our system of dysfunctional thinking. But we smile with a fig leaf while greeting others to cover our deception. The apostle Peter acted in a biased manner against the Gentiles whenever the Jews appeared on the scene!

The punishment and consequences have been laid out to the serpent (vv. 14–15). The woman was given her verdict, and today all women experience pain during childbirth as a reminder. There is no separation of individualized outcome (v. 16). Adam was dealt with accordingly for listening to his wife rather than following the command and precepts that God laid out. Today all of mankind survive by the sweat of their brow. The ground also became dysfunctional and produced fruitless and painful thorns and thistles (vv. 16–19). We should always remember that the action of one individual affects those who are around. Adam and Eve were now clothed and covered by God with garments of skin. Man was no longer allowed access to the tree of life. He cannot continue to be rewarded while living a life of infidelity. The attack of the serpent is also a reminder of the enmity between humanity and the spiritual entity.

Love is not how you feel, but what you know. Sometimes in a relationship, both individuals may be selfishly achieving their goals, so they are under the impression that they are in love, until one stops meeting the expectations of the other, whether by choice or by unpleasant circumstances; then reality is swiftly accepted. Jesus came not to condemn the world, but with His love to grant us eternal life. The prodigal son said to his father, "Let me be one of your hired servants." His sinful action left him with a sense of guilt and low self-esteem. He was willing to forfeit his future by dismissing success. His dad had to shake up his consciousness by reinforcing that "you are my son." Let us not judge and condemn ourselves or the world; neither should we think that we have reached a place of prominence.

Let change begin in me. Let us see others as God sees us, with a lens of love. My wife once said to me that she discovered that we often treat our kids based upon what's on our mind, and not by the actual situation. We do not go for resolution, but gratification. The last straw breaks the camel's back. The least of your problems can face the heaviest judgment. You could look at a thing and choose to love and appreciate or reject it. Your love, your happiness, your success, your peace, and your contentment are wrapped up in your mind. Your rationale could chew it up and spit it out or swallow to embrace. Stop thinking about revenge and feeling sorry for yourself. Every conflict should reach a place of healthy resolution. Let us outdo each other by overcoming evil with good.

As slavery was being abolished, a system was developed known as the Mississippi Black Code. This system was designed to recapture those who were pronounced and declared as free. It was meant to condition the free to accept a perception of enslavement. Wealthy men would hire slave catchers to "police" the neighborhood and hunt down these men as though they had committed a crime and bring them back into captivity. These codes are self-explanatory and lead to an almost guilty verdict if men and women were perceived to be loitering, were gazing in the eyes of Caucasians, or were simply reported to commit a crime even with baseless merits. In addition, there were written laws that considered slaves as subhuman or partial percentage of a person. Subsequently there were bills drafted that would later lead to mass incarceration and separation of family members. As the stronghold of these laws has loosened its grips over the years, it also acts as a powerful contrast to the obstacle of sin, until God steps in and dismantles the stronghold by giving the world His Son.

> For God so loved the world, that he gave his only begotten Son, that whosoever believeth in him should not perish, but have everlasting life. (John 3:16 KJV)

CHAPTER 6
SLY AS A FOX, SLICK AS A WOLF
(Power of Boundaries)

If I have no idea of the direction in which I want to go;
inevitably someone will lead or take me there.

– M. Reid

Isn't it ironic that the one who deceives does not appreciate being the victim of deception? Am I of the wolf or fox family? Will I ever encounter, engage, or marry a wolf or perhaps a fox-like personality and character trait?

Foxes and wolves are very intelligent and friendly. They can be assimilated among humans as pets. Foxes and wolves often display nonaggressive behavior and are said to possess the ability to develop strong emotional bonding. Foxes are flexible in transitioning from dens (holes) or burrows where they raise their young offspring. Foxes can be very subtle and nonconfrontational. When being disrupted by humanity, a fox just simply changes to a different hole or den. This display of inconspicuous attitude is usually not reflective of a flamboyant charismatic individual. A fox will therefore utilize its cunningness as opposed to sudden compulsive reaction to war or physical strength that warrants immediate attention. This attitude or charisma seems to resemble a person who is labeled "GQ," subtle in operation and occasionally lacks honesty or commitment.

Did you just put your foot in your own mouth? Can you imagine being in public with one of your feet in your mouth? This expression speaks of being in an undeniable and compromising situation or encounter. We have all experienced at least one unique occasion in which we were biased, spoke, or executed some regrettable actions witnessed by others. But what if this is consistently your lifestyle without getting caught? A person is considered very blessed if the fox gets his foot caught before he outsmarts you!

Encountering some form of interaction or associating with a fox or wolf is almost inevitable. A fox or wolf will come searching for you with a very subtle disguised operation. We are all relational beings. Falling in love is deeply rooted and connected to our emotional state of well-being. I have worked in the justice system for over a decade and have seen that the majority of individuals who are either incarcerated or rearrested are due to relationship issues.

No man or woman wants to commit his/her life to a relationship only to discover that it was disrupted or built on the foundation of deception. In every relationship, the husband or wife constantly questions in the realm of the subconscious, the potential or manifestation of wolf/fox-like traits. We have all heard stories or possibly experienced some of these interrogations: Are you cheating? Who were you speaking with? Who just called the phone? Why are you just reaching home? Did you stop on your way home? Did you go to the party when you said you were going to the party? Are you lying to me? These probing questions continue and also lodge in the subconscious. It's even more painful when victimized individuals know the deceptive acts exist, yet the other party is unwilling to change or engage in a conversation for improvement or reconciliation.

If you have children, no parents want their children to be wrapped up or embraced by a wolf/fox. We are all cautious of these exhibiting traits and symptoms. Anyone who has been exposed or experienced deception is likely to be very cautious and will be on the constant lookout for any similar signs or further manifestations. Forgiveness may have taken place, yet the feeling or emotional despair may appear dormant (potential to return). Your hurts will likely develop the inclination to live in constant worry, wondering if this volcano will erupt again. Fear perceived is fear lived! Insecurities stemming from hurts and pain will cause you to see things that do not exist. It is mental illusion and parallels insanity.

What better way to divulge in the character traits or symptoms deeply embedded within us over the course of time than to disclose the statement made by Jesus about wolves and foxes?

> Watch out for false prophets. They come to you in sheep's clothing, *but inwardly they are ferocious wolves.* By their fruit you will recognize them. Do people pick grapes from thornbushes, or figs from thistles? (Matthew 7:15–16 NIV; emphasis added)

> And Jesus saith unto him, The foxes have holes, and the birds of the air have nests; but the Son of man hath not where to lay his head. (Matthew 8:20 KJV)

The wolf possesses the personality trait of a charismatic individual who can aspire and ascend to a position of heightened status quo. This wolf therefore will be very cunning, which means it possesses intelligence, gentleness, and flexibility and is very tactical in social and emotional connections.

Let us dissect beyond the surface and see the different perspectives of what God is telling us. The first statement according to Matthew 7:15 is one of warning: "Watch out . . ."

God wants us to be very cautious and aware of the dangers in encountering someone with the personality or character traits of a wolf. God gave us the association in the person of a false prophet, someone who lends the appearance and perception of and portrays himself to be other than his authentic self. The second sentence conveys that he comes in "sheep's clothing." His job is to offer protection and spiritual guidance to those who have entrusted their lives in his hands, yet his true nature is inwardly a ferocious wolf! The question then begs the answer, why does he come or choose such outfit? Apparently, he knows the attributes of his prey and qualities of association that attract the victim into vulnerable conditions. Be very careful of exposing very sensitive information too early when developing close friendships. Your mind may be clouded and overwhelmed by emotional feelings, and the wolf breaks you down by flabbergasting you with gifts and pleasant surprises. The wolf personality has already premeditated and identified its target. The wolf has mastered the art of understanding, masquerading, camouflaging, and exploiting the personality of its intended victims in order to play the role. The wolf nature is dressed in camouflaged sheep's clothing, which indicates that the wolf knows how to mimic the actions and attitude enough to lure the sheep into its trap. A sheep is very tender, obedient, noncombative, submissive, and vulnerable especially when being alone. Studies reveal that sheep have a very strong instinct to follow the sheep that is in front. Sheep will follow each other even to the slaughter. If the sheep in front jumps over a cliff, the others are likely and will follow. From the early stages of birth, lambs are conditioned to follow the older sheep. The wolf will then become attractive, exercise patience, and be manipulative until the results are accomplished. The danger zone can be more elusive than perceived or understood.

There are many intimate relationships that are built on a foundation that lacks proper discipline or quality that will enhance and foster a healthy lifestyle or family orientation. What are the visions that I have for myself?

If I have no idea of the direction in which I want to go; inevitably someone will lead or take me there.

How well do I understand myself, my history, my experiences, and my family traits? What are my trigger mechanisms and ticking time bombs? Do I hold things within and then explode when it reaches that boiling point? Am I being dragged in my own net and entrapped in my web of pride? Do I refuse to express my pains and hurts, seeking healing and resolution, or do I simply hold out until the next individual initiates his/her viewpoint? How much do I understand the inner power of forgiveness? Do I have social and spiritual outlets? Do I have a well-balanced lifestyle and dimensions of well-being? *Am I insecure*, and if I am, what are my thought process and root causes?

The wolf, who has mastered his craft, will understand your vulnerability and exploit you by feeding into your relegated desire. The challenge in understanding the wolf is that you have entered a territory that offers and portrays something that resembles that which is genuine, but the wolf's selfish desire boycotts the process with ulterior motives. Oftentimes, it takes more than the natural sight or circumstances to discover the potential dangers. A person may only live to discover the true nature of a wolf through a negative experience. A person may escape being the victim of rape by deciding through intuition not to go out with a serial rapist who lends the appearance of being authentic. Usually you would not know the full extent of your escape unless you fall victim or learn from someone's demise. Unfortunately, it's always and almost too late to undo the detrimental effects. It takes discernment and establishing boundaries to escape the trap before ever living to encounter the extent of the possibilities.

By their fruits you will know them. (Verse 16)

You may not want to be in a situation in which you wait for the fruit or results of manifestation to evolve, to discover, or to live through the consequences of the prophet who is supposed to protect you, your goals, your asset, your vision, and your future because you may not be able to recover or get a second opportunity. Shame on us if we await the thornbushes to produce grapes or sit around expecting thistles to give us fig!

Healing Before Leaping

If you were in a toxic relationship or going through a bitter divorce, you may want to take some time and start the healing process before you seek solace or comfort from a high school sweetheart, past lover, or some memories of nostalgic encounter.

If you should go on your quest for a quick resolution, you may just be training a baby wolf in becoming better at his game.

A wolf sometimes will not understand how ferocious it can become until it has encountered a situation. You can't fully blame the wolf, because the wolf is developing symptoms of negative learned behavior.

Behold, I was shapen in iniquity; and in sin did my mother conceive me. (Psalm 51:5 KJV)

Frustration, anger, and stress will cloud your vision and thought process, hindering you from executing wise decisions. You may feel compelled to resort to your last memories or experiences of comfort. Many experiences of pleasure were not built or established on foundations of love and commitment. We can mistake a rotten wooden platform of infatuation for a solid foundation, not realizing that the platform was a temporal juncture and transitional point in our life. Such expectation is like visiting a childhood friend and not realizing that he is now an adult who has outgrown the concept and perception lodged in my memory.

Going in search of past pleasure to fulfill future endeavors is like telling your pet cat to safeguard an open container of butter.

Your values will be licked away and eradicated by an entity that cannot resist self-fulfillment.

105

I strongly implore you to be cautious; do not rush for expedient results and end up with permanent damage.

Let us reflect on the statement of the wise-man king Solomon as depicted in Proverbs 7:21–23 NIV:

> With persuasive words she led him astray; she seduced him with her smooth talk. All at once he followed her like an ox going to the slaughter, like a deer stepping into a noose till an arrow pierces his liver, like a bird darting into a snare, little knowing it will cost him his life.

> Do not lust in your heart after her beauty or let her captivate you with her eyes. For a prostitute can be had for a loaf of bread, but another man's wife preys on your very life. (Proverbs 6:25–26 NIV)

There are so many stories of infidelity that lead to individuals running, fleeing by jumping through windows to escape with their lives, physical and emotional abuse, murder, divorce, family feud, and turmoil. Let us reflect on the following real-life events:

Living in Spicy Deception

There is a story involving a woman who was married to a military man, and as a couple, they were unable to have a child that they both strongly desired. They went through counseling and sought a resolution. One day the woman met with the pastor and confessed by explaining that she was born a man but had a transplant to become a woman. "She" has not disclosed to "her" husband that he (husband) was married to someone who was born a man due to fear of losing him or "her" life. During one church service, the couple went to the altar, and the husband requested for the pastor to pray so that they could produce a child. The pastor refused and told him to have a conversation with his wife when he reaches home, and she will explain the complexity of the situation. The pastor did not want the responsibility and potential liability as a result of exposing the truth. The couple eventually moved out of town and settled in another state.

The ultimate question that demands a response is this: if the husband did not know that he was married to a man, does this constitute an act of homosexuality? Can God truly hold you accountable while you are oblivious, just like a judge in the courtroom telling you that ignorance is no excuse?

Let us conduct a parallel to see the verdict and consequences according to Genesis 20:1–7: involving Abraham being fearful that he would have lost his life to the king, so he said that his wife was his sister.

> Abraham moved south to the Negev and lived for a while between Kadesh and Shur, and then he moved on to Gerar. While living there as a foreigner, Abraham introduced his wife, Sarah, by saying, "She is my sister." So King Abimelech of Gerar sent for Sarah and had her brought to him at his palace.

> But that night God came to Abimelech in a dream and told him, *"You are a dead man, for that woman you have taken is already married!"*

> But Abimelech had not slept with her yet, so he said, *"Lord, will you destroy an innocent nation? Didn't Abraham tell me, 'She is my sister'? And she herself said, 'Yes, he is my brother.' I acted in complete innocence! My hands are clean."*

> In the dream God responded, *"Yes, I know you are innocent. That's why I kept you from sinning against me, and why I did* not let you touch her. [7] Now return the woman to her husband, and he will pray for you, for he is a prophet. *Then you will live. But if you don't return her to him, you can be*

sure that you and all your people *will die.*" (Genesis 20:1–7 NLT; emphasis added)

Based on the story presented that parallels the scenario depicted with the transgender relationship, being unaware, being oblivious, or lacking discernment to the voice of God does not constitute the lack or absence of a sinful act. According to verse 6, God kept Abimelech from sinning. But how many people are not discerning or perhaps rebellious to the voice of God? There are times when important elements remain undisclosed, but secrecy does not vindicate the consequences or the manifested results and effects. Many people today would rather hide from each other in secrecy and disregard the omnipresence of God. The Lord would have struck with vengeance on the entire nation. The decision made by leadership, fathers, and spiritual covering can have significant blessings or negative impact on others. Ultimately the scheme was designed by the devil who is the enemy of our soul. It is therefore important for the nation to walk in the accurate knowledge of God and in obedience to His Word. The devil plays upon our lack of understanding and disobedience. A significant segment of premarital counseling is recommending both parties to conduct a medical exam and blood test then openly disclosing the results with each other. This is highly recommended even if it's the first or sole partner for life.

Isaac also repeated the same cycle as his father, Abraham.

> When the men who lived there asked Isaac about his wife, Rebekah, he said, "She is my sister." He was afraid to say, "She is my wife." He thought, "They will kill me to get her, because she is so beautiful." But some time later, Abimelech, king of the Philistines, looked out his window and saw Isaac caressing Rebekah.

> Immediately, Abimelech called for Isaac and exclaimed, "She is obviously your wife! Why did you say, 'She is my sister'?"

"Because I was afraid someone would kill me to get her from me," Isaac replied.

"How could you do this to us?" Abimelech exclaimed. "One of my people might easily have taken your wife and slept with her, and *you would have made us guilty of great sin.*"

Then Abimelech issued a public proclamation: "Anyone who touches this man or his wife will be put to death!" (Genesis 26:7–11 NLT; emphasis added)

Isaac said that his wife was his sister out of fear of losing his life. The other party was unaware because of deception, but this does not alleviate the guilt spread over you by the devil's blanket of schemes by sending his agents of foxes and wolves. The king acknowledged that he along with the nation would have been found guilty just by association, even when being unaware of the facts. What hidden sins and secrecies in fear have we embraced and accepted as a regular routine part of our lives? What has God been warning us against and the needed actions to execute? Do we rather live with our feet caught in a lifetime trap? I can remember vividly having interviewed a nurse and inquired about any similar situation encountered. The nurse explains that there are male transgenders going through the process of change and wanting to know how come they have not experienced their menstrual cycle. I have observed male transgenders getting upset in having excessive facial hair, because it does not match the newly implanted breast. Humanity can be sued, but when nature takes its course, it cannot be accused of hatred and discrimination.

Job became the center of the devil's scheme not knowing the conversation that was taking place in the heavenly realm of the courtroom as the devil bargains his case. But Job lived in total integrity even when his finite mind did not fully comprehend the complexity of his encounter (Job 1–2).

Achan's action leads to the stoning of his entire household and family members, even though his dishonesty and lack of integrity were done in secrecy (Joshua 7). It's amazing how humanity willingly hides from one another while disregarding the Creator who is staring in our faces! We fail to realize that the mercies and compassion of God are keeping us, while we remain in a rebellious state and harden our hearts like Pharaoh.

Playing on the Ledge

There is a true story that was reenacted in a movie known as *A Girl Like Me* involving a young boy who enjoyed dressing up as a girl. During childhood, the boy's sister dressed him up in female apparel and put cosmetics on him. The young boy started wearing brassiere and was constantly bullied in school due to his high-pitched voice and appearance. Later in life, he went to a party, and his level of beauty while being dressed up as a woman made him the constant center of attraction. He met a few young men who thought he was a woman. The men were intensely attracted to him, became intimate, and had oral sex conducted on them. Two of the men desired to have sexual intimacy at different times, in which the transgender allowed only anal intercourse and claimed he was experiencing her menstrual cycle. Both men became suspicious after realizing the same reason was given on different occasions in a relatively short time. They challenged him to strip in order to prove that "she" was a woman. A young lady who was at the house went into the bathroom and force-inspected him and discovered that he was a male. The men became furious and prevented him from leaving. He was murdered, and his body was transported and buried four hours away. The men were incarcerated and served several years in prison. This result was a very sad and unfortunate situation.

What thoughts could possibly stir up vengeance in our mind as individuals who felt deceived? So often offensive words, financial dealings, tangible possessions, or undisclosed actions that later revealed to be dishonest can stir up such anger. The "righteous judge" within a man then rises up to sit on the throne and execute actions and guilty verdict with his gavel against others but himself. What rationale passes through our mind to punish others for their wrong, yet we seek indemnification for ourselves after doing worse? Is this why we are commanded to love and forgive, because it has the power to destroy evil?

> A person without self-control is like a city with broken-down walls. (Proverbs 25:28 NLT)

> Better to be patient than powerful; better to have self-control than to conquer a city (Proverbs 16:32 NLT)

> But the Holy Spirit produces this kind of fruit in our lives: love, joy, peace, patience, kindness, goodness, faithfulness, gentleness, and self-control. There is no law against these things! (Galatians 5:22–23 NLT)

The statement "sly as a fox, slick as a wolf" didn't just originate.

Victims who are vulnerable to sly foxes and cunning wolves are usually safer through self-awareness than to be on a quest to transform the mindset of such predators as wolves and foxes. Sheep are usually safer when traveling in groups than becoming distracted and drifting away. Sheep need to be observant and listen closely to the advice and the voice of the shepherd.

> My sheep hear my voice, and I know them, and they follow me:

> And I give unto them eternal life; and they shall never perish, neither shall any man pluck them out of my hand. (John 10:27–28 KJV)

Many individuals in life observe the early signs of the predator; however, they enjoy the ecstatic feeling of playing dangerously on the edge. Such individuals do not count the cost or factor the consequences approaching as fast as a ball falling by gravitational force toward a rapidly rising ground.

Life can become more intense and increasingly difficult when a wolflike character takes full control and dominate the entire herd of sheep. Such scenario exists when the people of Israel wanted a king with charisma, not counting the cost of rejecting God. According to 1 Samuel 8, the people of Israel asked for a king like the other nations, preferably than going directly to God. The prophet Samuel was displeased, and God reassured him not to become disappointed because the people rejected God from reigning over their lives. The story depicted in 1 Samuel 8 is quite self-explanatory. Verse 18 warns the people that very soon they will be crying out for help, to which they still refused and proceeded in rebellion. The people were informed that eventually they would suffer persecution and cry out for God but may not get a response.

Is It Fair to Blame the Victim

Oftentimes we can misconstrue the outcome and demise faced by the victim and overlook the process that exposed or made the victim vulnerable. The actions of the perpetrator are never to be condoned, but let's admit that steps are frequently implemented to avoid becoming victims of exploitation. This is definite proof that anyone can become susceptible to unfortunate circumstances.

Esau was very hungry and sold his entire inheritance to his brother for one meal that was cooked on the stove. He then became mad at his brother and threatened to kill him when the consequence could not be reversed.

God warns us to pursue peace and holiness; otherwise, we fall short from His grace. Interestingly, comparison was made to Esau as being a profane person for his actions. Esau subsequently desired his inheritance, pursued it diligently with tears, yet was rejected. Jacob is considered to be a trickster and deceiver, while Esau is perceived as the victim. However, God loved the mindset of Jacob and hated the thought process of Esau. What happens when there is no one in the process to be blamed, just nature or unfortunate circumstances of life! Could the victim be mirrored as the perpetrator for not safeguarding his blessings? Is there a parallel with the state of imagination because the inheritance was futuristic? How do we guard the gateway of our mind from allowing the foxes and the wolves to gain entry and sabotage our future?

How many times in life have we gambled with very poor choices? We drink irresponsibly, we drive recklessly, we engage in unprotected sexual encounters, we commit infidelity utterly destroying relationships, we get pregnant in uncommitted relationships, and we have abortions with little regard to the life of the unborn, increasing debts without factoring income and unforeseeable circumstances!

We have walked into the trap of the sly fox and hungry ferocious wolf. We are now angry because the wolf used us for its meal. And the wolf is expressing gratitude to you for satisfying its desires. Sometimes individuals are so focused on their accomplishments, they are not aware that they have hurt you in the process. How many relationships are experiencing turbulence simply because there is no common ground of reciprocity? Both parties are equally hurting when the condition could be resolved by a simple conversation. Communication is key to a successful relationship, instead of remaining in constant hurt and expecting the other to figure it out.

> Study to shew thyself approved unto God, a workman
> that needeth not to be ashamed, rightly dividing the
> word of truth. (2 Timothy 2:15 KJV)

If you are a sheep, and you keep friends with a wolf/fox character, you will eventually compromise. A fox/wolf steals, manipulates, and habitually expects you to give them answers on the test or conduct duties without their due diligence. This eventually progresses to greater issues, and you will backslide from the essential. The wolf/fox will always explain the necessity of their actions and find your sincerity humorous.

> Keep your heart with all diligence,
> For out of it *spring* the issues of life.
> Put away from you a deceitful mouth,
> And put perverse lips far from you.

Let your eyes look straight ahead,
And your eyelids look right before you.
Ponder the path of your feet,
And let all your ways be established.
Do not turn to the right or the left;
Remove your foot from evil. (Proverbs 4:23–27 NKJV)

The Anger and Rage of Samson

What would cause a man to catch three hundred foxes, tie their tails together in pair, attach bottle torches, and let them loose in a field with planted products? The first sign of trouble started when Samson became attracted to a Philistine woman who did not share the same vision as Samson or understood his anointing. Samson became the center of attention, and trouble started when he posed a riddle at the wedding preparation party and promised to give a major prize to the one who solved it. If the riddle was not solved in seven days, then the people would have to give Samson the gift. The prize was so enticing, the men of the town threatened to kill his bride and burn her and her father's house if she didn't pressure Samson and get the answer. The woman then cried tears and softened the heart of Samson, subsequently spilling her guts because of being blackmailed. The issue is that Samson did not even have the gifts that he promised, because he had to rob and kill thirty men to get the gift after losing the bet. His wife was then given away to the best man. Samson fumed with anger OR was enraged, he caught the three hundred foxes and attached the torch in pairs, and then all hell broke loose. His anger and rage was unresolved, then spilled over into a subsequent relationship in which he was deceived. The Philistines inquired about the damage to their property, and the people explained the situation and ironically led to the death of the woman and her father who were burned (Judges 14–15:8).

There will be times in life when the wolf/fox cannot get to you and will bribe or use the people who are closest to you.

> *The power of money can purchase the loyalty of friendship and sell it on the market of betrayal.*

Jesus was betrayed for thirty pieces of silver. The disciples criticized the woman who sacrificed the anointing oil on the feet of Jesus that cost a year's salary, because they would rather obtain the money for gain. Jealousy is very dangerous; the same principle of bribery is the same covetousness against what someone else possesses.

Unresolved Issues

Samson was appointed by God before he was born. Many of us are still trying to figure out our purpose, but God has ordained great things for your life even before your parents considered about you. God commanded Manoah, the father of Samson, to ensure that he drinks no wine, eats nothing unclean, and does not cut his hair. Judges 13:12 mentions that Sampson's father inquired of the Lord how to grow his son with wisdom in order for him to walk in the precepts of God. Manoah then made a sacrificial offering unto God to secure a future blessing over his son. Samson apparently forgot about his purpose! He was still searching for companionship and fell in love with Delilah. The Philistines bribed Delilah, and everyone promised to contribute eleven hundred pieces of silver if she could break Samson to the vulnerable state until he confesses the secret to his power and anointing. On numerous occasions, Samson gave misleading information to Delilah and almost lost his life even though he destroyed the Philistines when they thought that Samson had lost his strength. But Judges 16:16 declares that Delilah pestered Samson, cried, accused him of making a mockery of her, and didn't love her. Samson proved his love by yielding to her demands and confessed by exposing the truth to his power and anointing.

Approval of love, validation, and exposing the most vulnerable in-depth secrecy can be a very risky emotional transaction for love and acceptance. Whether in the Garden of Eden, privacy of your home, or intimate connection with God, the enemy will endeavor to persist with lucrative operation. It is vital to understand and know your purpose and calling. The enemy didn't stop until he derailed Samson. Can you imagine what the enemy may be doing with your gift if you fail to even be aware that you possess it? By the time you find out that it has been tampered with, you will be surprised like someone getting pulled over by a police not knowing where the title or vehicle registration is being kept. Hopefully you are not in possession of any illegal substance substituted by the devil for your anointing. Samson searched for his anointing and power, but the Lord had already departed from him. The wolf and fox are patient, so we should not mistake their gentleness and patience for loyalty. Unless we turn wholeheartedly to God, we fail by thinking that we possess the ultimate strength, not realizing that we have been disconnected from the source!

When Light Sheds on the Dark

During the catastrophe involving the collapse of the twin tower in NYC, a certain individual while being home was watching the news broadcasting the building under intense flames of fire. This particular individual knew that her spouse works in the building and being concerned made a call via telephone to check if he was still alive. The spouse answered the phone and conveyed a response that says, "I am at work." But when the wife asked if he was working in a building that collapsed and engulfed in fire, the spouse evidently was clueless because he had not reported to work as implied. The spouse was at another person's house in an alleged love affair when supposed to be at work. The marriage was immediately faced with divorce.

Whatever is done in the dark will eventually be exposed by the light. The execution of deception, filled with compromise, is action depicting lies that are preceded before the justification is verbally articulated. Many foxes go hunting, only to find rest at another place other than home. When the fox gets weary and tired, the fox will lay his head to rest wherever there is comfort. Man justifies laying his head by his state of tiredness and discomfort. The reality is that there will always be a reason to explain the trend of actions. The fox becomes the greatest Shakespeare when his legs are caught in the snare, and convinces self to believe his nonsense. You will ask the fox why the bed is wet, and he will respond that he had too much water to drink. He instantly believes what he concludes in his mind. The fox did not see the needs to be addressed and the real issue to discover that the root cause is a diabetic condition. What are the symptoms in our lives that manifest according to what we superficially conclude, not realizing that our perception is the issue and not the other individual?

There are so many siblings in the world who do not know that each other exists because of relationships of infidelity in secrecy and deception. One household is hoping that the fox will change his dwelling place address and move into the new "burrow" location.

The victim does not realize that a physical change in address does not radicalize a new attitude of loyalty within the fox.

A fox in one hole does not change or mysteriously transform because he switches his location. Very soon if the fox joins with you in a relationship scheme, by leaving the previous family, your expectation of the fox will introduce insecurities because you have been exposed to the brilliance of his toxic scheme. The fox advanced from an amateur to pro-college graduate with your assistance. While you contributed to his skill level, you failed to excel in wisdom. At the end of the rope, and at the dead-end street, when it's time to turn around the car, it may be too late to say, "I should have known."

Don't blame all the sheep and say that they are all wolves, because in the process of ripping off the wool, you may realize that you have just killed a genuine sheep or made him into a meal for someone else when he moves out. It's vital to address self and unresolved issues before moving forward.

Whether Abraham, Isaac, the transgender couple, or the young man posing as a woman, individuals who are internally ferocious at times

117

will execute unjustifiable actions against you because they felt deceived in the process. The consequences in the mental and spiritual dimension are just as real, like contracting a physical disease in poor decision choices, which neither party was privileged to have known.

Systemic Wolf Operation

When does life begin? Why would you abort or terminate something that is already dead?

Can you kill, abort, or terminate something without life?

The simple fact that you are executing the act of abortion simply renders the indisputable truth that a life source is in existence. Is it therefore not being irrelevant or redundant to ask or beg for a response to when does life begin? Are you rendering the implication that upon establishing the proof of life, the act of abortion shall not be executed? Are you therefore willing to embark on a journey for the quest for truth? The hard-core truth of the reality of life and existence! This is not about being right or wrong. Will you think independently, or will the court of law that changes its rules like a pendulum be the determinant factor of what you believe? Every reader of this document does not consider himself/herself a mistake. Every man came into existence by means of agreement, with the sperm cell meeting the egg and producing the irreversible process of the seed of life.

> The most successful educational approach to the Negro is through a religious appeal. We do not want word to go out that we want to exterminate the Negro population and the minister is the man that can straighten out the idea if ever occurs to any of their more rebellious members. (Margaret Sanger)

> Three generations of imbeciles is enough. (*Buck v. Bell*
> *[1927]*, Justice Oliver Wendell Holmes Jr., United States
> Supreme Court)

Do we need to look very far when the justice system that many individuals seek for a solution seemingly walks into a web of death trap? A man who should render fair justice, in his written decree and court ruling, permitted compulsory sterilization of those whom society deems to be unfit and intellectually incapable and disabled. This means forced abortion, sterilization, and segregation from society as was committed in the Holocaust via eugenics. How many times have we watched in the news where the leaders of this nation have met accidents and become victims of gun violence making them physically debilitated? Do we convert them to imbeciles?

The practice of abortion has been from the ancient times. Let's take a look at an event that took place in Egypt according to Exodus 1:8–9, 15–16, 22 NLT.

> Eventually, a new king came to power in Egypt who
> knew nothing about Joseph or what he had done. He
> said to his people, "Look, the people of Israel now
> outnumber us and are stronger than we are. We must
> make a plan to keep them from growing even more.
> If we don't, and if war breaks out, they will join our
> enemies and fight against us. Then they will escape
> from the country.

> Then Pharaoh, the king of Egypt, gave this order to
> the Hebrew midwives, Shiphrah and Puah: "When you
> help the Hebrew women as they give birth, watch as
> they deliver. If the baby is a boy, kill him; if it is a girl,
> let her live."

> Then Pharaoh gave this order to all his people: "Throw
> every newborn Hebrew boy into the Nile River. But you
> may let the girls live."

Could you or someone that you know be a part of this multibillion-dollar fetus sales scheme? Abortion has been widely used as population reduction and force control but is more lucrative than many may think. Focus is oftentimes on the male figure, the strength that interweaves the identity of society. Margaret Higgins Sanger, born Margaret Louise Higgins (September 14, 1879–September 6, 1966), was an American birth control activist, sex educator, writer, and nurse. She opened the first birth control clinic in the United States and established organizations that evolved into Planned Parenthood Federation of America. Pressures from the Roman Catholic Church and other religious organizations led to the new name due to many controversial issues and contraceptives were widely opposed by the Roman Catholics, church groups, and pro-life individuals.

In the case Roe v Wade with Roe being the generic surname given to a female individual (Jane Roe) to remain anonymous or hide her identity in a legal case, later became an avalanche into the legalization of abortion within the United States of America. In a similar manner, "Doe" is the surname given to a male (John Doe) in a legal case to remain anonymous. Wade was the district attorney representing the case. It was in1969 when at the age of twenty-one, a young woman known as Norma McCorvey became pregnant a third time. Norma McCorvey was living with her father and was working low-paying jobs. Society oftentimes rejects and views individuals negatively if they become pregnant out of wedlock. McCorvey's friends advised her that she should assert a false claim and concoct a lie that she had been raped and should obtain legal abortion under Texas's law that prohibited abortion.

This system then gave birth to a multimillion-dollar systemic wolf operation. Many delivery vehicles would be evidence of the process of selling (fetal) body parts and joining the lucrative operation on the procurement of specimen experiments and stem cell research.

According to penal law,

S 125.05 Homicide, abortion and related offenses; definitions of terms.

3. *"Justifiable abortional act."* An abortional act is justifiable when committed upon a female with her consent by a duly licensed physician acting (a) under a reasonable belief that such is necessary to preserve her life, or, (b) *within twenty-four weeks from the commencement of her pregnancy.* A pregnant female's commission of an abortional act upon herself is justifiable when she acts upon the advice of a duly licensed physician (1) that such act is necessary to preserve her life, or, (2) within twenty-four weeks from the commencement of her pregnancy. (emphasis added)

As we dissect this written law governing the regulation of abortion, many individuals will try to conform simply because it's written by those who are supposedly filled with justifiable wisdom. But very soon even without contest, you will discover that the law is rigged with so much compromises that it collapses under its own pressure. Not only does abortion oftentimes pose more risk than the birth delivery process, but this brings into question the twenty-four weeks from commencement of the mother's pregnancy. Abortion attempts justification necessary to preserve the life of the mother and within twenty-four weeks period. Many abortions are executed after this time frame, which is a violation of the law itself and brings into play the risk factor of the mother versus the delivery process of the child. Nonetheless, what is the logic involving the twenty-four weeks window?

The first trimester (three months = twelve weeks) simply means that twenty-four weeks is the equivalent of six months or the end of the second trimester (six months = twenty-four weeks). Many constitute this as being the state of viability, which means the child can survive independently outside the mother's womb when bodily organs are fully developed, thus becoming a person. Technological advancements and rapid improvements in medicine and medical care have proven beyond reasonable doubts that the newborn child can survive outside the womb of the mother as early as current record shows twenty weeks and five days and another child that survives after being born at eighteen weeks. This man-made law has collapsed miserably because it was constructed under the bridge and influence of false pretense.

Second, there are instances in which drivers were under the influence of alcohol and caused the death of the mother and the unborn child. Prosecutors attempted to charge the drunk driver with double vehicular homicide or manslaughter of the mother and vehicular feticide of the child. According to the law constructed for abortion, the unborn that is less than twenty-four weeks old is not considered a person due to the state of viability and therefore cannot be factored in the equation as a person being man-slaughtered. Otherwise, the law would be in conflict, and one of two would have to be overturned. The system then continues in motion while people with designed intelligence pretend as though it's perfectly constructed. Can one imagine the devastation of the surviving mothers who know that the life of a child has been snatched away and case proceeding dismissed as though the person was never in existence due to viability?

Third, the unborn children that have been aborted are used as part of a multimillion-dollar industry in the sales of body parts, "specimens," for stem cell research. This aids in the biases and influences of the rate of abortion. Many children are being coerced and influenced through a system that pretends to cater to their needs, yet it is largely in support of a ferocious racketeering and profit-making industry. Schools also collaborate by protecting children against disclosing the abortion process to their parents, oftentimes crossing state borders where laws are favorable without parental notification. Yet the system holds parents responsible in the event of the death of a child. Everyone claims and defends the right to his/her body, and many have acknowledged that the unborn child is undoubtedly a person. Yet individuals will stand on their right to survive while forsaking the right of the children without a voice in their womb with the act of abortion.

Systemic Wolf Operation—Abortion Conspiracy

The sole premise and defense for concluding that a fetus is not a person is simply the fetus's stage of viability. If the fetus lacks the independence of survival outside the mother's womb, can we dare conclude that an organism or disease that is a parasite lacks life? Even with a selfish attempt to deny this fact, it is evident that life starts not in the second or third trimester, but by the principles of defense, at the very moment of formation and conception. If the very cells in our bodies, without our visual recognition or understanding, may it be foreign bodies attacking our immune system or defending our body, can be construed as life-form, how much more precious an entity that is identical to my being and state of existence?

The judicial system has made twenty-four weeks the line of demarcation for the legality of abortion. Researchers have also concluded that at twenty-one weeks, the unborn is fully developed, and any present abnormalities can be detected. The judicial system has classified within the penal law justifiable act of abortion as preserving the life of the mother. However, an overwhelming number of parents on a yearly basis commits the act of abortion on the premise of financial forecast, disruption of family prestige, inconvenience to lifestyle, attempt at maintaining image and reputation, and a lack of fear of and admiration for God. Very rarely is the act of abortion due to abnormalities, which is usually discovered at the twenty weeks duration.

By definition, what constitutes threat? Threat can be perceived, imminent, or miscalculated and can change from one stage to a more or less intense level. Threat can be relative to one's interpretation.

If the unborn poses a threat to the life of the mother, can this factor be used to determine the basis for the death of the child?

Many parents, individuals, and citizens pose a threat to society and self. Many people have overdosed on drugs, robbed, violated, raped, and killed and still do not constitute or justify the taking of such person's life with the death penalty. The innocent unborn child who is perceived to pose a future threat at a stage of viability has been viciously eradicated on the virtue or basis of probability. Do we euthanize individuals for not meeting certain criteria of viability or threat to the other? Do we euthanize the mentally challenged, the crippled, the amputated, the ignorant, the lawbreakers, the elderly who is helpless and cannot survive on his/her own, etc.? Should powerful nations destroy the "baby" nations in the third-world classification that may rise up to be a major threat or danger of future world power as done with socioeconomic warfare? Has mankind failed to understand that no man exists independently? Like the unborn clinging for dear life, like a man deep in coma clinging on life support, is a man existing codependently? Plant life excretes oxygen and intakes carbon dioxide and mankind does the reverse. Does mankind fail to realize that man does not physically survive by money, but the intake of food oftentimes and naturally produced by the earth? The unborn receives food and oxygen from the mother the day before twenty-four weeks just like he/she does when the clock strikes at midnight to exceed and surpass the threshold of limitation inscribed by a judicial system thereafter.

During the 1970s, in the quest for exercising the "inherent" right of abortion, the defense is viability. Who is willing to reverse the law since viability shows babies can survive in the second trimester? But as technology increases, we mistakenly conclude that knowledge increases. Knowledge has always existed. Man discovers knowledge and information and is never the creator of such entity. He can never take credit for his wisdom any more than he rejects his ignorance. However, the knowledge that presumably increased undoubtedly became readily available and then made privileged to the world at large. Can we therefore contend that the leading nation was the originator of such knowledge, or did this leading nation come into discovery of this already existing possibility and availability of this vast wealth of knowledge? Can a third-world nation or a less fortunate nation use the lack of access to knowledge, exposure, or ignorance as their defense to the legalization of abortion? The same holds true for the United States of America and other nations that follow this trend.

During the 1970s, when a fetus could not naturally survive outside the mother's womb, it's not that it was impossible; it's just simply our default of shortcoming to the awareness, capabilities, and possibilities like many other nations that still lack the fundamental resources to enhance this capability. Can they conclude that the process is impossible? Or does the knowledgeable condemn the other nation for being ignorant, simply because the leading nation has discovered the facts a few years earlier, while pretending to be the originator? The court of law will slap you across the face with "ignorance is no excuse"! Nations that are competing to remain in power strive to obtain knowledge and improvements in development ahead of their competitors. Can we use delinquencies or mediocrity as a rationale for our failure to discover, like we oftentimes do to undermine others? Of course not! Then this begs the question: can the lack of technology be the main determinant or factor in determining the fate of another? Man can naturally justify the taking of one's life to suit his cause. We have seen it manifest through the eyes of wars, religion, racism, slavery, discrimination, insanity, law enforcement, euthanasia, and more.

Many individuals believe that abortion is a woman's right to her body (the Scripture does not grant individuality in a marital relationship). Upon proven facts that a fetus is a person capable of surviving outside the mother's womb, such right to one's body should then be transcended to the unborn baby, even though such right already naturally exists! Or perhaps we should await the court to let the pendulum swing back with equal force and reaction like Newton's law. If abortion holds true, then with today's technological advancements and the discovery of survival in the second trimester, abortion should be strictly prohibited at this stage. This would then be classified as murder, simply because it is the taking of one's life. It would also defy the very claim pursued—one's right to his/her own body. If you indeed inherit this right by merely entering life, then a fetus at the stage of viability should be entitled to this inherent right, which by no means can or should be taken away, not even by the mother any more than a drunk driver. It is appointed for man once to die (Hebrews 9:27), so can a judge on the Supreme Court bench grant the authority to live or deny access to life? Didn't such individual walk into the same inherent divine favor from the womb of a mother? Who gave such high and exalted authority to presume and preside over others by that which he so favorably enjoys?

Does mankind fail to realize that his spirit man and sense of existence, spiritual life, breath that he breathes, heart that pumps, peace of mind, analytical processing, and designed intelligence are upheld, sustained, and orchestrated by God? This right is inherent and is naturally obligated to the child and cannot be taken away by any force. Not even the mother has the power to alter such right, or else the mother and the doctors collaborated and become a greater threat to that child's well-being and safety. Do we perceive the child not to be a person and treat such individual as property with a slave-master approach? Do we get the father's input to procreate but reject his perspective when it's time to eliminate? How long will we devalue and place the limitation of death on entities not within our scope?

Do we not know that the same doctors have been monitoring the child's heart rate and physiological function from as early as twenty-two days?

Does the same doctor accept payment to deliver, as much as he accepts payment to abort?

The common factor seems to be payment! Do we not know that the child's mind and intelligence is formulated and functioning at its best?

> When Elizabeth heard Mary's greeting, the baby leaped in her womb, and Elizabeth was filled with the Holy Spirit. (Luke 1:41 NIV)

Don't psychologists inform us that within the first five years of birth will be the most indelible and formidable years of survival that will determine the child's personality? Will we shred the physical body and deny the fact of the mind and the impossibilities of being able to touch the spirit and internal existence and consciousness? Isn't this why juveniles are not placed in solitary confinement for an extenuating period, because researchers and lawmakers agree that this impacts the brain that is not fully developed at this age? Are teenagers less of a person or subhumans as deemed for the unborn? The IRS polices and monitors the financial aspect of society. Should advocates quit being biased and ensure that not only the rights are exercised to the extreme of taking life, but that lives are being preserved?

Do we really hold these truths as the Declaration of Independence states?

> We hold these truths to be self-evident, that all men are
> created equal, that they are endowed by their Creator
> with certain unalienable Rights, that among these are
> Life, Liberty and the pursuit of Happiness . . .

Babies are being slaughtered on tables after twenty-four weeks of conception. Should the judicial system forcefully form advocacy groups that will enforce laws and policies against doctors who religiously break these laws that are established and upheld by the Constitution? Doctors can determine full-term births and the weeks of pregnancy but seemingly become blind when it's time to abort. Are doctors falsifying documents and usurping their authority? Shouldn't this be classified as unjust gains when doctors kill these babies for monetary gains? Doctors are not working free of charge! Isn't the life of the mother at a greater risk during the abortion procedure itself than carrying the child that the body is naturally designed by God to uphold? Who is defending the Constitution after its amendment? Or do we settle after a temper tantrum by society has accomplished its agenda?

If a mother should say to the abortionist doctor that she changed her mind and is now willing to have the child, how many doctors will say to the mother, "No, for you shall surely die in the natural birth process"?

Whenever a person destroys a home, makes threats, defaces buildings, verbally states threats, endangers educational institutions, or destroys a generation, these elements are being treated as a hate crime. If you break into a house and remove a television or scratch someone's car, you will be liable and possibly face prison time. Is the unborn of a more dangerous terroristic threat, with mother and doctor bypassing due process and presenting the child to face capital punishment instantly? Once out of the womb, we are willing to spend millions of dollars for survival against all elements of destructions that are contrary to life. We spend to combat diseases, depression, anxiety, racism, prejudice, apartheid, social injustice, social segregation, and fight against terrorist groups. We also spend to conduct research projects, perform heart transplant, facelift and treat our psychological well-being especially against negative/suicidal thoughts. On a yearly basis budgets are implemented for dealing with drunk drivers, malpractice, food consumption, racial symbols, potential threats, wars, mass incarceration and other legal entities. Destruction to life and the quality of survival shouldn't be swept to the side and treat the unborn as a lesser value. Perhaps payment for preservation of sperm cells, egg implant, or watching and monitoring the fertility process for sperm to be infused with the egg of a surrogate shouldn't cause anyone to rejoice in advance; apparently life is useless according to the wise judges.

Some individuals sue doctors for failing in the process. Some sue the surrogate mothers who fall in love with the unborn and start to claim ownership. Many prospective mothers who face the challenges of pregnancies invest millions in the preservation of eggs and sperm cells to maintain survivability and life-form. How can society spend and maintain such billion-dollar industry to sustain cells, preserve the process of fertility, and watch and monitor sperm fusing with the egg, DNA evidence, yet go to the extent to despise, reject, and forsake and destroy the unborn like discarding garbage in a dumpster? Or is it because one of the greatest marketing and sales industries is the selling of specimens (fetus's body parts) for stem cell research?

Does a disease have life, but the unborn child doesn't?

The news media has reported multiple cases across the United States, Europe, and other countries involving men who knowingly have human immunodeficiency virus (HIV) (the virus that causes acquired immune deficiency syndrome [AIDS] by weakening the cells that fight infection) and deliberately spread the disease by sleeping with multiple women. Some men would rent luxury vehicles and go to clubs to lure women into their trap of spreading the disease. Many of the women had just one encounter and were unaware that they are now carriers of the disease. Some of the men are caught, arrested, and charged with felonious assault. When you consider such cases, there are multiple factors that are at play for the context of this topic and life principle. We have two parties involved, namely, the man and the woman both having different motives and deceit. Without a doubt, there is also an indisputable entity that is alive and destructive; this is the HIV. Though rape is not involved, neither a child that will be aborted, but unfortunately a disease that will linger, causing emotional pain and regrets. The life and future of the innocent mother or future child has been impacted because of the consensual decision made by two adults. Without the existence of the disease factor, one could clearly walk away and easily forget that an action was done that gratified my desires and is now behind me. But the evidence of the disease has stamped and embedded an indisputable image. The disease is evidently inseparable without intervention, although on the other hand, we may treat the unborn as though the blood flow and oxygen from the mother are isolated. Unfortunately, this type of lifestyle has been the norm and has become prevalent and highly accepted in society as the standard of living.

Should a parent or two adults take offense for divorce, adoption, or rejection but take a casual approach when being one unit in pregnancy because the unborn is unable to articulate offense in rejection? Should the perpetrators be told not to sleep around because they have a disease, while everyone else has the right to reject your opinion by asking, "Who are you to tell me what to do?" simply because they feel qualified to the right to their bodies? Having no disease seems to exempt others from being told to exercise precautionary measures! Do we only see the problems and the high risks upon discovery of the results or consequences of the actions? Is my action highly acceptable as long as there are no visible devastating effects? Is it your choice to protect yourself when you feel like doing so, then only to subsequently discover that your actions do impact society and disrupt families? Isn't it obvious that there is a moral law at work, whether it's engraved on the pages of the Constitution or rejected by the government? Does the government now quarantine the neighborhood due to a new epidemic, or do we live by the law that states that "I can do whatever I want with my body"? Do I now rebel against the government, or does the government override my rights to exercise freedom?

What happens when the doctor cannot abort the disease like the way he legally aborts the fetus?

What do I do when my life is in danger, and I cannot make the growing fetus the perpetrator? The perpetrator is now a disease or HIV, and not a fetus that can be easily discarded. Do I then tell myself that there is no life in the fetus, but there is life in the disease that is ravaging through my body? Will I find a way to live even with the threat of the disease in my body? Do I acknowledge that the partner is equally responsible for his action, or perhaps not because he was not included in the process of abortion? Do I claim the disease as right to my body, or do I include others in my misery because it's beyond the scope of human control? Is it an illusion to believe that I can terminate the life of an individual but not eradicate a disease?

Does the government now entertain a debate and ask at what stage did life begin in the disease? Do we now wait for twenty-four weeks when the disease becomes viable and quickened, or do we tell the victims to report to the clinic immediately? Perhaps the sperm cells that were ejected into the uterus have no life until it reaches the eggs. Maybe there is no consequence to the choices made since you were not raped or gotten pregnant in the process. Why bother feeling guilty when you have to explain to your husband that this is proof of infidelity? Why bother explain the risks to my children when the school system distributes contraceptives to bodies that are not fully developed? Do we consume foods that are not ripe or fully edible? Do animals run around mating outside of a fully grown and developed companion? Maybe the government could develop a curriculum that convinces humanity that the animals are compatible and ready irrespective of the sociophysiological stages of development. Who has the right and authority to tell these women what to do when they have the legal authority in the First, Fifth, and Ninth Amendments to walk into danger because the right to your body supersedes natural law? Who has been granted the authority to take such step and risk being sued for the violation of women's right? Wouldn't this result in court cases and battles that would create new laws that would be implemented across the fifty states? Perhaps not—that's too close to church and state conflict! Let's just continue along a clear path of acceptable danger. After all, there's only one life to live; your choice matters. Who is now your advocate when the life that is started in you is a life that is outside the power and control of an abortionist doctor? Will he admit that you have no other option but to approach this challenge by faith? Can you now pretend on paper that your life is at risk in order to stay on the legal side, or will you face this challenge by looking to a greater source?

Will the mother find ways to live with a life-threatening disease trapped in her body, or will she give up and conclude there is no other option like she did with a child that would exit her body in few months?

Maybe we could put our trust in a system with contraceptives that are designed to fail in order to boost the abortion market sales and the fetuses that are sold as specimens.

There are many factors outside the scope of our control, which we all have to deal with to different extents. Some actions are inclusive of rape, infidelity, incest coerced or forced, spousal rape, exploitation of the mentally incapacitated, or even Immaculate Conception. The ultimate outcome may not necessarily be limited to pregnancy nor restricted to the female gender, but entails physical birth defects, diseases discovered or unknown or emotional scars. We react and execute decisions by our awareness, but we are limited finite beings. All the negative factors can be outside the will of God but are under one category, namely, *sin*. If your mind fails to comprehend this fact, then refusal to change or gain resolution is inevitable. What a great nation this would be if we as a people would fight the sinful nature as we do to gratify the carnal!

Doesn't the unborn need to be treated with greater dignity like we would cater to the effects of a disease? Are they not celebrating life? Are the doctors monitoring the dead in vain? Is the womb a morgue that after twenty-four weeks mysteriously stimulates, resurrects, and incites life? When mothers naturally mourn after accidents and miscarriages, are they shedding tears as though out of touch with reality?

Is this why it is extremely difficult to convict a drunk driver for hitting down a mother who is less than twenty-four weeks pregnant, because your contradictory law states that the mother is not carrying a person?

Is this why birds, eagles, and reptiles guard their nests and sit on eggs throughout winter and severe weather conditions to sustain life in their unborn?

Is this why the very ants create a nesting and colony underground larger than the average-size house, for survival and giving birth? Is this why the ants create an area in their colony just for reproduction and a separate place for food storage, sleeping, and waste?

Is this why snakes, reptiles, and animals guard the pregnant female and attack any signs or perceived threats of danger and predators, even at the early stage equivalent to the first trimester?

Is this why man has established laws prohibiting fishing certain times and seasons for mating, reproduction, and sea preservation? Is this why you can't hunt or become limited to the quantity of animals you can keep? Is this why farmers take a break so that the soil can replenish for quality production? Do we sit back and watch the forest and plant life become extinct and dormant, or do we regulate rules and laws restricting the cutting down and planting of trees?

How different could this process be for the children that are the future generation? Children that will not only physically exist but, with designed intelligence and purpose, will also impact the world. Is this why people go into a state of shock when children with autism excel above those who should function with excellence? Do we preserve every other life-form, information, history, precious memories, pictures, movies, books, gadgets, and memorabilia but have total disregard for life? Is a doctor willing to trade prestige and monetary gain for the termination of life? Do I face incarceration for making verbal threats against life, burning down a forest or building, but not execution of the life of the unborn? Do I abort dreams, visions, and business decisions—and it costs great wealth, political status, and priceless entities—yet apply logic while denying the great resources of a life that can change the world and is unable to fight this evil force? A child crying behind closed doors in the womb, entrapped by the mother's decision and the hands of a doctor tied to greed and business contract!

A child walking into death penalty without a trial, without a voice, without a representative, defenseless! An individual who is a victim of rape can regain hope, can face the perpetrator, can live to talk about the painful experience, and can make a difference. How can the taking of an innocent life ever justify any action done or conducted against another? In the extreme rarity of a perpetrator raping and impregnating a victim, how does the killing and rapid eradication of an innocent child justify, liberate, or be the consequential penalty for either the victim or the perpetrator? Will the memory, guilt, and conviction be the perpetual evidence against those attempting and having the inclination to act oblivious?

Would this measure also validate the epidemic of fathers who manipulate, abuse, and impregnate our women of society then go missing in action? In no way this is an attempt to equate rape with irresponsible fathers. A father who forcibly takes sex, manipulates, and victimizes women is just as destructive as a perpetrator who rapes or may not be in his sound mind, regardless of the process resulting in child production. Many of these children, inclusive of incest, are surviving and enjoying the freedom of breathing fresh air and oxygen like those who would want to suffocate them on the abortion table of death. Where is the justice when slave masters raped and forced family members to breed each other while covering their heads? Where is the justice when the vulnerable are being constantly raped in hospices, incest against minors is committed, and children are sodomized? Do we turn against the unborn, or do we confess that there is no trace of evidence? How selfish can one be to enjoy life while dictating to the innocent that he does not deserve to live? Is this not worse than oppression, prejudice, and racism? Can we even compare this vicious act to destruction of property?

Have you ever experienced a loved one becoming extremely sick or know someone who has been taken to the hospital and clinging to life at the brink of death? Can you envision visitors in the sick room with internal turmoil having an outward expression of sorrow and grief? Everyone is sad at the face of death even when it's caused by a natural disaster.

Should we honor or entertain your plea from the death penalty or execution after you raped or murdered someone? Or is it innocent until proven guilty? We fight for the life of robbers, rapists, and murderers and oftentimes conclude that they do not deserve the death penalty. Years later, these individuals are granted forgiveness for early release after committing various heinous crimes. On the other hand, the innocent unborn child who is fully functioning is introduced the penalty of death at the introductory stage of life, while the perpetrator lives and pleas his case for life.

Should we honor your request to live if you are an elderly or aged or stricken with a disease on life support, when loved ones produce all rationale why they think doctors should "pull the plug" (disconnect life support)? Is this also justifiable at the other end of the table, since you are old and dependent on life support like a fetus attached by the umbilical cord? Do the opinion of the doctors and the decisions made by your loved ones without your input qualify you for death sentence? Should your life end simply because as an elderly you are solely dependent on others for continuum of life and considered a major inconvenience to their lifestyle? No one seems to know that death is appointed for man once to die, and everyone is yelling and believes that the elderly and unborn should be put to death, apparently unaware that your day is also fast approaching. We are like a flower tossed in the wind awaiting a grave like an open ocean that is never satisfied. Who has the power to reverse death when he knocks on the door? Perhaps the same judge who decided the fate of the unborn! Show me such judge so that I can make my appeal in advance.

Will the victim of rape be free from pain and sorrow if there is no child to abort? Or is it justifiable to say, if rape had resulted in pregnancy, abortion is justifiable because being born would prolong the painful memories of the act committed? Should a victim of rape become married or continue to sleep with her spouse? Because without a doubt, unless you have developed the power to overcome this potential defeat, you will be reminded of such heinous experience at every lovemaking session. Abortion does not erase the reality of your past or eradicate the natural ability of mental processing and memory. Abortion is not the solution to a psychological trauma.

With or without being pregnant or the act of abortion, there is an action committed that is not conducive to the standards of society. The action of sexual engagement is preceded by the manifestation of the consequences or damages. So the one that luckily escapes pregnancy or diseases has committed an act that should be under the microscope or scrutiny of society. The problem is not found in the results of the actions, but the decisions that lead to the outcome. Do we turn to the victims of accidents while negate those who drive with negligence and potential dangers and threats? Do we make laws for deterrent in all other factors of life, holding both parties responsible, while turning a blind eye toward family dysfunction by silencing the church and pro-life groups? Will advocacy groups shout for rights and then become utterly silent when discovered in the wrong? Will you shout for your right before the stage of viability yet turn your back thereafter? Something is terribly wrong with women's rights. Martin Luther King Jr. made a profound statement when he said that our lives will begin to end on the day that we become silent on important matters and issues.

The phenomenon of life is initiated at a sexual agreement, even without the awareness of pregnancy. It has always been this way in God's design, and not through evolution. Many individuals attempt several times to get pregnant and may have missed it due to complications or the ovulation cycle. Many individuals are hit with a surprise, after wondering why they have missed their menstrual cycle. Some female entrap males by getting pregnant without their consent like in the case of Lot and his daughters (Genesis 19:30–38). Some males were not prepared for the consequences after the gratification, then try to persuade their partner to terminate the pregnancy.

Parents oftentimes warn their children about engaging in premarital and unprotected sex. Life will begin with or without your consent. Doctors can tell you within twenty-four hours if you are pregnant through various methods and tests. Pregnancy is defined as carrying an embryo or fetus over a nine-month period from your last menstrual cycle. You can pretend as though you are not pregnant and life has not been initiated at that point of sexual agreement, but give enough time and the evidence will grow and manifest, erupting like a volcano. Provided you wait long enough, the child will exit and enter this world without your permission. You can interview the many different women who did not know that they were pregnant and thought that they were just gaining weight. They may have experienced an irregular menstrual cycle due to the effects of birth control or dysfunction within their body. Many women felt the urge to urinate, then panic when another individual mysteriously exited the birth canal. This can be a traumatic experience sending shock waves like you are engaged in a world war. Some mothers try to run away from the child still lying in the toilet. Some mothers scream and utter words they never thought were in their vocabulary. Many are not prepared to express to their spouse that there is a new addition to the family, and this is not through adoption measures, but through a sexual agreement. For individuals who are engaged in infidelity, they hope that the sperm of the husband outran the sperm of the infidel partner and made a successful touchdown. Life when initiated has no boundaries, limits, or discrimination. Life will honor your choice and executed decisions. The evidence of life will manifest itself regardless of the definition that the Supreme Court tries to assert.

Have you ever asked someone who believes in God, "Who created you?" The response will always be "God of course!" The response will almost never be my parents even from the mouth of a child. There is no child that will ever know or understand the process of their conception unless it is brought to their awareness. Every human being knows that he lacks the capacity or potential to create another individual. Such individual therefore undeniably knows that he came into existence beyond the capabilities of his parents. Such individual therefore has no knowledge of the initiation or agreement that initiated or transpired in such existence. The information conveyed to such child may not even be accurate, but one that covers up shame or guilt. Many young parents got pregnant out of forced sex, duress, coercion, date rape, intoxication, being under the influence, multiple participants and abusers, prostitution, one-night date, spousal rape, incest, underage sex, and the list goes on. Many of these young ladies are ashamed to confess that they did not consent to the sexual activity and are afraid to convey the truth to their parents, who gave endless warnings. They are afraid to tarnish their reputation and to face the complexities of the consequences awaiting the perpetrator. Many young ladies are at a dilemma and internal conflict, knowing that they desired the gratification and trusted the display of integrity from the one who became the perpetrator. Nonetheless, the mother has courageously faced the reality of such unpleasant circumstance and made a decision to raise her offspring going against the odds of abortion. Today, such mother has never disclosed the inner boundaries of her mental prison but watches her child grow above the status quo of society and the temptation of abortion. The average bi-racial couples can confess that they have experienced some form of toxic behavior in this nation due to racial discrimination. Today, we can salute these mothers who acknowledge that only God gives life and takes life, Whom can erase or reverse the hands of death when it knocks at your door.

> For in him we live, and move, and have our being; as certain also of your own poets have said, For we are also his offspring. (Acts 17:28 KJV)

The commencement of life does not equate to a nonexistent state. Animals, birds, and reptiles will guard their eggs with their life; there is no question if the liquid form will transform and become a replica of the parent.

> Just as He chose us in Him before the foundation of the world, that we should be holy and without blame before Him in love. (Ephesians 1:4 NKJV)

If Jesus died for humanity, why would mankind assume the position of declaring death!

> For I am persuaded, that neither death, nor life, nor angels, nor principalities, nor powers, nor things

present, nor things to come, Nor height, nor depth, nor any other creature, shall be able to separate us from the love of God, which is in Christ Jesus our Lord. (Romans 8:38–39 KJV)

God has the desire and redemptive power for every man to dwell in His eternal kingdom. Martin Luther King Jr. expresses that injustice in any location is a threat to justice in every place, because we are all affected in one way or another.

The United States is emulated by many nations that are either sanctioned or feel compelled to follow.

In a recorded documentary on the issue of abortion, Justice Byron R. White of the United States Supreme Court stated, "I find nothing in the language or history of the constitution to support the court's judgment. The Court simply fashions and announces a new constitutional right for pregnant mothers and, with scarcely any reason or authority for its action . . ."

White later argued that the Court should not establish constitutional barriers to protect life and grant constitutional power to mothers and doctors to exterminate life. The Supreme Court stated if it had not been ruled on before, they would have ruled otherwise.

So why not apply this principle to the homosexual community and not change the law and the right to life according to the Fifth Amendment and Fourteenth Amendment? Didn't this community argue its way until the laws were changed to facilitate their needs?

Fifth Amendment

No person shall be held to answer for a capital, or otherwise infamous crime, unless on a presentment or indictment of a grand jury, except in cases arising in the land or naval forces, or in the militia, when in actual service in time of war or public danger; nor shall any person be subject for the same offense to be twice put in jeopardy of life or limb; nor shall be compelled in any criminal case to be a witness against himself, *nor be deprived of life, liberty, or property, without due process of law*; nor shall private property be taken for public use, without just compensation. (emphasis added)

Are we depriving the life and liberty of a child by accusing that child to be of a great danger and threat to the mother? Is there a trial with due process, or is it just the mother's undisclosed opinion and a contract killer known as the doctor conducting same-day execution?

Fourteenth Amendment

All persons born or naturalized in the United States, and subject to the jurisdiction thereof, are citizens of the United States and of the State wherein they reside. No State shall make or enforce any law which shall abridge the privileges or immunities of citizens of the United States; *nor shall any State deprive any person of life, liberty, or property,* without due process of law; nor deny to any person within its jurisdiction the equal protection of the laws. (emphasis added)

Is this the great United States speaking on behalf of those she claims to naturalize to citizenship, as though the Constitution can speak on behalf of the Creator while confusing geographical location with a universal law of supernatural birth?

Didn't the homosexual community argue that according to their X-Y chromosomes, this behavior is found within their genetic design, and therefore, they are predestined for such lifestyle? Is this why the leading nation sanctions the other nations to emulate her decision?

Will you be homosexual from conception yet cannot be a person until after twenty-four weeks even though your heart is already beating at twenty-two days?

Did humanity fail to realize that the growth process continues even after we exit the womb and birth canal, and is not just confined to the physical and physiological realm? Self-induced stress, the environment, and behavior of the parent also impact the mental, spiritual, and emotional well-being of the child.

The ACLU, which is the American Civil Liberties Union, that pledged "to defend and preserve the individual rights and liberties guaranteed to every person in this country by the Constitution and laws of the United States" was very vocal in the rights of a mother according to the law of the land. Where are you when the lives of the unborn are being brutally eradicated even after the twenty-four weeks cycle? I can't see any protest or picket signs against such injustice. Or maybe we will continue to hide behind the glass door of a nonprofit organization.

For further information, you can review the case that has been provided below:

"*Planned Parenthood of South Eastern Pennsylvania et al. v. Casey,* Governor of Pennsylvania, et al. certiorari to the United States Court of Appeals for the third circuit." No. 91-744 argued April 22, 1992, decided June 29, 1992.

As we honestly ponder this reality, it may be debatable to conclude the time in which life begins, but it does not require much effort to know when a life truly exists. Humanity will talk themselves into almost any action that they wish to execute whether in prosperity or walking off the ledge of their own demise. The Supreme Court has definitely granted mankind a false hope of law and rulership over their life.

Carol Everett is said to be the founder of the Heidi Group, which is an antiabortion nonprofit organization. Carol Everett, at a pro-life sponsored workshop, gave her testimony of how she made a pivotal turn in her life from being a former independent practicing abortion clinic owner to a radical pro-life activist. Below is a portion of her testimonial as she became transparent about her experience as a victim of abortion and also as a promoter before her radical transformation:

> What I'm telling you is that this man offered to do an illegal abortion in the State of Texas and, yes, indeed, we did it. I was looking for someone to tell me not to have the abortion and I ran into an abortion salesman. And that's what happens in our nation today. We're going to talk a lot more about that, but let's go back to my story and what happened to me.
>
> Let's talk about those kids when they find out that they are pregnant. They may not want an abortion; they may want information. But when they call that number that's paid for by abortion money, what kind of information do you think they're going to get? Let's remember, they sell abortions. They don't sell keeping the baby. They don't sell giving the baby up for adoption. They don't sell delivering that baby in any form. They only sell abortions.
>
> And then they say: Is it a baby? No, it's a product of conception; it's a blood clot; it's a piece of tissue. They don't even really tell them it's a fetus, because, you see, that almost humanizes it too much. It's never a baby.
>
> So they get this girl to come in the clinic, and many times they just get her to come in for a pregnancy test, and if that's the case then they greet her at the door and they say, Oh, Linda, I'm so glad you're here. I've been waiting for you. This girl doesn't know they have an

appointment book and each counselor has to schedule their appointments an hour apart so she has plenty of time to spend being their "friend" while they're there. She takes them back; she does the pregnancy test; it doesn't really matter. If there's any way they can convince this girl she's pregnant, she's going to be pregnant. But they go through this test anyway. She tells her she's pregnant, and the girl might cry. She may get upset. But they take her into a separate room; they don't want anyone to see anyone crying in there; it's supposed to be a great place; we're supposed to help people in the abortion clinic.

There are two problems that are going on that we might be able to do something with, too. That is, that abortion clinics, if they have someone that does present themselves thinking they're pregnant and of course the test show they're not; that they're going to sell that abortion to that non-pregnant woman.

Carol Everett has led many movements by exposing secret clinics being operated by doctors who commit abortion and hide the truth from their own family members or create illusion in their neighborhoods. Abortion clinics are strategically placed within the parameters of schools. Children who are victims of abortion according to statistics are said to likely abort a child three to five times before graduation. Scripts are written to overcome the objections and oppositions of students in order to compel them into the act of abortion. Contraceptives are designed to fail and created with low dosage that will increase the potential result of pregnancy leading to abortion. Is this really a surprise when clinics deceive you into thinking that you are pregnant and officiate a false procedure for monetary gain?

Foxes will lure you into a trap and convince you that what you are doing is right and the ethical thing to do. The fox then desensitizes you to perceive your parents as the enemy who will launch an attack of character assassination if the truth is revealed. Yet the one who lends the notion of caring is the one with ulterior motives for monetary gain and racial alienation and identity destruction. The fox has multiple holes and will go creeping into another dwelling place until it finds rest. Since you cannot tame or recondition the fox, it's incumbent upon you to exercise wisdom in avoidance of a systemic scheme.

The wolf will become very friendly and warm in its sheep's clothing and cause a young lady to express her love and obligation by committing abortion as proof. The wolf will tell you that we are both not ready for this journey as a family while taking no form of precautionary measures to prevent pregnancy. The true internal ferocious nature of the wolf erupts when the young lady decides she will face the odds of life and bring her child into the world.

> I will praise You, for I am fearfully *and* wonderfully made; Marvelous are Your works, And *that* my soul knows very well. (Psalm 139:14 NKJV)

CHAPTER 7
STOMPING ELEPHANTS
(Power of Preparation)

One of the greatest victories to be won is to conquer the obstacle of self.
—M. Reid

Still Standing

It was Thanksgiving night; we just enjoyed a variety of food at our family gathering. As the time was getting late, I drove my sister to her home about one minute away to retrieve clothing items for her son. As my sister and I proceeded along the main road back to my aunt's house in my Toyota Highlander, I could see my destination approximately one hundred meters, less than thirty seconds away. I put on my left indicator in anticipation of my very next turn. My sister saw a fast-moving object of a bright light approaching from her immediate right, then she yelled, "Look out!" Before I could observe this mysterious speeding object, my vehicle was already spinning and spiraling out of control. Both airbags were deployed. The front of my vehicle started folding and caved in. In my peripheral vision, I saw a vehicle proceeding and went out of sight. My vehicle came to a full stop. I was disoriented and tried to gather my thoughts wondering where we were. I was in an accident. I could smell burning chemical as the airbags deflated and appeared to be on smoke, with a possible fire igniting. My first instinct said I should evacuate the vehicle. There was now a huge crowd assembled like elephants running to the rescue. I opened the driver's side door, unbuckled my seat belt, and quickly exited the vehicle. I told my sister to exit the vehicle. She climbed over into the driver's seat then exited the vehicle and lay on her back in excruciating pain. I urged her to remain calm. I examined my vehicle; it was hit from the right at a perpendicular angle. I finally realized that my vehicle was struck by a speeding car that failed to obey the stop sign. The car was going at such forceful speed, not only did my vehicle spin around but the speeding car went over a ditch and came to a stop on the lawn of a neighboring house. The driver was a young man who subsequently sat on the grass and appeared to be in a state of shock.

The closest depiction of this scenario is a video that I had watched earlier before the incident. It is as though this became soothing medicine to appease my soul from this anguish and incomprehensible encounter. It was a jaguar standing in the bushes at the edge of the water, observing a crocodile on a small plot of land in the middle of a pond. The jaguar then repositioned itself in perfect alignment behind the crocodile, got into the water, and swam across the pond to the edge of the plot of land. The jaguar then slowly crawled onto the edge of the plot of land, then crouched while sneaking closer toward the crocodile in a very inconspicuous manner. The jaguar then stopped and got in position as though in preparation for a hundred-meter sprint. Before the crocodile could observe the sprint and speed to plot its escape, the teeth of the jaguar were already grasping the crocodile in the back of its neck. The crocodile was instantly immobilized, as the jaguar carried the crocodile and swam back across the pond to dry land for a great feast.

> Be alert and of sober mind. Your enemy the devil prowls around like a roaring lion looking for someone to devour. Resist him, standing firm in the faith, because you know that the family of believers throughout the world is undergoing the same kind of sufferings. (1 Peter 5:7–8 NIV)

I can only imagine as I drove along the main road; the other driver and I, inclusive of occupants in the vehicles, were like that crocodile unaware of impending danger. First Peter 5:8 encourages us to be vigilant and of a sober mind. This means that the enemy can get into our thought process and cause us to execute irresponsible and inappropriate actions that can become self-destructive and detrimental to others. As the speeding car awaited (like the jaguar), ready to sprint toward the Toyota Highlander, I can imagine the thoughts going on in the mind of the driver of the speeding Ford Focus. What was he thinking? What was his mind and body coordination as he stepped on the gas pedal, and the speedometer increased with acceleration? I can imagine the calculation of speed, time, and distance. I can recall physics and calculus classes in college when I did instantaneous velocity. The roaring lion (devil/spiritual adversary) was calculating the pace of the Toyota Highlander, while factoring the distance travel versus speed and time of the Ford Focus, which will meet at the central point, called the intersection of collision. I can recall decreasing my pace in preparation for my left turn a little earlier than usual because the street was like a cul-de-sac with the same name of the previous street. It was that split-second thought of my destination being closer than anticipated, which resulted in the speeding car hitting the front section of my vehicle as opposed to the direct center. It was indeed a miracle at this monumental site, as God pulled us out of the jaws of death. Many have asked how am I doing? Still standing!

The enemy may have ordered my coffin, but God did not authorize the transaction; death was canceled and returned to sender!

The Scent of Death

Whenever I smell the scent of steam while showering or cooking, it reminds me of the burning chemical reaction in the Toyota Highlander—the scent of death. In the scent of death, there is life. This experience has given me a greater appreciation for life. I find myself reflecting and praying with a heart of gratitude. The simple things of life make perfect sense to me. The smiling faces of my family, the touch of my children, and even the emotional hurts have blessed me with heightened sensitivity. Earthly possessions seem to diminish in their significance.

147

As I reflect on the title of a famous book, *Everybody Wants to Go to Heaven, but Nobody Wants to Die,* it seems to encapsulate my noble experience and vastly highlights the notable discipline and lifestyle of the elephant. How are elephants able to dismantle herd of lions and constantly stand firm against the odds of life?

Elephants are herbivores, which mean plant-eating animals. Obviously this naturally renders the point that elephants do not need to hunt and rip apart the flesh of other animals for food. Elephants therefore are consumed with peaceful thoughts and preoccupied with finding noncombative elements for survival, as opposed to the daily stress of a fierce encounter to feed its hunger and physical desire. Nonetheless, elephants are always ready and will defend self, other elephants, as well as other animals that are in distress against predators. If a man becomes hungry and desperate, that energy could be channeled in either productivity and life or utter destruction.

Elephants are concluded to be extremely intelligent and exceptionally wise creatures. Elephants in comparison to other animals are said to possess the largest brain. Their neurons are used to control their gigantic bodies and the amount of their neurons is said to triple to those of human beings. Elephants are also impeccable in their mental state and verbosity. The bulls (male elephants) are significantly different in terms of certain social needs. Studies also reveal that the young elephants upon reaching sexual maturity either leave the herd or are forced out. Males initiate leaving while others are pushed out. This means the older and more mature elephants recognize that there may be elements of fear and getting too comfortable in overextending their stay. Though detaching may be painful, elephants refuse to cripple the potential of the offspring by a system of enablement. Male elephants develop, strive, and formulate independency, which frequently resorts to living alone. This is a great reflection for humanity to understand that being alone does not mean lonely. Elephants are assured of themselves and embrace confidence. Commitment is also readily embraced by both parties without fear of manipulation. When love becomes pure and sincere, it fosters self-growth and understanding and aids in great preparation for life. Love is not determined on the basis of our fluctuating emotions.

Cultural Epidemic

There is a cultural epidemic in the lives of many male figures when they have reached the age of adulthood. Many men reach a point of turbulence. They have reached a stage of awakening and realize that in order to start a family, they will have to take on a wife and detach themselves from their current family or home.

The man can physically leave his current geographical location but will soon encounter an emotional shock and trauma, because he has never been taught or prepared to depart from his mother.

Many homes may not have a father to affirm and reassure our young men that they have what it takes to survive independently. The confidence of the men in society has been shattered by doubts, disappointments, and frustrations. Men are silent, because men have recognized the dysfunction of missing elements. Men are confused not knowing where to find the source of help without embarrassment or feeling ridiculed. Men are searching for instant result, because they are at the finished line of boyhood and the starting point of manhood, yet not prepared for the transition. They are then overcome with fear. Men apparently have been put in a position of parachuting after reading the manual, but no mentoring or practical reference point for safe landing.

The elephant at an early age has been prepared to exit at sexual maturity, whether by means of a forceful measure or voluntarily; nonetheless, it has to come into quick acceptance of its new reality of departure from its herd. The elephant from an early age has to develop the skills of survival in advance of adulthood in order to be the leader of its newly formed herd.

In society, we spend a lot of time in school in preparation for a career and a job that will bring in financial income and stability. However, there is not as much emphasis or institutional establishments in teaching young men how to lead; how to be a husband, a father, a positive role model; or how to handle the responsibility encountered in adulthood. As a result, many men turn to violence and take by force that which they have never been taught to attain and endure beyond their point of frustration.

The elephant cannot run back to its herd in search of its parents when in conflict. Too many men run back to their mothers' house when they encounter conflict, crying, "Mama! I am coming home." Parents who are still emotionally connected, especially single parents/absent fathers, leave the door easily accessible for a return. Parents are hesitant in telling their adult sons that the door is closed and to stand up as a man and develop the resiliency to conquer this inevitable feat. Parents simply condone the adult son who is going through his cocoon stage and cripple the butterfly of a great man. We then produce a society of physically grown men but underdeveloped in maturity and mental fortitude.

The adult son then starts a family and resorts to a flight response when he comes into contact with or engages in emotional turbulence. The adult son then leaves behind his newly formed family in a vulnerable state and go in search of "better," not knowing that the problem is the man in the mirror. The adult son now goes in search of a solution, not being able to find it because he is on the run from his own self. The adult son never graduated from his common problems, so he has to repeat his courses on issues that he needed to overcome in order to be qualified for the next levels of responsibilities. The elephant has to now learn how to blow his own trumpet and be a protector and scare off his predators.

The female elephant has to learn how to affirm, embrace, and validate this newfound young elephant who is trying to disconnect his "umbilical cord" from his mother and join his wife. The female elephant should not destroy the male elephant by telling him that he is just trying to blow his trumpet to sound like his father. A man can never isolate himself from the qualities that have been embedded and imparted unto him. A man can utilize these qualities in the most positive manner and future endeavors, even if they were negatively imparted and experienced.

The female elephant has to ensure that there are no father wounds that will impede negatively in the way that she perceives her male companion. She will be prone to embrace the gratifications but despise his presence.

Many women are fearful of the physical presence, because it reminds them of the abusive experiences that they endured in childhood. They then have mixed emotions and dysfunctional thoughts, because they enjoy the emotional and sexual fulfillment but mentally reject his physical existence. Many women therefore seek alternative measures and go in search of fulfillment in ways that substitute the male figure. This can be inclusive of lesbianism or sexual artificial devices, or they can simply be crippled by fear and dwell in singlehood.

Some men are encouraged to get married and start their family in their late teenage years. Some cultures would treat you in contempt as though you have just committed a crime and you are naive and in search of possession, status quo, and sexual fulfillment. On the other hand, if you are excelling academically above your peers or ahead of the average, you are celebrated.

Why do we celebrate young millionaires, young celebrities, entertainers, and movie stars and embrace educational geniuses but despise the potential of our youths when companionship is being formed? Is it that we have modeled a weak infrastructure in healthy family-oriented development and cannot trust the foundation for our young generation to survive? Do we equate inadequate preparation with lacking capability to conquer the odds of life by our young generation? Are we cumbersome in our trust for our youths, because society and social media have drenched and infiltrate our thought process with curiosity toward unhealthy living and vices?

Many individuals learn to drive motor vehicles at the early stage in life but have never been taught what to expect in a relationship. Parents are now worried to trust their young children in the arms of a person who may not be able to drive a relationship, steer with love, or maneuver with compassion.

Parents are left worried if this relationship will foster growth with love, or is it just an idealized fantasy for carnal fulfillment through the lens of curiosity? Arranged marriages built on principles seem to outlast those built of love and passion. Can you imagine if society invested in principle during childhood? We would produce a world of well-disciplined individuals who would be excellent when ignited later with newfound love.

Parents can also be fearful and judge their children's success or failure based on the memories of their own personal discipline and experience during their years of development. If a parent lacked the discipline during childhood, such parent will likely to be strict and overprotective in shielding the children from his/her own past painful experiences. Such parent will constitute his/her love and concern for the children as proper parenting, not realizing that he/she is hindering the children from developing in the greatest years of formation due to fear. Elephants are goal oriented; they plan thoroughly for their future success.

Family Structure and Model

So this brings into question, what are elephants doing to walk into such constant success? Elephants in general are very unified close-knit family groups. This matriarchal system is frequently operated under the leadership of the largest and oldest female. With this established systematic order of leadership, it will likely model and naturally demand discipline and respect. The elephant has developed a positive system that produces productive and beneficial results, bringing into greater appreciation the asset and value of the older and experienced elephants. Potential conflicts are likely to be diminished, and younger elephants will be obedient and less likely to deviate when the older elephants are unified and consistent to the set pattern. This usually provides a greater level of safety and longevity, maintains family values, and keeps each other accountable. At the presence or sound of any threats, the elephants sound their trumpets to warn others of impending dangers. Younger elephants apply what has been modeled, utilize effective communication, and refrain from drifting. The male specie survives after leaving the herd, which means the same tactical measures are implemented and evidently a sign of good structure passed on to the next generation. It is therefore striking to observe the level at which humanity kills and tears down while elephants sustain and preserve. The close bonding of elephants causes them to survive against any threats. If you have "elephants" in your family, it's a sign of a healthy family. Your family life will have a greater propensity to stay within the home and church family while constantly growing healthy together. School friends look out for each other, pray for you, and correct you when you go astray.

> Because the Lord disciplines the one he loves, and he chastens everyone he accepts as his son. (Hebrews 12:6 NIV)

Living on the Ledge

Living in a relationship without long-term commitment is living life on the ledge. It is like a banquet or a party in progress and a passerby who is curious stops by, grabs some food, drinks, and partakes in the amenities then continues on his journey. That passerby then tells how great the party was.

How often individuals who are facing turmoil in their relationships are pulled into the attraction of another relationship like the illusion of a banquet or party? Individuals enjoy the pleasures of romance, dinner, movies, surface conversations, and fun activities.

The passerby who stopped at the banquet has no attachment, neither can he identify with the hours of preparation, frustration, planning, disagreement, hurts, pains, sweat, tears, heat in the kitchen, possible burns, sacrifice, forsaking pleasures, and compromises for the benefit of others.

The passerby is a particular person seeking refuge or solace in the home, who unrealistically expects the same demands to reap or resort to the same results.

Such individual has to admit to self that any long-term commitment will inevitably require the passerby to forsake all his duties and ways and become totally engaged. The passerby will have to willingly acknowledge that the flight response is not an option for the pilot in the cockpit. But such passerby will have to forsake all other missions, become wholesome in submission, share, partake, and experience in the pain of the journey before embracing the fruition of the amenities.

Such individual will have to come to grips with reality and realize fully and wholeheartedly that every man is inescapable of himself. The status or quality of your relationship does not matter; it will require a common walk of life that is foundational to mankind and immune to none. Otherwise, such man will forever fail and run the risk of perpetual searching, like a hamster in a treadmill motion, constantly repeating a lesson in unlearned pattern and behavior.

One of the most common misperceptions in life is to believe that holistic and successful individuals have life easy. We then develop the preponderance of self to believe that a person who struggles with hardships has a difficult life. Becoming successful in the broad spectrum and the different areas of your life requires self-discipline.

One of the greatest victories to be won is to conquer the obstacle of self.

The struggles faced and engaged are often due to a distorted thought process. The art of mastering oneself requires self-understanding and discipline. This also means that one will have to endure pain and hurt, without reacting to a battlefield that is more detrimental in comparison to wisely enduring the temporal storm.

A soft answer turns away wrath, But a harsh word stirs up anger. The tongue of the wise uses knowledge rightly, But the mouth of fools pours forth foolishness. (Proverbs 15:1–2 NKJV)

The grass is greener on the other side holds true in the concept and imagination of the beholder, until such individual crosses over to the other side and quickly realizes that the grass withered the moment that he/she arrived. In other words, a man can never escape himself. Perception and reality are found in the scope and realm of his/her mind. Humanity has to come to grips with and face their reality while eliminating the desire for denial. Such a man/woman has to refuse the comparison syndrome.

How many individuals wish and hope to have the physical strength and mental and spiritual fortitude of an elephant? But when shown what it takes to attain to such height and status, we eradicate the mere thoughts, much less to embrace the possibilities. Our level of humility lets us serve with excellence. But it can also condition and delay us to lead and step out in our blessings with confidence. We judge ourselves critically in advance and become crippled by what others may say and think. Oftentimes, they may not think what we perceived or may be jealous because they desire the path that God has laid out for us. We are enslaved and conditioned, so we pray like Lot and say, "Bring me to this little town because I'm tired," instead of Jabez who says, "Bless me indeed and enlarge my territory." Be careful, because God answers prayers. Let us not be afraid of Sanballat and Tobiah; it is time!

What are the debilitating factors that cause us to reach this point? Quickly identifying our hurdles is essential!

Obstacle 1: Becoming intimidated by the finished line, we miss the feasibility of the capable steps.

Waiting and delayed progress are some of the greatest robbers of future opportunities. One of my mottos over the years is Just Start! Or Just Do It! In life, there are so many wasted energy and doubts that develop in justifying ourselves from doing what ought to be done. The moment I open my eyes, I put my feet on the floor and debunk every opposing thought that would cause me to remain in bed. Let us not judge the future by our current resources. God will and has laid out provisions further on the journey.

Obstacle 2: It's unwise to compare yourself with others.

In the military, we oftentimes have to maintain our annual qualifications by running 1.5 miles in a limited time. Entertaining the thought of the distance to the finishing line or comparing self to those who are ahead will cause your mind to prevent your feet from moving. Your breathing then becomes heavy, and your thought process seems to attract every opposing force. But as you begin to visualize the short interval, manage your breathing, and develop the technique of positive thinking, and most important your training, you begin to realize that you are just as capable as everyone who started out and embarked on the journey.

Obstacle 3: Believing the fire is meant to destroy you rather than to preserve you!

God is a skillful user of fire. The three Hebrew boys were kept safely in the fire, yet the enemies on the outside were destroyed. Some of the greatest enemies are the elements found within self. To become the best that you can will require the skillful use of fire like a surgeon utilizing laser beams to destroy destructive elements. Sometimes we cannot see or understand the depth, nature, or condition to the extent and future potential roadblocks. This is why we have to embrace the present condition and rejoice in an appreciative manner, not only in self-gratification but through perseverance during hard times.

We will embark upon the understanding of self through encountering and socializing with others. But firstly, let us examine the process of change—going through the fire!

God says that you are like precious gold. But before gold becomes precious, it goes through a process. The goldsmith holds the gold in the fire. How many of you are going through some fiery circumstances and wondering how long before your change comes and how long before you see results? But the gold is held in the fire, until it reaches close to a melting point, like clay in the hands of the potter. All the impurities disappear from the gold. And when the goldsmith sees himself in the gold, he knows that the gold is ready to be removed from the fire and pliable to be conformed to whatever shape he desires. Could it be that you are still in your fire, because God is not through with you yet? Your circumstance may propel you to develop the inclination to question God, "Why am I going through the things that I am facing?" Job asked God why, and God quickly responded by rhetorically asking Job where he was while the heaven and the universe were being measured. When the apostle Peter realized the nature and prediction of his death, he asked and wondered what will happen to John because he was very loved by Jesus. When it was very close for Jesus to be crucified, Jesus said, "If at all possible, take this cup of suffering away, but nevertheless, let your will be done." No one enjoys suffering, but it is a necessary ingredient for our life. In your situation, you may feel like you are the long-forgotten son or daughter, friends may have turned their backs on you, people may have spoken negative words about you; but when Jesus was on the cross, He granted you access to salvation and broke the chains of death! This too shall pass.

Beware of these four individuals:

1. The person who commits his/her life to the end, and challenging circumstances cause him/her to break the commitment (Luke 9:61–62).

2. Persons with inflated egos.

There is a famous statement that says you are full of yourself. A man/woman who believes that he/she has everything that he/she needs usually leaves very little room for improvement. Be very careful of the man who finds contentment in his possessions, because his heart will be at the center of his attachment. He becomes empty when his possessions decrease in quantity. Therefore, he does not find contentment in giving away, and jealousy pricks at his heart with another who excels.

3. A woman who quickly tells you that she can live all by herself!

Be careful of the woman who quickly tells you that she can live all by herself. She has not fully mastered the art of reciprocity. She has not mastered the principles of selfless giving, which will powerfully transform others as a change agent for improvement. Such a woman strives on satisfaction and fulfillment. She is caught up in a quid pro quo—you do for me, then I will do for you. If she feels as if the man is not living up to her standards, the man becomes automatically disqualified. If the man sacrifices his life to ensure that she grows and becomes empowered, she quickly forgets the journey after she surpasses him on the path of success. She believes that he is not growing and is therefore irrelevant and burdensome. A man out of fear will be tempted to sabotage her journey and evolve into a controlling monster. This relationship then quickly spirals into turbulence mode, when it could have been prevented if both parties selflessly outdo each other in satisfying individual needs in a quality manner. Keeping scores quantifies the relationship and becomes destructive. There will be low and high seasons. Love and patience have to persevere.

4. A man who leads others astray.

Be very careful of the person who is quick to say, "I will forgive but not forget." A heart of flesh is better to have than a heart of stone. A person who finds it hard to forgive is a merciless individual. Such person enjoys the compassion of others and often feels like he/she is obligated to such extension of kindness. Such person keeps storage units of hurts to the point where he/she believes others should just "get over it" with their hurt because of all that he/she has been through. He/she may listen to the pain of others, but the comparison syndrome is saying, "I have been through worse. You will be all right." Be very careful of the advice given by such individual, because you will have a "bitter" ending and revengeful attitude. This is the beginning of struggle. Naturally, the human heart is meant to dwell and socialize in love and harmony. The struggles then evolve when the mind is pulling your heart in a direction contrary to its fundamental design. The mind that does not forgive into freedom will constant err in search of justifiable measures.

> Then He said to the disciples, "It is impossible that no offenses should come, but woe *to him* through whom they do come! It would be better for him if a millstone were hung around his neck, and he were thrown into the sea, than that he should offend one of these little ones. Take heed to yourselves. If your brother sins against you, rebuke him; and if he repents, forgive him. And if he sins against you seven times in a day, and seven times in a day returns to you, saying, 'I repent,' you shall forgive him." (Luke 17:1–4 NKJV)

A person who finds it hard to forgive will inevitably become a stumbling block and lead others astray. Hatred is a dangerous and deadly weapon hurled at the life in the direction projected. (Oh Lord my God, may you caution my soul to do right, in the name of Jesus, amen!)

Elephants enjoy and embrace the challenges that they face. Elephants see challenges as a stepping-stone that elevates them to the next level of growth. Elephants set new challenges for themselves and offspring while sticking to their long-term goals. The older and more mature elephants push out the young elephants from the herd. This is a notable and very noble condition. The experienced elephants do train, validate, and believe in their next generation. Elephants know that the world is real, and they will be faced with life challenges and dangers, so it is imperative that the family is equipped and united. Elephants assemble in times of attacks, and all stomp together, destroying anything that is brave enough to venture underneath such forceful weight.

To become this great elephant, not only does it require a great deal in the understanding of oneself, but it takes enduring painful measures in correction from deviation and also the debunking of negative and mediocre thinking. How much more could I have accomplished without processing doubts? What would my life be without fear?

Elephants don't quit when things don't go the way they expected. Elephants know that when you go through the fire and the testing of life, it's not meant to kill you. Elephants know that the fire is not a destructive element; it's just a tool that brings transformation. When hell breaks loose around you, James 1 says count it joy because the testing of our faith gives us perseverance. Like Job, we will get the opportunity to show off the love and grace of God. Job knew that if God blessed him before, He will bless him again. Job declared, "Naked I came into the world, and naked I will leave, but I will serve God." You may feel like the situation is about to kill you or you are surrounded by angry lions with roaring circumstances, but if you stand strong and obedient, you will make it through. You may not have a job and be dating someone, but don't compromise. Desperation will cause you to offer your body to keep the relationship, but in the process, it only undervalues your perception in the mind of the other.

Elephant: Life is built on the principles of preparation!

I want to jump, but I am not prepared to swim.

Since we cannot survive by avoiding people and jumping over hurdles, preparation is paramount. A lot of people want to retire but are not prepared for the future. Not being thoroughly prepared for life will shatter our image and self-understanding, which inevitably leads to an excess of hurts and disappointments. We will self-victimize, label others for our painful experiences, develop misplaced anger, and in the process ultimately blame God. Statistical reports reveal that the greatest threat against elephants is the human specie.

Researchers have concluded that elephants can recognize their image in a mirror and have self-awareness identical to that of human beings. The elephant is an animal very well known for its memory, especially treatment of cruelty. The fact that the elephant remembers and launches an attack on the source of its pain reveals that the elephant has not regained trust and fears a reoccurrence of the situation. The elephant is seeking closure and has not become convinced by mere remorse or apology. Many people look in the mirror daily and despise the image that they see. This can be a very dangerous element against thorough preparation in order to maneuver and swim through life. The elephant is very transparent (visible) and obviously doesn't hide too well. We can't pretend like there's no elephant in the room. (Our pains, expression, and reality are undeniably huge and obvious even when we wish and hope others cannot see them). Sometimes it as simple as hugging or asking someone, "What is bothering you?" then the tears rain like shattering glasses. We can't turn a blind eye like the elephant doesn't exist. The elephants of life are real.

It is important to truly know who we are. The overwhelming feelings of guilt, regret, frustration, and disappointment can reshape, fashion, and change our outlook of inward self. On the contrary, how many of us have some friends or self-confession of overinflated egos? How many times do we find faults in others when similar faults are in the blind spot of self? The Scripture reminds us to first remove the plank from our eyes before we attempt to judge others about the speck in their eyes.

This speaks of the direct correlation of man and his reality of the deeply embedded thoughts, hurts, pain, temptation, etc., that are lodged in the subconscious and control our actions even when we try to push away or forget unpleasant circumstances.

The thoughts entering the memory of a man that seep into the depths of his emotion are like smoke from a fire escaping underneath a door.

We cannot pretend like the situation or the rationale of his reality doesn't exist any more than an elephant cannot turn its back on a roaring lion and then pretend as though it is just mere thoughts. In a similar fashion, we cannot turn our back on the voice of God in order to embrace the pleasures of sin and indulge in a variety of desires, then act as though the repercussions and consequences are nonexistent because I am not looking at the lion.

The elephant that is experiencing painful bites will apply the full scope of its rationale, and its defense mechanism will activate in survival mode. The elephant will fight off the ferocious attacks of bites from the lion.

But ironically a man will attempt to shut off his rationale and disengage his moral conviction when desiring to enjoy the pleasures of wrongful doing or unethical actions amid biting consequences. Man seemingly activates and adjusts his level of sensitivity to reach a state of remorse, as though it guarantees forgiveness and access to the grace of God. King David cried many tears over his sin, and God reassures him that his sinful actions will not escape consequences even though he will receive forgiveness.

Man has a tendency to confuse forgiveness with needed reprimand.

Only if such a man would realize and recognize that this subsequent and consequential hurt as a result of his action is far greater than the physical pain inflicted upon the elephant. This is death (separation from God) of his soul.

We can all attest to having deflected our thoughts in order to challenge and oppose our moral conviction, which is in fact drowning out the voice of God. After yielding to the forces of temptation, whether financial, sexual, hurtful words, or other actions, we then refrain from wrestling and admit that we have erred. Being faced with guilt, we then attempt to use the same mental energy that was used defiantly to then muster up the strength and courage to confess inwardly. In the process, we presumptuously demand instant forgiveness. The thirsty soul cries out that there's indeed a God. Not allowing ourselves to hear the voice of God's direction does not dismantle our scope of wisdom and judgment.

Will a man jokingly laugh himself to mockery, not wanting to be right if wrong is engulfing in heightened ecstasy and pleasure?

Will a man walk into the abyss, allowing the door to close behind him, only to realize that he is entrapped in the darkness of his ignorance?

He is now outnumbered and surrounded by lions as they evolve more and more visibly with a ferocious look and dripping saliva on their faces. Nowhere to run, no place to hide! It is over; his mind beckons to his soul. His soul refuses to believe, but his mind and rationale admit and manage to convince him that with such evidence of impending death and danger, mere rationale cannot deny, delay, or push to the side in a desensitized manner. The elephant that spots the lion in a distance yet decides to stop and eat the last straw of grass is like a man stopping to engage in his sinful actions while failing to factor the speed of the lion. Obedience is the carrier of blessings and the vessel of life. Do you have it? Well, use it carefully!

CHAPTER 8
DAZZLING ZEBRA
(Power of Agreement)

*The hidden thoughts in a man's heart are not always
reflective of the smile on his face.*

—M. Reid

Will we stand together like zebras in times of crises?

Have you ever been in a situation where you have been victimized, yet
you walked away admitting that you have no one to blame but yourself?
Instant acceptance of one's responsibility results in immediate self-
empowerment. In the process, you have just formulated mental fortitude
and established boundaries and fortresses for future self-defense. In
fact, you almost want to express gratitude to the perpetrator because
you have been schooled in a very expensive yet life-worth lesson. The
letter of gratitude will be signed, sealed, and delivered with a stamp that
says, "Thank you for the gift of a radical transformation." What great
classroom to sit in, what great curriculum to study, but to be empowered
by zebras who sleep standing up and confuse the horseflies, lions, and
other predators by their mere stripes, presence, lifestyle, character traits,
and attributes. Let us join in this classroom for a great lecture on our
VIP (*v*ision, *i*ntuition, *p*erception).

There was a study conducted on zebras and wildebeests, during the night
when it was extremely dark. The videographer filmed the wildebeests

by utilizing a starlight intensifier, which has a special scope used to see in darkness. Zebras are horselike creatures that have black and white vertical stripes along their bodies, which act as a visual camouflage from predators. While the videographer was filming, the wildebeests were very visible since they were black shapes against the grass, which was relatively pale in the background.

As the researcher continued in the process of filming, the wildebeests would occasionally disappear or instantly go out of sight. To the surprise of the field researcher, it was later discovered that the zebras were walking across the path of the wildebeests and were undetected by the camera without a clear view. This created an illusion because the zebra was the same intensity of light as the background.

Many predators choose to hunt at night, because they are able to spot their opponents before being observed. The stripes on the zebra grant the advantage of remaining invisible at night, which naturally aids in protection against its prey.

The zebra is our VIP. The zebra has great *vision*, *intuition*, and *perception*. The zebra has great *vision*. The eyes of the zebra are located on the sides of its head, instead of in the front. This enables a greater peripheral view and visual to the rear without repositioning its body. The zebra has great *intuition* and listening skills. The ears of the zebra can rotate 180 degrees like a radar satellite. The zebra can also rotate one ear while the other remains still. This gives the zebra a heightened sense of awareness and intuition to detect sounds, threats, or danger without panicking, becoming exposed, becoming overly alarmed, or becoming more vulnerable in the process. The zebra has great *perception*. The skin of a zebra is said to be black. The zebra then grows black and white mixed striped furs. In addition to aggressive predators, there are also horseflies that can be a nuisance by biting and also transmit diseases. The sight and range of visibility by insects and other animal predators may be impeded upon by the camouflage effects of the zebras' stripes. The reflection of light and poor visibility as demonstrated with the camera help to explain why the horseflies find it difficult to land on the skin of the zebra, even though the horseflies are a major pest to all different animals. The horseflies would fly past the zebra, finding it difficult to land due to the distorted image of depth perception. Like the zebra, we are all born with natural gifts and attributes. Some gifts are developed, are acquired, and are all bestowed to us by God. The irony is that we are oftentimes prone to being attacked for the gifts and characteristics that are a natural part of our lives. How beautiful is it when you can defeat your enemies by just being your natural self!

Vision

In life, you may not always have a clear vision of your journey, neither a mapped-out path to your destination. One thing for sure is that you will have to safeguard your sense of purpose and existence until the darkness fades away, giving you greater clarity in your direction. During your time of waiting, you cannot compromise your value and self-worth or manipulate your boundaries.

Joseph was hated for his vision, dreams, and coat of many stripes and colors that represented royalty (Genesis 37). The zebra will possess its fault, but your enemy will join together in the dark and attempt to expose your mess to other people. These individuals will be unable to see what the haters are trying to expose because you are covered by stripes of divine grace. Don't try to retaliate due to gossiping lips, because when others cannot see the negativity that the enemy is trying to expose, your enemies will then be perceived as the issue. The zebra does not need to believe that the enemy is seeing the things and flaws that you feel or know that you may possess. The zebra owes no one any explanation and has great vision that sees the enemy long before he arrives on the scene. The predator will prowl casually into your presence. But your peripheral vision has already extracted wisdom from their body language and social behavior. The zebra is so vigilant, the zebra sleeps standing up. The enemy is not sure whether you are sleeping, praying, meditating, observing, listening, or about to open your eyes. The zebra is unpredictable and cannot be studied by a usual routine.

> Put on the whole armour of God, that ye may be able to stand against the wiles of the devil. (Ephesians 6:11 KJV)

> Keep watch and pray, so that you will not give into temptation. For the spirit is willing, but the body is weak. (Matthew 26:41 NLT)

The zebra has a great vision for the family. The zebra understands that predators such as lions will wait all day until one of the zebras, especially the young, drifts away from the group. It is therefore vital for the family to stand together and empower each other with knowledge and establish boundaries.

The research showed the zebra appearing on the scene of life walking through the dark, minding its business, being itself, and becoming undetected by cameras or the visual recognition by predators. What is so special about the zebra that it possesses such unique gift to defeat the enemy by just being itself? When David was about to become king over Israel by just being himself, Saul, the king on the throne, attempted to kill David, his successor, even though it was destined for David to become king. How many predators have we developed just by the mere attributes that we possess? Have you become enemies, being constantly watched by predators in the dark, simply because of your intelligence, beauty, character, or charisma, or hated for your gifts? Do we become complacent by taking for granted the liberty of our stripes of covering?

The zebra cannot take credit for remaining invisible from the dangers of its enemies, no more than the children of Israel cannot attribute survival from the plague of death in Egypt to their homes or castles. We have to be deliberate and give credit to God for His covering against the spiritual warfare, dangers, and catastrophes of this world.

Vision will allow us to see the enemy from far off. There is no reason to overreact to the grand entrance of the enemy. This does not mean a casual approach on my behalf but rather simply confidence in my Creator. The mind oftentimes processes, analyzes, and calculates the situation and establishes self-control, eliminating the need for panic.

The zebras that are standing strong usually stand as a group and fight off ferocious lions. Sometimes part of the herd occasionally walks away, leaving those who are willing to stay with no other option but to flee as well. The injured zebra while being in pain is not likely to acknowledge that its poor decisions may have caused the unpleasant outcome or possibly the near demise and risk of others. If a man is hungry, it may not be the best time to tell him about a job. The zebra will speak from its place of pain. It will perceive life differently and according to the immediate need. The zebra will wonder how can everyone be so selfish and walk away at such a time and leave it to die? Others logically and realistically may ponder how come the injured zebra failed to understand the others' perspective?

To successfully reach those who are around us every day, we have to empathize and see life from their perspective. Otherwise, we become the irony of the hypocrite who fails to understand, while we are just as guilty with this common factor of humanity. The woman who was caught in the act of adultery was about to be stoned by those who are equally guilty (John 8:1–11). Jesus had to quickly disarm this hypocritical explosive attitude and behavior by exposing their secret filth. This behavior was worse than zebras teaming up with the lion to destroy its own. This is expected from your enemy, not internally from the ones you love and have relinquished your trust.

The hurting zebra is likely to speak from a place of pain, and through the lens of hurt and distrust, and tarnish your reputation. But don't get twisted out of character; you have just encountered a wounded zebra. Do not take ownership of the offense, nor react with hatred or anger; otherwise, you have just become the very thing that you despise. How many times should I forgive within a day, seven times or seventy times seven (unlimited)? Forgiveness is beneficial to oneself and allows you to constantly walk in freedom. How free do you want to be?

Lesson of Self-awareness

Are we willing to sacrifice ourselves, reputation, and self-glorification to support and surround our hurting brothers and sisters, in order to ensure that they become fully restored from their hurts and painful life experiences? Or do we rather enjoy and take pleasure in the suffering of others by walking away and watching them being devoured by "lion" circumstances?

The hidden thoughts in a man's heart are not always reflective of the smile on his face.

We can learn from our own blood cells and physiological and bodily makeup along with its protective function. The sperm cell or seed of a man, when it enters the egg of a woman, instantly develops a protective coating; and nothing else is allowed to enter or to penetrate the walls of that egg. The coating or shield is to protect from attack and forbid any compromise, because the result of a great fruit has been created. Multiple surveys, research, and documentaries reveal that whenever a zebra is hurting or injured, all the other zebras form a protective circle around the hurting zebra and fight against the predators by delivering powerful strikes of kicks and deadly bites.

But how can *we effectively stand together against the wiles of the enemy* if we constantly react in the natural realm rather than recognize that there is a spiritual warfare at hand?

No wonder the psalmist David according to Psalm 119:11 KJV writes, "Thy word have I hid in mine heart that I might not sin against thee." We have to surround our hearts with the Word of God to protect against all intruding forces of lies and deception.

Say No to Domestic Violence

Your mind is like a pond: when it becomes calm, all kinds of junk and toxic measures surface to the top and forefront of the subconscious. It affects your response time, judgment, and the quality of content that protrudes from your mouth and permeates the atmosphere. Vision and boundaries start in the concept of the mind.

Our children can be like observing a vibrant baby zebra casually drifting off toward the bushes. The parents then inquire the propensity that leads to such decision. The baby zebra may give a simplistic response stating that "I am going to munch on some grass that I saw looking very luscious." The suspicious and caring parent may ask a probing question and implore the baby zebra to stay closer because there is no grass that can be so much tastier that is worth the risk. Upon further observation, the adult zebra sees danger lurking in the bush in the person of a lion. It's not a strange phenomenon to occasionally see two animals who are enemies by nature play together. To the surprise of the adult zebra, that is exactly where the baby zebra is heading, and the baby zebra tells the parents, "Stop overreacting. The lion is not as dangerous as you might think. He is just a nice guy. How about you take some time to understand the lion?"

(There is an old proverb that says, "The piglet asks the mother pig, 'Why is your mouth so long?' The mother pig said that 'you are growing, so in due season you will understand.'")

The issue is that many of us in life are not willing to learn from the growth and experiences of our parents and others. We would rather endure the pain rather than avoidance through words of warnings and wisdom. Very soon, the angry lion leaves the zebra with a swollen face and bruised eye. The zebra is so ashamed and has been conditioned in an incompatible relationship of domestic violence rather than eradicating self-pride and returning to a loving home.

> *Pride and wealth are a dangerous combination of dilemmas. It is like driving on an oily, slippery road, and you ponder whether to step on the brake and spiral out of control or let momentum take its course.*

Pride will let you drive continually into danger, while wealth deceives you into believing that you can purchase your way successfully against the odds and forces of momentum.

We have to teach our children and loved ones the true values of life. Otherwise, we are prone to search for perfect solutions in our wealth and earthly possessions instead of from imperfect experienced individuals who are willing to steer us away from the dangers that they have encountered. We will never arrive, so we have to remain humble. One exit door is an open door to another field of opportunity, so there is no need to dwell in a constant state of regret. Man is attached to his possessions but needs to brace for landing. One of the greatest downfalls for humanity in the last days will be a low resistance against the opposition of the world government, simply because we are attached to earthly possessions. Whatever we are not willing to let go, we are willing to possess and contain. Every thought that is preoccupied and possessed by the mind is an element of either distraction or productivity. Most people in life encounter detrimental experiences because of mental distraction.

> He said, "Listen, all you people of Judah and Jerusalem! Listen, King Jehoshaphat! This is what the LORD says: Do not be afraid! Don't be discouraged by this mighty army, for the battle is not yours, but God's. (2 Chronicles 20:15 NIV)

To guard the mind is to guard the heart and protect your life. A zebra collectively stands together in unity and uses its stripes to confuse and weaken the strength of its prey. This tells a lot and speaks great volume of the mindset and thought process that would resort to such unified power of camaraderie. The zebra does not rely solely on its physical strength but combats the enemy and wins the battle without brutal force. To win this battle, it is important to purge the mind of obstacles, maximizing on concentrated energy. Let us examine where we stand!

Intuition

Sometimes in life, our journey can be like driving a vehicle on a very long trip to our destination while our occupants in the vehicle are sleeping. Our wife, children, or any individual who embarks on such trip eventually wakes up to the beauty and amenities of the destination. Everyone enjoys the beauty of the destination but forgets the process of the journey.

Perhaps you are in the driver's seat of life because of the purpose that you are meant to serve. Whether we are on a military battlefield, a firefighter putting out a blazing fire, a doctor in the emergency room with a scalpel, or a parent at home teaching morals and values, we are equipped because of the war we will face. People will want to travel our journey but don't realize that we are equipped differently. What the zebra survives may be the demise of the wildebeest.

Do we glorify in the arrival but lack the gravity of the gratitude simply because we were never involved in the pain of the process?

Can we truly genuinely and realistically expect others to fully understand the journey of our personal experiences?

Do we blame others for the faults they contain or the magnitude of their capacity to err while we internally admit and confess to be equally limited and at fault?

Do we unrealistically expect or assert responsibilities and obligations unto others due to our selfish approach or pain in which we hope others could identify or empathize?

Was my journey truly meant to be experienced by others or perceived equally from my concept?

Whether the driver or passengers, was God guarding our hearts from distraction, conflict, or confusion?

Was God protecting the occupants and granting their minds from the pain or weight of the journey?

Do others find comfort or simply experience peaceful rest in our presence? Will others share equally or partake in our journey simply because of their company in the process, because their awareness is engaged, because they are awake, or because of their state of consciousness?

We have established that zebras are one of the most fascinating creatures and teachers on the face of the planet. Not only do they teach and mentor their offspring, they can also teach humanity self-developmental skills and relationship improvement. We at times study our children through observation; we learn habits from social media, books, movies, and articles and are influenced by friends. How much more could we learn if we observe and understand zebras beyond the surface of zoo entertainment?

Lions are oftentimes depicted as fierce predators that come to destroy. What are the lions in our lives, and how can we remain vigilant and alert in order to guard ourselves effectively and bring out the zebra within us?

What may have been the self-drive and initiative that led to the straying of the baby zebra? Could it be that the zebra has not been validated by actions of love, neither was it reaffirmed with verbal words of expression? The lion then lured the zebra toward the bush by its masculine physique while the zebra has not grown the experience of "the long-mouthed pig" with wisdom in order not to overstep the boundaries into a field on the playground of chances.

Can we suspend our desires and fulfillment that come through instant gratification?

Pleasure before establishing a loving relationship is exploration on advanced credit.

We are destined later to regret not being able to recompensate or pay the debt of a hefty accumulated liability! The mind of a man has to be developed like a film and into a clear picture to overcome his fears and uncertainties. There are too many homes with absentee parents because pleasure was prioritized over the endurance of pain and commitment.

Domestic violence did not originate on the day of finals like in an exam or sports game. It was birthed in the pattern of thought process and embedded in our discipline and low state of resistance a long time ago. There is a key and trigger switch that unraveled a trend of thoughts like a runaway train or broken faucet without control. The same mind of a person that unleashes adverse reactions is the same mind that should be able to properly rearrange thoughts that result into a peaceful and safe outcome with proper discipline.

A second factor that may impede upon the stages of maturity is that we may never grow up in the mind of some individuals. Our parents will always see us as their children. Our parents and older relatives can cripple our growth by their language, choices of words and usages, and constantly perceiving us as a burden that has never matured. If this perception bares true for the offspring, then the spouse of the offspring will also experience the burden and biases of such expectation from the parents and in-laws. Any shortcoming of the offspring can leave the spouse inadvertently to be blamed. This can push or force us prematurely into the arms of exploiters and predators. A zebra therefore has to grow through the pain, while making preparations with proper timing to transition from this environment into independence. It's important for the family structure to be maintained, and there is no detachment through animosity and separation through this time of transition. Otherwise, there will be internal revenge, animosity, and strife. Later in life, as parents get older, there may be a role reversal; and the painful memories may evolve, leading to neglect of parents by the offspring.

Choice of words can be a mental cue or key that unlocks the door of choices and decisions. Our choice of words in response to one's actions against us is also a mental cue to our state of resistance. Does man have the capacity to carry the weight or bear the load of his burden?

The lion hunts and watches the state of our resistance. He watches certain cues and assesses whether we are surrendering or resisting. The lion can test the character of a naive zebra and unlocks its mind with jokes and cunning innuendos. The lion then adjusts its tactical approach based on our laughter or offensive reaction. The lion hunts to fulfill its desire. The lion roars and uses aggression for its victim to crumble internally and surrender.

When we think of this dark world, it becomes like a lion with a loud roar instantly crippling a small animal with fear. Many supervisors and figures of authority abuse this character trait of a loud roar to take advantage of subordinates. People are overworked, underpaid, treated unfairly, and in toxic relationships of infidelity; and many "zebras" get pregnant in the process. When the lion roars, the inexperienced, fearful, and vulnerable zebras go into shock mode. While in a freezing state, the zebra inadvertently surrenders to the leader's authority and charisma. While in shock mode, our mind can operate in a dysfunctional manner by attempting to justify poor decisions because of previous hurts and betrayal by someone we trusted; and before long, our protective walls and state of resistance are far gone and come crumbling down. It's like waking up in your car after a long sleep to find out that the wheels were removed and the vehicle is left inoperable on cylinder blocks. You are left stranded, waking up in a sober mind with no way of secretly driving away from your mess. Your location reveals your state of compromise and exposes your condition as you rely on help from limited options to rescue you. In refusing to accept and face responsibility or make the perpetrator accountable, we are likely to constantly rebut our guilt and shame. We run the risk of accepting and persuading ourselves that the encounter was consensual. It is important to stay away from pleasurable and attractive wrongful conditions. Parents should not be fearful nor compromise instructing children because they may have made poor past decisions.

It's okay to process our shame, which can be a useful tool and reminder for wise future decisions. This is why communication and forgiveness are so important. Communication clears up a lot of misconstrued and major misunderstandings. The power to resist is a strong mental cue against the opponent. It comes with a demonstration of strong willpower and is reflective of our drive and attitude. It is important to lock away and secure ourselves in a room of faith and play a vital role in the mentorship of our offspring. The more we resist the prowling lion, the greater the chances that it will eventually flee.

We have to equip ourselves relative to the battle that we will face. Let us equip, mentor, and instill discipline of strong self-esteem to our future generation. We can tear down weak walls and develop strong infrastructure of self-esteem by showing love and appreciation. So many times our children drift in search of these fundamentals while the foundation is being developed. A zebra will be naturally hated for its gifts and talents, causing a void and desire for acceptance. We will undeniably and readily discover that humanity possesses a lot of self-hatred and resentment.

A lot of individuals will ask questions, not to uplift but to formulate claims to discredit others. We search earnestly for information and scenarios that will further validate and substantiate our claims of hatred and ill feelings, often fueled against each other.

We then utilize this as a tool negatively, yet creditable information, to execute character assassination. Self-improvement will let us understand that being right with information does not necessitate appropriate attitude or display in behavior. A zebra has to be confident and understand that it is not responsible for the unhappiness and distasteful behavior of others.

How many individuals in life do you know, associate with, or can identify that become jealous, become envious, and exhibit extreme anger and frustration just by you being your own positive, productive, independent, and optimistic self as natural as a zebra's stripes? You will show up at a social gathering with a smile on your face, and people become disgruntled wondering why you are so happy this early in the morning. You say a pleasant good morning, and the response is "What is so good about the morning?" You say hello, and the same breath of response to say hello is used with more energy to tell you that "it's early, and I am not in the mood," or "I am still waking up and gathering my thoughts together," or "I need a cup of coffee."

If simple distracting elements dominate, preoccupy our minds, and destroy our state of productivity, then the strength of our mental platform and spiritual fortitude is highly questionable.

Humanity contains double standards. We will condone and justify the negative attitude of the one that we love and adore, even willingly forgive them. Yet, on the other hand, we condemn those who are of less significance in our lives, while holding them hostage for doing the same thing. We are professionals in categorizing, associating, and magnifying faults! The Word of God is indeed profound when it tells us that love covers a multitude of sin.

One of the most common elements that cause individuals to drift away into danger is the lack of validation or the feeling and *perception* of not being loved, leading to search for a place to belong.

Don't run into the arms of the lion for protection and expect not to be eaten.

Lions observe disunity and lurk around until they find the most vulnerable, distracted, and isolated zebra. The preoccupying thoughts in our mind can be detrimental like a person walking with a cell phone distracted and falling into a ditch, as much as a zebra walking into a lion's jaw. Our state of awareness and alertness has vanished and removed our boundaries and protective borders.

> Listen, my son, to your father's instruction and do not forsake your mother's teaching. (Proverbs 1:8 NIV)

Where there is a gathering of people of God, family, or any unified body, rest assured that strife and divisive elements are lurking around. Instructions can be a lifesaving mechanism when followed.

Matthew 24 challenges us to know the signs of the time and end-time. We would do ourselves great justice by understanding the important lessons and survival skills taught to us by zebras as mentors and professors. Like it was in the days of Noah, it will surely be in our lifetime.

> From the tribe of Issachar, there were 200 leaders of the tribe with their relatives. All these men understood the signs of the times and knew the best course for Israel to take. (1 Chronicles 12:32 KJV).

Perception

There is a story about a man who was looking through his window and trying to observe what was going on in his neighbor's house. The man could not see clearly through his neighbor's window and wondered to himself why his neighbor's windows were so dirty and caused major distortion. A short time later, the man started to notice that as he touched his window, dust particles were disappearing. The man then cleaned his window and realized that the distorted image he saw was a direct result of his own view that was obstructed by the dust on the windows in his house.

How many times have we misjudged others by our faulty outlook and misconception? How many times have we seen our neighbors with the latest model vehicles, grand houses, prestigious colleges, clothes, items, jobs, spouses, etc.; then we develop this increasing desire to possess, to purchase, or to attain the same not knowing the means by which they were acquired?

We look in our neighbor's yard and think to ourselves that the grass is greener on the other side. Until we visit our neighbor's yard, and with a close-up look, we realize that our grass is of a better quality. Our perception is obstructed by our own biases.

The success of the zebra is not found in the comparison syndrome. (2 Corinthians 10:12 tells us that it is unwise to compare ourselves with others.)

Most of our mental and emotional fights on a daily basis are exhaustive and lead to frustration and unnecessary verbal altercation, simply because we have not mastered the art of relinquishing our struggles to God. Matthew 11:28–30 tells us that we should come to God with our burdens, and He will give us peace of mind and rest in our spirit. There are so many different avenues that God has provided as sources of help and intervention, but as Jesus said, "I have come so many times, but you refused to realize." Jesus came in need of clothes, food, and various assistances; but we lacked the compassion and turned away those who are in need. Husbands and wives should live in understanding of each other; otherwise, we block the path to answered prayers. We are searching for the supernatural manifestation, missing it because it is not in the storm but answers that came in a silent whisper.

The zebra knows that instead of allowing differences to trigger malice and conflicts, the magnitude of our success is predicated upon our unity and the efficient execution of strategies to achieve our goals. The zebra develops healthy boundaries and lifestyle. Zebras eat together and master the art of influence toward healthy living and survival skills. Establishing and building boundaries allow the young and vulnerable zebras to develop a holistic way and pattern of thinking that will prevent them from being exploited. Working and eating together causes the predator to think twice or evaluate if it's really worth the fight of risking its life. Predators know that to choose a fight against one zebra will result in a fight against many.

Zebras are naturally born with stripes, or the innate physiological traits to grow and develop stripes. Stripes serve the core purpose of camouflage against predators. Since zebras are naturally born with this protective measure, not predicated, predisposed, or imposed by its environment, it simply means there is a supernatural phenomenon that implemented such protective design before the existence of the zebra.

As parents, there are principles and precepts we have developed and go in preparation and legacy mode in order to pass unto our future generation even beyond our life span. As a family structure, it's incumbent upon each and everyone to ensure the preservation of life against all predators. Humanistic behavior could resort to a predatory outcome. Naturally we are abusive emotionally, financially, mentally, socially, physically, and spiritually. We should use our zebra stripes and be protective of each other. We should not cripple the spiritual growth of our young generation by our lack of discipline and negate toward the principles of spiritual success. Being constantly busy and preoccupied should not substitute or prevent the progress for a rudimentary family or developmental structure for our children. Our children need to develop their stripes for proper use toward future survival. Being busy should not impede upon prayer, devotional, meditation, and spiritual formation. According to Luke 10:28–32, Martha was busy preparing meal in the kitchen while Mary sat by the feet of Jesus listening and conversing. Martha began to complain and said it's unfair to be doing all the work while her sister just sits around doing nothing. At least that was the perception of Martha and many of us, until Jesus said Mary has discovered the key to life, and it will not be taken away from her.

Living in a "rat-race" society abusing ourselves with being constantly busy has given us a perception of healthy life, while it is like chasing after the forbidden fruit not realizing it leads to death!

Zebras are loyal to their surroundings and do not usually drift away out of sight. Parents and role models ought to teach our teenagers to set boundaries. Teenagers should not allow themselves to become vulnerable, drifting out of sight in the arms of sweet embrace, or linger in the confinement of homes with individuals who lack accountability measures. Adults and experienced individuals are usually able to detect or observe unhealthy signs, which the immature and amateur are not aware or prepared to handle. The injured zebra puts the entire family at risk by demanding attention, supervision, and constant protection.

Avoiding Misconceptions

The thoughts of a man are like looking into a mirror; it is descriptive of self.

My thoughts, visions, passion, desires, actions, love, and other attributes are subjected to the beholder and ought not to be projected onto others. This aids in avoiding misconceptions and distorted thought patterns.

Zebras stand together in agreement and commitment. Many individuals in life looking from the outside in the life of others oftentimes believe that your life is different and free from conflict and problems. The highlight of the matter is whether we are seeking resolution or revengeful conflicts. The highlight of the issue is to recognize that in a relationship, we are not enemies but one force. The highlight of recognition is to realize that the faster we come together and choose the most effective mean to resolve the conflict at hand, the less time the problem will linger. A relationship that develops effective measures in conflict resolution will be less likely to encounter a severe crisis.

If we can defeat three particular elements, namely, curiosity, expectation, and desires, we will likely conquer life. Defeating curiosity is the inner strength that prevents us from yielding to temptation. We do not need to treat dissatisfaction of our curiosity as a major loss. Sometimes in life, it does better not to know. Second, expectation is an anticipation usually attached to some form of pleasurable results. Having the proper approach of expectation will protect us from disappointment. Our anticipation should be healthy, practical, and realistic, knowing that we are limited beings that do not control the possibilities of every outcome. Third, desire is a force that takes growth and spiritual maturity to control. Desires can be attractive, exciting, and pleasurable even when sinful and detrimental. Exercising self-control over our desires will grant us fulfillment and anchor us from seeking gratification in unwarranted and unsolicited areas. Too oftentimes we feed depression with food craving. We numb our pain with sexual gratification, drugs, food, video games, multiple partners, spending, etc.

As we enjoy the enticing elements of life, we become more engulfed and engaged in its pleasure. Our attention is likely diverted from the pain of reality; we then compromise and lack strategy to face and overcome pain and temporary battles. Before long, we find ourselves pulled further into what seems to be a suitable solution yet a major demise. Emotional ties will lead to mental and spiritual connectivity. We will mourn for our pets as much as a lifeless object that we possess. Before long, we discover that we are attached and anchored to sinking stones. Low self-esteem and adventurous desires can cause the mind to play dangerously. Thoughts are like a cue or keys that unlock and get into your mind to control your actions. Thoughts will preoccupy your mind with distractions, allowing you less time to process thoughts of resistance. If the actions are pleasurable, some individuals leave the door open or leave hints suggesting the door is unlocked. Some people pretend to be on the defense as a facade while others are perceived to be on the offense. When sin occurs against the nature of our spirit, the outer influences against the inner influences can incite the desire to depart this world. We have never been to that place beyond death, but pain and suffering will cause you to embrace it in a reassuring way as though it's a familiar place previously known, and it has to be better than your current circumstance. Life experiences will cause you to let go of the things of this life. Contentment is a common factor to defeat all three synonymous enemies. Even when we increase in resources and physical assets, may our hearts be forbidden from becoming attached.

Do I Have the Right to Blame Even When I Am Not at Fault?

One of the greatest stories in history and downfall of King David was when he stole the wife from the main military leader then placed him on the front line of the battlefield so that he could lose his life. David thought that he got away until God sent Nathan to David with a parable (2 Samuel 12:1–13). Nathan was very fearful of approaching David but nonetheless told David that there were two men in a town: one was very rich, and the other was poor. The rich man had acres of land filled with animals. The poor man had a little lamb that he took care of like a child. But one day when the rich man had a guest at his home, he killed the man's lamb and made a feast. Nathan then asked David what should be done with such a man. David got intensely angry and said such a man deserves to die. Nathan then confronted David and said, "You are that man who has all the riches and opportunities, yet you murdered Uriah and took the only wife that he had. God will reward you accordingly with deserved consequences."

Accountability factor is a major part of the pruning process. To prevent a plant from dying, the gardener has to constantly cut away the bad part. The cutting-away process is very painful, but far more rewarding and fruitful after the healing. Can a man truly change or become effectively influential if he does not recognize his blindness or his own equal state of guilt? Nathan was very afraid to approach King David.

Do we have friends in our lives that we would love to tell them the truth, but we may lose them in the process?

Am I that person who finds it hard to accept the truth when I am being exposed, causing others around me to remain a hypocrite in silence out of duress? Our children will become conditioned to remain in silence with frustration, instead of communicating the truth in a loving atmosphere if parents fail to model this type of discipline in harmony. We find and spend more time in battle pointing out the faults of each other, rather than accept the pruning and flourish. This behavior will also lead to outburst and retaliation if there is no established model of operation to express each other's point of view. Our children will absorb this type of attitude like sponge then become the lawyer and judge to tell us that we are also guilty in doing the same. How hypocritical and devastating to punish the child for exposing us by telling them that they are disrespectful for undermining your authority. We will find ourselves surrounding a wounded zebra if we do not prune them from constantly walking into devastating positions.

Can I quantify the weight of faults and guilt found in others, to compare, rationalize, or justify the faults recognized in myself?

Do I have a tendency to reject the truth that is meant to improve me, simply because the messenger has similar faults?

As parents, we should not blame our family for their action, neither our feelings of neglect. We have to quickly realize that our lives are parallel to our relationship with our Abba Father who has created and blessed us in abundance. Everything, and everyone, inclusive of myself, spouse, and children, belongs to Him.

One of the first scripture verses that I learned in Sunday school:

> The earth is the LORD's, and the fulness thereof; the
> world, and they that dwell therein. (Psalm 24:1 KJV)

We have to quickly come to grips with and realize that there is no need to complain or apply irrational blame. An unhealthy, carnal, or negative thought process would translate this experience into faulty coded entries in the mind to believe that the relationship is in trouble beyond reconciliation.

A jealous heart or neighbor would tell you that where there is smoke, there is fire (referring to signs of problems in the relationship). A carnal mind will advise and reassure you that there seems to be trouble ahead. That's why when there is turbulence in a relationship or situation, be careful where we go in search of "wise" counseling!

But zebras, by their actions, demonstrate openly and transparently that they have their own faults, yet with a healthy approach and discipline, we all have to stand together in love, and success is guaranteed. A zebra does not operate on the horizontal (carnal) plane. A zebra steps in the realm of the vertical in total reliance and the full scope of unity and power in the might of the Creator.

Living on the Vertical Plane

Sometimes zebras will start to assemble and stand guard around their offspring. The zebras are now on high alert, even the ones that are clueless to what is going on.

The book of Job chapter 1 tells us that one day the members of the heavenly court came to present themselves before the LORD, and Satan the Accuser showed up as well. The Lord then inquired where Satan is coming from, and Satan said that he is just patrolling back and forth and observing what is going on. God then rhetorically asked Satan if he has been thinking about his righteous son Job.

Satan is like a lion looking for the opportunity to devour the zebra that might be vulnerable. The author of the book of Job was able to beautifully capture the essence of the conversation in the heavenly realm between God and Lucifer. The conversation was not with Job, as the devil was plotting his demise. Job, however, was able to discern the attacks of the enemy and refused to curse God as was suggested by his wife. The zebra with sensitive ears, listening skills, and discernment is able to detect the motives of the predator even before he appears. The zebra will not ask where is God when there is so much evil. We all have freedom of choice, and no parents like the feel of being blamed when their baby puts on a temper tantrum in public. It's a warm feeling when someone comes to assist when you are in need and preoccupied with an important agenda.

Sometimes God reveals or exposes to you the plot of the enemy so that you can guard, protect, and confuse the enemy upon arrival.

The zebra does not fight solely in its strength or natural ability. The zebra utilizes its inherent stripes and listens distinctly with discernment with those 180 degrees rotating capability. The zebra has great sensitivity and does not react with sudden emotion or initial *perception*. The zebra understands social behavior and knows that there is often an underlying condition that is triggering movement of the bushes or rattling of the leaves. A zebra knows that if the young babies are scared, they may not know how to eloquently articulate their emotional frustration. But as parents, if we listen long enough, we will see beyond the surface of perception. We will understand that there may be predators in the midst that want to molest, sexually abuse, steal, gossip, cheat, impregnate, or present peer pressure that insinuates suicidal and drug abuse thoughts.

A zebra willingly develops maturity and knows how to survive the fight by relying on external strength. Humanity has to rely on answers through prayer. We have to obediently let go, knowing that the fight belongs to God. Have you ever seen someone trying to part a fight or separate multiple individuals involved in a conflict? Oftentimes, there is at least one person who persists in fighting and tries to push past in order to take a wild swinging punch or even negative words. So it is when God is fighting our battles, and we refuse to relinquish full responsibility from our mind, heart, or actions!

When crisis, confusion, and conflict arise, it's not time to malign, blame, fall apart, and hope and wish someone gets devoured by the lion.

Desensitized emotional turmoil, sabotage, and coldhearted insensitivity have no part or tolerance in family unity and bonding. Neither is it time to recognize the danger yet walk away with close circles of friends and act as though the lion is just taking a casual stroll.

In life, we can turn a blind eye or pretend to be oblivious, but as the famous adage says, "Today for me, tomorrow for you."

Having a negative or ulterior motive is like having the gallow that Haman built to hang Mordecai that became the same gallow that was his demise, making Haman a public spectacle (Esther 7:9–10). If the lion recognizes that it can devour one set of herd, then naturally a different set of identical herd will be pursued and perceived as easy target.

Victory Over Opposition—"Celebrate others!"

Were we ever disciplined to share in the joy of others, or were we rather conditioned to be the center and focus of attention?

Have you ever seen a child that is hurting, and as you kiss that child's fingers, he/she smiles and runs away forgetting that the pain even exists? What a great source of healing when we can pause long enough to express deep love and compassion to someone in distress. If humanity can walk away after clearly observing someone in need, how much more the overlooked with hidden and deep underlying weight submerging underneath the sea of distress? Romans 12:14–21 implores us to weep with those who are weeping, refrain from executing evil behavior against those who may have done us wrong, provide for those who may be against us, and if at all possible try our endeavor best to live in peace with each other. Naturally the mind is inclined to accept these terms. But those who are in a position of leadership know that there is no greater joy but to do good to those who may try to undermine your authority. It's not a fear of retaliation but to see the transformation when you are being lovingly sincere to another. It causes the person to conduct a self-interview and assessment, which propels a change and clears up the dark clouds of misplaced anger. Our mind is like a fertile ground; anything that we place in it will grow.

> Guard your heart with all diligence, for out of it is the
> wellspring of life. (Proverbs 4:23 NHEB)

Matthew 18:21–35 tells a parable of the unforgiving debtor who lacks compassion and forgets the journey of life. He was forgiven of millions of dollars in accumulated debts that could have landed him in prison. But very soon after being forgiven, he refused to forgive his servant who was very poor a few thousand dollars and placed him in prison. There are so many times as parents we have purchased homes, gifts, and other entities and provide for our children, friends, or someone in need. We then make phone calls, desire company and time, or want to experience the beauty of their fellowship but seem nowhere to be found. We can only imagine what it felt like when God would visit Enoch who lived and fellowshipped in a close relationship with God until the age of 365 when God took him (Genesis 5:21–24). There is no greater feeling than to be flooded with sincere and genuine love from someone equally desiring you and reciprocating the same love! As parents, friends, and spouses, we have expectations like our Heavenly Father with Enoch. But very soon the relationship may begin to feel like Genesis 3:8–11 when Adam and Eve hid from the Lord in the cool of the evening among the trees. The Lord then inquired, and they responded that upon hearing the Lord coming, they went to hide because they were naked and ashamed of their disobedience having eaten from the forbidden tree.

Our relationship at times can feel like our families are hiding in the garden, even when we live in the same house. Our children are preoccupied with their gadgets, video games, telephones, iPads, and all the other devices that were meant to bring us closer. But like the forbidden tree, the pleasure of the fruit has created a wedge of distance and hiding place. People in society will just talk long enough to tolerate the voice of others, but not long enough to embrace the quality of love and their presence. We constantly give the blessings that each of us desires but become neglected and forsaken in the process. People are searching for fulfillment, which is a sign of societal breakdown. One of the main issues is that as parents, we weren't privileged to a lot of opportunities, so we begin to overcompensate and flourish our children with excessive gifts. We in turn and indirectly conditioned their hearts and mind into a spirit of ingratitude, into failing to understand the true value and sacrifice of what it takes to accomplish.

> Instead of buying your children all the things you never had, you should teach them all the things you were never taught. Material wears out but knowledge stays. (Bruce Lee)

Second, children will begin to despise the less fortunate as though it was some mishap by their parents why they have such shortcoming. The false notion is that if my family can do it, your family should be able to do it as well. The disciples asked Jesus, "Why is this lame man sitting by the gate? Is it because of some evil deeds that were done by the parents?" Jesus responded by stating that it is neither evil done by the individual nor the parents, but it is to transform the hearts of the people who will observe the miracle that is about to be performed. How ironic are the stripes of the zebra, when you discover that your perception is different from the revealed and concluded truth.

When zebras stand together and their stripes are multiplied like a field of interweaved blankets, the lion experiences massive distortion and cannot visualize any starting point to attack or penetrate. Deuteronomy 32:30 tells us that one can chase a thousand, but two will put ten thousand to flight. Zebras become a greater force in unified agreement. Matthew 18:18–21 encourages to claim victory on earth, and heaven will bestow the results. If two individuals come together, much more a greater number in agreement asking God for a great intervention, it will be like encountering love or protection from the wrath of a father manifested when rescuing your child from imminent danger.

Why Does the Zebra Sleep and Eat Standing Up?

There is a great victory in the mind of the prepared. The one who lacks alertness is a grave liability! We confuse the direction of the crowd with the right path of travel. Gideon thought that he would have won the battle with a great number according to perception. God then told him that the people are too many and will claim the victory and glory according to their own strength. God then showed Gideon how many individuals were not vigilant and were very distracted. Distraction will be a great demise. Twenty-two thousand men were scared and went home. God then told him to carefully observe the men by the riverside while they were drinking water. Only three hundred men out of remaining ten thousand were ready and alert by drinking while watching. The other men all knelt down and drank water in an oblivious state (Judges 7). How frightening that would be to rely on such a small number to win a battle. But in fact, they did win! When they moved into the camp with loud sounds and musical instruments, the perception by the enemies caused them to launch an attack on each other. There are so many times the hungry lions turn against each other, simply because the zebras stood together and refused to be devoured. Nehemiah, the cupbearer, reveals a similar parallel. Nehemiah and his team while building the Jerusalem wall worked with their tool in one hand and a weapon in the other. Nehemiah refused to become distracted by Sanballat and Tobiah (Nehemiah 4). One ounce of distraction in thoughts or actions is like texting and driving.

The zebra knows that celebration starts before any signs of victory. Your praise will confuse the enemy! When the lion or any predators approach the zebra, the zebra forms prayerlike circles, running back and forth creating distorted imageries with their stripes, utterly confusing the perception of the enemy with a Judah "crazy-praise" type effect.

The zebralike person chews on the Word of God, while having a weapon of praise and shout of victory. Have you ever seen someone surviving an encounter that could have been fatal? That person becomes ecstatic while crying and rejoicing, forgetting who is in their midst. If we hold back our expression of gratitude, we have a distorted perception of the magnitude of God's grace over our lives.

Do we say, "Thank you, Lord," when it's a major close call to home, while we fail to recognize the small steps of the bridge that brings us safely across the deep?

The zebra knows how to return with a praise and thanksgiving after receiving the victory, knowing that this completes the healing process like the leper who returned, instead of running off to celebrate (Luke 17:11–19). A zebra that recognizes its faults returns to the flock and maintains a sober mind and admits that isolation can lead to depression like the prodigal son (Luke 5:11–32).

Zebras have developed a common boundary and mastered the art and principle of living in understanding with each other. God, according to 2 Peter 3:7, encourages husbands to give honor to their wives and live in understanding as they live together so that your prayers will not be hindered. Prayer does not necessarily mean I ask or request with a certain petition then there is an instant result. The answer to a prayer can be a perpetuating daily result. Living in understanding does not mean there will never be any conflict. The occurrence of conflict is usually a great opportunity for discovery in a relationship. In fact, to live in understanding is impossible without conflict. However, the result of our accomplishments is to acquire and utilize the wisdom of problem solving, confidence, and application of faith beyond our natural comprehension. We ought to grow and strive not to hurt or repeat unhealthy action, which will inevitably lead to potential relationship hazards.

The power of exponential growth rapidly transcends as the numbers increase linearly. What one person can do by himself increases the potential result like ten thousand joining forces together.

How much more is the merging of our mental faculties, thought process, energy when we merge together our potential? Ecclesiastes 4:9–12 tells us that two are always better than one for success and assistance when in need. The verse went on to tell us that a triple-braided cord is able to bear the weight exponentially when compared to a double-braided cord.

We can, as a group, stand together to accomplish great things or be defeated and destructive by yielding to corrupt motives. This is why the Lord confused the men by giving them different languages when they started to build the Tower of Babel. When humanity stands together, whether to do evil or good deeds, it will happen (Genesis 11:5–7).

As I was in the process of folding my clothes, there was a sweater with stripes resembling the zebra. As I looked at the sweater and began folding, the stripes distorted my vision, and I became slightly disoriented. I began to reflect on the power of the zebra, bringing confusion to the enemy by just being itself. The Holy Spirit started ministering to me with a probing question, by asking how many times we have brought confusion to others unknowingly by just being ourselves. We can disarm opponents by yielding to the voice of the Holy Spirit.

Our silence can be most profound.

How many times have people become frustrated in trying to predict and analyze in order to either understand or perhaps even control and manipulate us?

The Word of God declares in James 4:7 KJV, "Submit yourselves therefore to God. Resist the devil, and he will flee from you."

Resistance to temptation, and obedience to God irrespective of our motives, justifications, or reactions in thoughts and defense, is forsaking our will to abide by the righteousness of God. "Be angry and sin not" is a direct command from God. My motive may be to retaliate, but obedience is to the utmost. Too many times we justify our actions, motives, and unhealthy thought patterns by saying, "I refuse to have anyone walk over me." The question then becomes, did the Holy Spirit caution you?

A soft answer turneth away wrath: but grievous words stir up anger. (Proverbs 15:1 KJV)

Zebras will come together when one is hurting. This is an exemplary and practical attitude demonstrated in the discipline of Jesus. Jesus asked if one sheep is lost, would you not leave the ninety-nine and go searching for the one that is lost? If one zebra is hurting, will the others not surround? If your brothers and sisters are hurting, will you not set aside judgmental attitude and declare that I did not come to condemn you? (John 3:17 NKJV: "For God did not send His Son into the world to condemn the world, but that the world through Him might be saved.") He that is without fault cast the first stone. Will we assemble like zebras and with the inner strength that says and recognize that I was once at this place, and neither am I invincible from similar attacks? When I discern spiritual warfare, I have to recognize that my brother or sister is hurting, and he/she will complain or possess misplaced anger, but we can't walk away. We must understand that my hurting brother and sister are speaking from a place of frustration and pain. There can also be great underlying root conditions that is drowning out proper judgment.

> Putting confidence in an unreliable person in times of trouble
> is like chewing with a broken tooth or walking on a lame foot.
> Singing cheerful songs to a person with a heavy heart
> is like taking someone's coat in cold weather
> or pouring vinegar in a wound.
> If your enemies are hungry, give them food to eat.
> If they are thirsty, give them water to drink.
> You will heap burning coals of shame on their heads,
> and the LORD will reward you.
> As surely as a north wind brings rain,
> so a gossiping tongue causes anger! (Proverbs 25:19–23 NLT)

And when you are brought to trial in the synagogues and before rulers and authorities, don't worry about how to defend yourself or what to say, for the Holy Spirit will teach you at that time what needs to be said. (Luke 12:11–12 NLT)

But in your hearts revere Christ as Lord. Always be prepared to give an answer to everyone who asks you to give the reason for the hope that you have. But do this with gentleness and respect, keeping a clear conscience, so that those who speak maliciously against your good behavior in Christ may be ashamed of their slander. For it is better, if it is God's will, to suffer for doing good than for doing evil. (1 Peter 3:15–17 NIV)

I cannot walk away, not being accountable, and ask rhetorically, "Am I my brother's keeper?" In times of crises, I can't ask what you were thinking and add to the weight of pain when logic is not at its optimum to the one who is hurting. I have to recognize that the passion that I have or desire to see you improve may require the maturity to suspend all judgment and delay the need for lecture. My mistiming may destroy a great field of opportunity to influence effective changes. Zebras keep their eyes on the lion that they want to destroy and do not become distracted by the wounded soldier by asking them what they were thinking. It's not time to tell the hurting zebra that it got us in this mess. Otherwise, we run away to watch the lion tear the zebra apart and with a heart of stone complain that the zebra brought such destruction upon itself. At no time should a victim of rape be accused of provoking the results of the action because of what he/she was wearing. Every zebra has walked through the valley of potential misfortune, like the sleeping occupants in the vehicle who fell asleep on the journey as described earlier. We have survived and made it this far on a journey of success due to interdependency! We all have faults and are all in need of each other.

CHAPTER 9
WISDOM OF THE ANTS
(Power of Unified Now)

Education is our passport to the future, for tomorrow belongs
to the people who prepare for it today. -Malcolm X
Cast your bread upon the waters, For you will find it
after many days. (Ecclesiastes 11:1 NKJV)

(The Wise Lecturer)

Building Success through the Ants' Colony Model

In a recent trip to Alaska while on a military assignment, I have been baffled and taunted by a phenomenon that has left my heart and mind pondering with a certain question. I will never forget it; it was during the summer months, on June 21, which would be called the longest day of summer. The sun would apparently stand still for approximately twenty-three hours in the day. The extra hour to complete the cycle would be a slight dimming of the sunlight, which then mysteriously brightened and intensified. For the Alaskan natives, this may perhaps be a monotonous encounter. But I was left pondering with one question resonating like a theme in my mind: "What is time?"

I then read an article that spoke about a passenger airplane that departed the airport on January 1, the first day of the year; but when it arrived at its destination, it was December 31, the last day of the previous year according to the time zone of that country, which was few hours behind. It's like reliving the past or experiencing the New Year twice. Filling out certain documentation would lend the appearance of time travel into the past. Nonetheless, I was left pondering, "What is time?"

Whether I put my vehicle in reverse, fly an airplane in an opposite time zone, or watch someone driving in the wrong direction, time apparently is neither phased nor impacted. Why do some people have the capacity to accomplish twice as much in half or significantly less time than others? Is it mere luck, more grace, self-discipline, limited according to geographical location and culture, or just predestined in our conceptual thought pattern?

Well, what better way to start than to introduce you to the ants!

Let's get the greatest genius on earth and put him in a classroom with an ant. Such a genius would encourage you to go pay the ant a visit. Ensure you bring gifts like when the queen of Sheba went to see King Solomon. In fact, auditoriums would be filled to capacity; stadiums would be overbooked without exaggeration even in inclement weather conditions. Can you picture the size and potential of a computer microchip? Can you envision the algorithm and the nanosecond speed of its execution? How about the size of the brain of an ant? How does it function with such intuition, creativity, and excellence?

How much more successful would I be in life if I was lectured by a group of ants? How much more advance can I become if only I follow the advice of one of the wisest men who ever lived, invest some time to learn, apply the way and attitude, and model the habits and discipline of the ants?

There was a group of scientists and engineers who came together who wanted to study the way of the ants' colony. As the ants would make holes in the surface of the earth, the scientists were curious to see what was below the surface that was so oblivious to men and women, even though their feet would trod it every day. The scientists poured cement to make protective concrete casing of the path traveled by the ants. They were amazed to discover that the ants' colony was over a one-fourth acre of establishment and can extend to over six hundred acres.

The ants are very meticulous in their operation and function in a distinct system of unity. The ants designed what would be a five-star architectural complex establishment. This design was advanced, both in physical development and in functional execution. Leading below the surface of the ground was an oxygen intake chamber to furnace the underground infrastructure. There were different compartments designated for specific purposes. Areas were separated in rooms for resting, reproduction, and early stage of birth; larvae chamber for the laying and storage of eggs; compartment for food storage; compartment for waste disposal; and other necessities.

As we analyze this ant institution and study at this college or ant university for higher learning, let us keep at the forefront of our minds that this is just the finished product in operation and possibly expansion. How many thoughts and organizational processes were implemented as far as the chosen location, dimensions, troubleshooting, weather condition, economy, work time, rest time, transporting of food, attacking live enemies for food supplies, weight and size to fit and carry supplies, possibly loss of lives, mourning, resiliency, man ("ant") power, etc.?

What could possibly be their thought process that would enable such success and productivity?

Let us closely examine what the wise man Solomon has to say in his writings, as he encouraged his son to study the way of the ant and be wise.

My son, if you have put up security for your neighbor,
if you have shaken hands in pledge for a stranger,
you have been trapped by what you said,
ensnared by the words of your mouth.
So do this, my son, to free yourself,
since you have fallen into your neighbor's hands:
Go—to the point of exhaustion—
and give your neighbor no rest!

> Allow no sleep to your eyes,
> no slumber to your eyelids.
> Free yourself, like a gazelle from the hand of the hunter,
> like a bird from the snare of the fowler.
> Go to the ant, you sluggard;
> consider its ways and be wise!
> It has no commander,
> no overseer or ruler,
> yet it stores its provisions in summer
> and gathers its food at harvest.
> How long will you lie there, you sluggard?
> When will you get up from your sleep?
> A little sleep, a little slumber,
> a little folding of the hands to rest—
> and poverty will come on you like a thief
> and scarcity like an armed man. (Proverbs 6:1–11 NIV)

Let us dissect these verses cautiously!

Verse 6: The lazy individual is being implored to visit the ant and adapt its ways. Have we become complacent and stagnant, not being productive or reaping the benefits of our labor? What does it mean to be lazy? The wise man Solomon in *Proverbs 12:27* declared, "The lazy man does not roast what he took hunting, but diligence is man's precious possession."

In other words, a lazy man will work, but what does he do with the raw material that he hunts? Does he sit around and watch the meat spoil, without processing, preserving, or roasting it to a converted state in which it is edible and can be repackaged for further profit? Do we convert raw material from the status of consumerism to a finished product as a supplier?

Verse 7: The wise man gave us an inside view and tells us that the ants execute due diligence and do what is expected without being micromanaged; neither do they abuse time while the clock keeps ticking. Time is just a categorized element in the realm of the mind. The ants are not defeated by procrastination or elements of excuses. There is no monitored system of supervision or leadership to ensure that each ant does what is expected. There is a natural state of initiative and compliance to exercise diligence. The ant is not discouraged by the absence of validation. Validation for productivity is simply awaiting an antidote, like an addict searching for a dose of motivation.

The law of diminishing returns tells us that if we constantly add one more factor to the process of productivity, it may eventually slow down productivity and yield less returns. For example, while I was carrying my grandmother's coffin at her funeral, there were supposed to be six men, in which three were on either side of the coffin. I soon found myself walking and bumping into another individual, only to realize that a seventh person came to assist. Adding more of one factor can diminish the outcome or the intended results. Humanity oftentimes reaches a turbulent state, not because we increase in number, but because our minds have not been disciplined and conditioned to synchronize for the vision and common accomplishment. Humanity instead struggles and is more inclined to eliminate and prone to sabotage for preeminence and kingship.

The ants, though large in number, seem to naturally synchronize and maximize their level of productivity. The ants do not appear to increase in anger to the point of eradicating or sabotaging each other. In other words, the level of return is consistently found to be at its maximum productivity or output, unless there are extreme crises.

Do I possess or have friends with a "blender" mindset?

When we enter the presence of certain individuals, their mind becomes like a blender. Their mental processor shreds, chops, blends, mixes, and reduces you to pieces. They feel empowered within themselves by reducing your significance as you pass through their mind.

How can I improve on conflict resolution with others while pursuing my long-term goals? How can I increase my self-satisfaction and become more passionate in the things that I pursue? Is it possible that I may have to change my outlook and rearrange my thought process?

Verse 8: The ant stores its provision in the summer and gathers its food at harvest. Why do I need to store, save, and safeguard my assets, information, time, friendship, conversation, accumulated resources, and eternal life? Why do I need to gather food at harvest time or maximize on these opportunities instead of saying tomorrow will provide for itself? There are so many unforeseeable conditions such as being laid off, being faced with a tragedy, sickness, health issues, tornados, earthquakes, hurricanes, foreclosures, robberies, marriages, family, college funds, education, inflation, recession, financial stability, retirements, etc.

Verse 9: How long will you lie there and sleep? Sleeping excessively is remaining in a state of dormancy and being robbed by procrastination. How many unfulfilled agenda do we have on our daily to-do list, which has grown from a list to a booklet? Time is a very precious resource and commodity and should be spent wisely. Excessive sleep is the equivalent of debt accumulation and is equally destructive as spending with high interest rates and allowing our debts and expenses to eat away at our savings. Is it possible that we are restless while awake, yet we are in sleep mode? Is this why we emphasize on stop wasting time or spend time wisely? Money does not purchase time, but time is a supernatural resource that converts to any commodity. Our minds are overly consumed, stressed, disarrayed, and mentally disoriented. We fail to execute effective thought patterns and lack clarity in our direction. We are ineffective and detrimental, being in a constant state of sleep deprivation, which is as destructive as intoxication.

Verse 10: "A little slumber, a little sleep, a little folding of the hands to rest." This verse is not implying that you should not get proper and adequate rest for the well-being and good health. However, there is a caution sign, and one is implored to be very sensitive and aware of factors and habits that are adverse to our discipline for success.

Verse 11: Poverty will come on you like a thief and scarcity like an armed gunman. Poverty has been used as a euphemism and in the context of a bandit and dangerous gunman. Poverty comes in unaware and creeps upon the vulnerable. Poverty will rob you and walk away with your precious resources. Encouragement has been given to remain vigilant or alert and walk in constant awareness. In the end, even when the problems and perpetrators of our issues are identified, the results and consequences are the same. Blaming the obstacles that are identified will not justify or rectify the problems. A thief could take away our possessions just as much as a natural disaster. Do we exhaust energy against man as the opponent and surrender the fight against the disaster? The concept is in the mind of the beholder. Am I stuck in a groove simply because my thought is affixed to a self-created enemy, like secret hatred in my mind?

I can be enslaved by anger against a person who accidentally damaged my car, but not the pothole that punctured my tire.

The effects are the same, but my mind attributes its thoughts and energy against a self-created enemy. I instantly offer forgiveness to the pothole or inanimate object, but not a person warranted of my love.

Do I allow poverty to overshadow and wrestle my finances by keeping my savings in the bank system while accumulating less than 1 percent, when inflation and other expenses are over 7 percent? This means that though my account balance reflects a certain amount, the reality is that the value has already reduced significantly like stocks and bonds plunging. Try holding $500 in your bank account for ten years, and you will realize that what would have been a down payment on a car ten years ago, today you would be lucky if the same amount can buy a meal on a date. Do I pay the minimum balance on my home loan, having high interests that cause me to purchase the house at twice the value? Diligence in extra payment would refill my pocket instead of scattering my finance on interest to the bank like sand dust to the ground. I then sell the house later in life a little higher than the cost price and become deceived to think that I made a profit when I have already paid twice the amount and could have owned another home.

Today the ants want us to recognize that one of the greatest investments is self-investment. Build your debt-free colony by evaluating the rate of holding on to your savings, or pay off the debts and benefit from the returns that you are constantly giving away. Isn't it easier for four family members to each contribute fifty thousand and purchase a debt-free colony for two hundred thousand? Each person then develops a vision and repays each other over a four-year period, rather than each renting a single room over a two-year period costing more than fifty thousand. Not only will you be debt free, but now the ant is able to expand from one-fourth acre to six hundred acres as the family grows and the finances stabilize. This systemic and progressive move will likely reduce potential conflict that is usually the bedrock of our fear to start with others. Spending money on interest rate is like spilling milk to the ground, while the baby cries for a drink against thirst. Study the ants! Let's synchronize. Let's build our "now"!

The Ant as a Flotation Device (To Victory)

In this age of technological advancements, social media hype, gadgets, and computer devices, humanity has lost its sense of urgency and sensitivity in assisting each other in the preservation of life. Many individuals have been seen utilizing their cell phone camera to capture people drowning, dying, or crying for help, instead of being the helper. There is a major disconnect if we do not recognize each other as a friend, family member, or relative or prioritize in a deliberate expedient time factor. We are divided by humor, race, age, significance, time factor, or expectation placed on the other.

There are many educational videos, documentaries, and pictures that show thousands of ants interconnecting their bodies during a flood and ultimately becoming a flotation device. The ants, even when they appear to submerge, refuse to let go, remaining interconnected until every ant has made it safely to shore. There are so many different object lessons to learn from this experience, so let us conduct a practical and multifaceted lesson.

Recent and current events undoubtedly show that storms and hurricanes are a common reoccurrence. Individuals will watch the storms approaching, disregard all warnings to evacuate, and then cry for help when the water starts to rise and beat against the dwelling. There are a few that may lack the quick adaptability to evacuate and attempt to get a boat, life jacket, life raft, or some form of flotation device.

What would cause ants that are as fearful of water like human beings to all survive in times of crises and emergency evacuation? Can my sense of urgency and planning be the very thing that saves and preserves life?

Miracle on the Hudson: If ants could be pilots and fly an airplane, I believe this would have been the same miraculous experience and result!

It was January 15, 2009, when "Miracle on the Hudson" occurred. Many individuals were amazed to find out that an airplane with 155 people on board conducted an emergency landing in the middle of the river, and everyone on board made it safely. As depicted in the news, history being told, US Airways Flight 1549 A320 took off from LaGuardia Airport in New York City and was struck by a flock of geese approximately five miles away. Both engines shut down, resulting in a gradual descent as the plane lost the necessary power to gain altitude. One of the pilots was a trained US Air Force fighter pilot who took control, being experienced with the A320, while the copilot who was also very experienced utilized the checklist. The pilot radioed Mayday and also explored different landing options to nearby airports by communicating with the control tower. Realizing that the airplane would not make it to the airport, the pilot did the unthinkable and told the air crew to brace for impact. The air traffic controller communicated with the United States Coast Guard to caution all vessels in the Hudson River and to be in preparation in the help and rescue mission. The plane was said to make a hard landing, without bouncing, with the tide drifting the airplane southward. An inflatable slide was deployed. The pilot opened the door and ordered an immediate evacuation. Many crew members climbed through the windows and exited to the inflatable raft. There were reports of rising water inside the rear of the airplane, resulting in passengers climbing over the seats and moving forward waiting to be rescued. The boats rescued many individuals who were on the detached plane wings that were used as a flotation device. Assistance was rendered from the rescue helicopters, divers, firefighters, police officers, coast guards, vessels, and other agencies. Some individuals had serious injuries, but all survived.

As I watched the interview that was subsequently conducted with many of the passengers, they gave testimonies such as the following:

> I saw the flames and said, "This is not good, this is not what I want to see . . ."

> We are crashing. What are you going to do? I kept thinking. I thought pray or send my wife a message, do I call her, or what do I do? So I quickly typed out a text. I said, "You know, plane is on fire, and I love you and the girls"; and I hit send and remember looking at the phone and seen the indicator light that the message got out, and I just kind of felt a sense of relief at that point that, you know, I got a chance to say goodbye.

> I felt sad that I may be leaving the family so young . . .

> Life goes by instantly. It's like will I see this person, will I ever talk to this person again? If this was the end, was I the person that I really wanted to be all my life? I was not ready to die yet. I have too many things to do . . .

> The possibility of not surviving was not a thought in my mind, but neither was the thought of living. It was just a peace that was over me, and I was ready to accept whatever was going to happen.

I and a lot of others thought this is it, this is the end . . .

I reached over and held the hands of a lady next to me and prepared to be a dead man.

We survived the crash, but now we are going to die.

I remember the gentle man sitting in grabbing my arm and saying, "We are going to die, aren't we? We are going to die."

I am thinking to myself, *This cannot be happening. This cannot be real. This is like a bad dream.*

After the plane landed in water:

I was giddy with excitement. We are not dying today.

You could see the fear and terror in her face, and I said, "Miss, don't give up." I actually slid down into the water off the wing and grabbed her and pulled her unto the wing yelling all the time, "You are going to make it! You are going to make it!"

He was just kind of standing there, and he was the picture of calm, and he just crashed the plane, and here he is, and he is wearing his captain's jacket, and he is just telling people to get into the raft.

It was the worst sickening-pit-of-your-stomach, falling-through-the-floor feeling I have ever felt in my life. (Pilot)

The crash changed lives:

I know there are other things I am supposed to do with my life, and I think there is 154 other people that also have something that they are supposed to do with their lives.

I see it as a second chance for life . . .

I have questioned everything now. Is this the type of work I am supposed to be doing? There is so many things that you can't help but to question and wonder what's next!

Enjoy life. Live for today. Don't live for tomorrow. My life has been touched by a miracle, so I have to give back some sort of, to something.

I was supposed to be a dead man. I try to get up every morning and look at my wife differently, hug my kids differently.

I remember I paid attention to the safety instructions . . .

Intentional and Purposeful Living

Is it possible for humanity to live life intentionally and purposefully, with such heightened intensity, without such external bearings or life-threatening experience? Was this mere luck or miracle with the absence of planning? When you board a plane, ship, or vessel or enter a car, how many individuals pray and pay attention to the instructions given? Do we give enough mental energy to be attentive and overcome this monotonous and lackadaisical attitude and approach? Or do we leave everything by chance mixed with poor planning and panic, scramble for help, and blame others for failure? Or perhaps the answer is staring us in the face by the self-probing catastrophic interview, which analyzes and surfaces the indisputable self-wrenching truth from the deep pit of our soul to the forefront of our consciousness.

How could the ants react, assemble, and become one unit so swiftly in the midst of unexpected flood? The ants were not running to steal bread crumbs, pick up baby eggs, search for sticks to build another colony, or look out for their own baby ants. Every ant moved together with the same effort, purpose, thought process, meeting point, location, and end goal in mind. The ants, upon reaching shore, each disconnected in an orderly formation and walked to safety on dry land. It was amazing to see and behold in the mind.

It is a strange thought to rationalize because humanity has never elevated to function at this supernatural and intrinsic level of design or organized system of emergency operation.

Let us now view this swift thinking of precautionary measures in times of great catastrophe. As working-class men and women, we conduct many fire drills, emergency precautionary measures, escape procedures, and active shooters exercise, in the event of any impending, potential, or actual dangers.

How much more the influence of love, self-worth, and value would be upon each other and manifest throughout society, if we truly cherish and put others first and before self.

Greater love has no one than this: to lay down one's life for one's friends. (John 15:13 NIV)

If you are familiar with a Jewish soldier known as Paul, who was a very influential leader, you will discover that he killed many Christians because at the time he thought he was doing a righteous deed. However, Paul had a spiritual encounter that left him physically blinded. Paul then regained his sight with the intervention of one of the very individuals whom Paul would have murdered if he had crossed his path. Paul was imprisoned and was on his way to Rome in chains on a ship transporting prisoners to face trial in the high court, when suddenly a storm ripped their ship apart. The irony of the story is that the 276 passengers on board a ship (Acts 27:37), with many who were unable to swim, all survived. How did this happen? Could it be an "ant-like" operation? Let's see!

According to Acts 27:37–44 NIV,

> Altogether there were 276 of us on board. When they had eaten as much as they wanted, they lightened the ship by throwing the grain into the sea.
>
> When daylight came, they did not recognize the land, but they saw a bay with a sandy beach, where they decided to run the ship aground if they could. Cutting loose the anchors, they left them in the sea and at the same time untied the ropes that held the rudders. Then they hoisted the foresail to the wind and made for the beach. But the ship struck a sandbar and ran aground. The bow stuck fast and would not move, and the stern was broken to pieces by the pounding of the surf.
>
> The soldiers planned to kill the prisoners to prevent any of them from swimming away and escaping. But the centurion wanted to spare Paul's life and kept them from carrying out their plan. He ordered those who could swim to jump overboard first and get to land. The rest were to get there on planks or on other pieces of the ship. In this way everyone reached land safely.

Paul implored everyone to stay on board, which is essential for survival. The power of unity and agreement can alleviate a whole lot of problems. In these two encounters involving the airplane and the ship, it left humanity with no other option but to stick together until the end. The ants have no leaders, yet they function as one core group that accomplishes the same common goal.

The pride and ego of humanity was diminished; nobody wanted to assume the leadership of this non-glorified position of liability.

Nobody would dare try to claim the fame and glamour in the experience. The mind and focus of man was shifted and concentrated on the task like a laser beam, even amid fear and anxiety, and not self. Man could not panic and flee with his feet, in the absence of solid ground. Man had to throw all excuses and justifications overboard. Man had to shift his ability to total dependence on the implementation of others. Whether soldier or prisoner, everyone had to put differences aside and swim together.

How much more can we achieve in life as a family that sticks and prays together even when the storms of life beat against our ship? Could our marriage perhaps survive the rough waters if we hold on together and acknowledge that rough raging waters will push us in different directions, but we are never the enemy; otherwise, we will not survive the journey.

Before I got married, I was offered words of advice from one of my church elders who was married for approximately forty years. He shared some of his experiences in life and reassured me that it will come my way, but when it does, I should embrace and understand that it is a natural part of life. Today those words of wisdom have anchored my mental fortitude. It is like a person being able to swim left me a plank of wood to stay afloat and navigate safely to shore. I embrace and cherish these challenges, because it brings richness by discovering the inner soul and thoughts of the one that I have pledged to forever love and adore. How can someone who loves me cause me pain was no longer a reason to jump overboard in deep waters.

The ship that is a lifeless earthly property and possession will be lost, but more importantly everyone will survive. (At times, it takes drastic measures and circumstances for humanity to put their differences aside and recognize the ultimate need for interdependency in each other.) The soldiers were about to kill the prisoners fearing an escape, but the centurion wanted to ensure that Paul was kept safely, and prevented the massacre. How many times in life have we experienced favor based on the merits of others? We therefore should never develop the slightest inclination to attribute any credit to self.

When the storms of life hit and all you have to survive is a piece of plank and each other, priority and purpose will undoubtedly birth instantaneously.

We do not have time to gossip, fight, or highlight differences. We have time to hold on and utilize every moment wisely. The instant elimination of negative thoughts will give instant birth and strength to our lives. I once challenged the congregation to treat negative thoughts like holding on to a hot iron. Allowing negativity to ponder in my thought process beyond two to three seconds would be like refusing to release a hot iron smearing the palm of my hand.

Proverbs 24:25 tells us that the ants are a people not strong, yet they prepare their food in the summer.

We need not look any further than the seven years of famine that struck Egypt. The country was saved from this devastation simply because the king at the time had a dream about seven meager cows eating and swallowing seven fat cows. There was a man of wisdom known as Joseph, who was able to interpret dreams and explained that there will be seven years of abundance in crops and food products symbolic of the seven fat cows, followed by seven years of intense famine. The wisdom of the ants prevailed, because enough food supplies were stored up to outlast the impact of the famine. Other nations and families were able to depend and survive through the assistance of Egypt (see Genesis 41:1–36). The ant is a group that constantly and proactively increases in wealth and supplies, because every season is approached like there is an impending danger!

Do we wait until there are problems in our relationships before we communicate and establish boundaries? Do we watch others and wait for failures to justify the launching of an attack to gain credibility on behalf of self? Do we utilize our calendars and insert dates intentionally for medical checkup, social life, emotional well-being, and spiritual and mental health and guarantee the balanced life within our family? Or do we oftentimes feel sick and shut away by treating our family members like they are the storm?

A chain is as strong as its weakest link holds true and reminds us to stick together and get rid of the comparison syndrome. It does not matter how great is the next person's strength or how limited or excellent I might be; we are all limited in our capacity and in need of each other.

The Ants as a Bridge—The Power of Now!

Let us carefully examine the importance of a bridge. A bridge is used to connect one point or entity to another in order to overcome or defy the odds and obstacles posed by a gap, void, or empty space. This void, gap, obstacle, or opposing element is usually not possible to overcome by the sole ability or potential of the person, thing, or entity that is on a quest to accomplish the feat. This could be a vehicle, ship, space shuttle, or person traveling through space, on land, on water, or on various other dimensions. More importantly, if an attempt is made without bridging the gap, death, defeat, and destruction are usually inevitable. The unwise is prone to inherit the results of his/her actions and demise. A bridge is therefore necessary to close the gap.

A bridge is first and foremost a mental concept, which can be instantly constructed and defy the laws of an opposing dimension. What mental scope or bridge do we need today or perhaps have to construct because I am at the end of my journey? Am I standing at the cliff or the edge of a deep precipice seeking an immediate ultimatum? Perhaps I need to look no further than the loyalty of ants that will not deceive us with ulterior motives. Please stick around in the classroom, because this section can be the next major breakthrough in my relationship, finance, self-growth, or life-making decisions!

Many inventions are created through the observatory function of birds, reptiles, and animals. The airplane was designed by studying the way in which birds would glide across the sky. The helicopter was designed by studying the way that the hummingbird would maneuver and apparently suspend in a standstill motion or position in midair while flapping its wings over seventy beats per second. Researchers and engineers utilized cameras to obtain visuals, conducted aerodynamic testing of the blades, and measured the drag and lift at a variety of angular airspeeds similar to the motion of the hummingbird's wings. The process of learning is not confined to lecture or limited to verbal dictation in a classroom. What can we possibly learn from the ants that become a chain formation bridge upon facing a variety of conditions, to successfully cross deep precipices with zero casualties?

If you are familiar with certain countries or states with major cities, you will appreciate bridges especially when they are not congested. For example, in New York City, unlike traditional or conventional bridges that have columns to support the weight, there are also suspension bridges such as the Verrazano-Narrows Bridge and the Brooklyn Bridge that have the weight of the deck supported by vertical cables. Humanity has become more creative and has designed and invented movable bridges. One of the most fascinating bridges of all time throughout the millennium is the drawbridge.

There are many reported catastrophic events in the collapse of bridges due to human errors and failure to incorporate or calculate certain factors. There are many buildings that have movable foundation, wheels, or bearings in order to absorb forces of nature, vibrations, or earthquakes. Vehicles are made with shock absorbers to lessen the impact of bumps, heavy loads, and ditches. How many factors, experiments, damages, and casualties have we encountered before these criteria were factored in the equation?

Many bridges were designed several decades ago, with the vision of far less vehicles than we have today. The bridges were tested with the vision of upholding constantly moving weight and heavy loads. The absence of proper maintenance and the increase of congestions have led to concentrated forces and loads at a standstill, resulting in the collapse of multiple bridges across the globe.

There are several experiments conducted on ants to factor and monitor their expertise.

The ants constantly use their bodies and conglomerate to form bridges by interlocking their feet, and they systematically transition by suspending between two entities such as leaves or tree branches. As the ants interlock their legs in a chain formation, they strategically detach as each ant carefully made it safely from one side to the other intended point. The experiment revealed that the distance of the gap was constantly shifted and manipulated, yet the ants instantly readjusted their position and grouping in real time. The ants obviously calculated weight and balance, enabling each ant to make it safely across. Do ants possess the architectural knowledge, geometric design, and ability to execute decisions that would take humanity several attempts as they return to the drawing board in the business room? Is this like the movie *Hidden Figures* depicting the true story of few black women, where the human mind demonstrated more powerfully than a calculator analyzing orbit? This granted real-time major breakthrough for astronauts in space. We refer to people as genius when we can't comprehend the possibility of their thought process, yet the ants consistently and naturally operate in this realm.

Although this ant experiment shows the results in a unique and real-time adjustment, what are the thought process and brilliance in the mind of the ants? How are ants able to have zero casualties at a moment of constant emergency? Humans, cats, and dogs sometimes walk in danger, causing the mind to wonder how one could be so oblivious; it's like volunteering for disaster. Not one of the ants was seen either aborting the plan or standing still to blame the obstacles and the moving branches. The ants seemingly operate in a very unselfish/selfless way, with each ant desiring to socialize and live a life of servitude, ensuring that everyone crosses safely to the other side. The ants were

213

not fluctuating in search of family members, but all moved together as an identified group accomplishing the same task.

Let us now examine closely the actions of the ants, communicating and synchronizing to accomplish the possible and the great. This task can become less complex to accomplish when many work together in unity, but the impossible task for one or a lone ranger. An ant that travels alone will not survive very long, but the ant that travels in its colony endures the struggles and obstacles of life. There is a famous saying, "If you want to go fast, travel alone; but if you want to go far, travel together."

> Two are better than one,
> because they have a good return for their labor:
> If either of them falls down,
> one can help the other up.
> But pity anyone who falls
> and has no one to help them up.
> Also, if two lie down together, they will keep warm.
> But how can one keep warm alone?
> Though one may be overpowered,
> two can defend themselves.
> A cord of three strands is not quickly broken. (Ecclesiastes 4:9–12 NIV)

Knowing Your Purpose—Drawbridge

A drawbridge is defined as a movable bridge usually seen at the entrance to a castle or a tower that is surrounded by a moat (deep ditch/pond). The drawbridge can be raised to prevent enemies or people from crossing or prevent vessels from passing underneath. In life, many of us were on our journey, destined to cross to the other side of greatness. But someone who was observant of our progress recognized our potential and manipulated our drawbridge. Something shifted the distance and lifted the connecting platform, derailing and diverting our path of divine purpose. Our temperament, reaction, and tenacity toward success have been tested. Discouragements have conditioned us to stand still like a dysfunctional bridge. Without a vision, we will perish and lack the proper direction of travel. Am I stuck in the vacuum of my mind? Did someone plant weeds among seeds or reconstruct a diverted bridge in my mind?

Learning from the ant, one would begin to self-actualize to the realization that it's not time to turn back or rely solely on oneself. It's not time to blame the moving parts of the bridge and write definitions and complaints for our failures. The same mental capacity that can be occupied with thoughts of failure can be utilized, substituted, and fully occupied with thought patterns of possibilities. Eradicating all doubts will refine our purpose of existence, reveal avenues, and activate intuition and creativity. Surrounding ourselves with friends, family members, and loyalty association will bring us to places of great success and accomplishment. You have been a bridge for many people. The person that you are today is not a result of what you have just accomplished, but a mentor became a link and invested quality time with care and love. Many people have joined together and have brought us over some troubled waters. Someone has spoken words of bridges into our lives that have anchored our discipline that resulted in success.

> Education is our passport to the future, for tomorrow
> belongs to the people who prepare for it today. (Malcolm X)

Our parents have also pulled up some drawbridges that separated, prevented, and protected us from harms, dangers, and some friends who were leading us astray. You can sleep peacefully when you can trust the anchoring of your bridge. Some of us have even joined together like ants to cross over some ditches not recognizing the enemies and dangers. Others have held hands to the wrong ants while suspended in midair and luckily had Ur and Aaron to hold up the hands of Moses (Exodus 17:12–14). Others have listened to friends perhaps who meant well yet influenced us to hook onto the wrong person. Our parents spoke to us in parables and told us birds of a feather flock together. We responded with a rhyme that says, "Whatever!" Our parents told us to "show me your company [friends] and I will tell you where you are going." We thought they were just being philosophical. But not long after, many were making telephone calls from prison or the hospital, and others could not because they are silent in the grave.

A bridge is a mental concept that can carry us to safety. Respect and character can be a great platform and bridge for life's journey. Many people who have met their demise in life have committed some actions that led others to resort in revenge. Many nations that have risen to a state of independence and great wealth have the lingering historical memory of oppressive nations that have sanctioned and derailed them with socioeconomic warfare.

> Cast your bread upon the waters, For you will find it after many days. (Ecclesiastes 11:1 NKJV)

This was the case of a woman who did cast her bread of good deeds upon the water. The woman was at home and heard rattling sounds, unknowing that there was an armed robber looking in her face through the glass. The robber left and subsequently confessed that he decided not to do her any harm, because he realized that she was the woman who fed him at the food pantry when he was in need. You can secure your future with good deeds, and it will find you in due season after many days, like planting a seed that returns fruits.

A reliable bridge will carry you safely from one point to the other. One of the greatest bridges to be trusted is a mother. She has brought us from one dimension, safeguarded us in the womb, and transported us throughout the world, then delivered us into the physical phenomena of a manifested embodiment.

The one who refuses to learn yet becomes conformed to his/her environment will be treated like a drawbridge. Unfortunately, the loyal people in life are often perceived as being naive and also get treated and used like a drawbridge in the process. People access you at the point of their need, to cross from one point to another. Some people wait for you to lie flat just to trod, roll, and drive over you. They then keep going, leaving you looking at their back and toxic fumes from their exhaust.

They later return for a favor, with a bright smiling headlight, waiting patiently in expectation, as though it's your obligation to be in place for their grand arrival and safe crossing. If the drawbridge has any malfunction, the true character of the awaiting party will come to light. They will react with loud honking sounds, reacting to the congestion of others behind, instead of empathizing with your brokenness. *How can the bridge break at the point of my greatest need?* many will ponder and wonder. They will render petition for you to go out of service, claiming to pay favors in their toll to travel over you as if that's your total cost and lifetime value. The drawbridge may need to develop the courage and take a break by staying in the upright position. Some drawbridges may need to deactivate the switch, get some rest, recalibrate themselves, and stop responding to every telephone call. Some drawbridges listen to honking sounds and offer favors by operating after hours, only to find themselves in a glitch and state of bribery and compromise. It's important not to allow fear and manipulation to dominate your life. It's okay not to be liked by everyone!

Though the purpose of the bridge is to be traveled upon, people will do just that, oftentimes without any thoughts, permission, or consideration. Ants will use you according to your purpose, to accomplish their goals. If you should break, the ants will intuitively create another path of travel or pursue alternatives. Ants develop emergency plans and create redundant systems (duplicate) to activate in case the main system becomes dysfunctional. This is proactive thinking! We have to develop the self-confidence and understand who we are as an individual. We cannot live through the scope or definition placed upon us by others. Don't tell your friends that they have become rich and switched. Don't develop resentment in your heart while others are succeeding. Join with the force and move in the direction of progress. Time is a present continuum, with a vacuum to occupy the unlimited resources that are accessible in the infinite.

What does it mean to exist in time? Am I able to spend, utilize, or exhaust time? Time is a convertible resource! How can I exhaust an indispensable source? Can I drink off the ocean? What does it mean to live in a world without end? If there was a physical measurement or ending to the dimension of the universe, then what would be beyond its ending? The world can debate and deceive us of many things, but the heavens declare the indisputable truth. Let's not occupy our present continuum with thoughts of the past. We will just recreate an imaginative future. We cannot escape the web of now. Now is the time! Now is the time to build! Now is the time to build and create bridges for our future generation. It doesn't matter how far we choose to run; we are in the inescapable now. The web of the present is here. Either the ants eat the spider, or be eaten in the web of this world!

> The earth is the LORD's, and the fulness thereof; the
> world, and they that dwell therein. (Psalm 24·1 KJV)

> If I ascend up into heaven, thou art there: if I make my
> bed in hell, behold, thou art there. (Psalm 139:8 KJV)

We can't escape our thoughts; we can't deceive ourselves. We are calibrated with divine truth and a built-in compass of our conscience and conviction. If we build our bed in hell, God is there. Wherever I go, I am there! Whatever I think, it is in the realm of the now in the presence of God. If I create a car yesterday, it is still in the now. The car is not yesterday as much as it is not tomorrow. Our family is now. Our opportunity is now. All there is and will be is forever now.

It's not that the ants are insensitive; they operate at the highest level of priority, the tyranny of the urgent.

> Another of his disciples said, "Lord, first let me return
> home and bury my father."

> But Jesus told him, "Follow me now. Let the spiritually
> dead bury their own dead." (Matthew 8:21–22 NLT)

Many would perhaps think that a funeral is of a very high priority, so I should be able to give my final respects before anything else could take precedence. Would I find ants at a funeral grieving, or do I rejoice and celebrate a life that was well lived? Do we mourn because someone has died, or do I mourn in a state of regret and attempt to find closure? Did I burn all the bridges with some toxic words in my lifetime and then try to find help to take me back across to the other side to speak to a lifeless body? Do I scream that I am sorry and ask why, when the mental faculty and logic of the dead are clearly gone?

Would the ants look at you and wonder what irony of wasted energy in a living person seeking resolution from the dead?

It takes ant-like love and discipline to build progressive and life-giving bridges. Give the compliments now and forgive others immediately. Whatsoever things that your hands find to do, do it now in love. Just do it!

How many of us have become broken and "inoperable" because people have used us after recognizing the purpose that we are put in place to serve? We become disappointed because we desired attachments and recognition. We have lost sight of the vision and the bigger picture; now we are in the dark searching for the entry point of the bridge. The bridge is not there to function as a garage for others to park, neither to entertain the buildup of congestion, lingering of toxic fumes, and the stress of heavy weight resting on us until we collapse. Enemies are sometimes more predictable and less exhaustive than some friends. Though enemies may hide out in the bushes then rush across the bridge when given the opportunity, friends will show up to the party at random times and contribute nothing but stress and liability.

Then one of the teachers of religious law said to him, "Teacher, I will follow you wherever you go."

But Jesus replied, "Foxes have dens to live in, and birds have nests, but the Son of Man has no place even to lay his head." (Matthew 8:19–20 NLT)

The ant defines its territory and is constantly moving forward. It does not have time to exhaust on waiting and gathering. It is not afraid to lose the crowd. It is sure of its direction in life. Ants understand that a vision is not confined by a lateral direction on a two-dimensional axis. A vision is like a fighter jet; it will rotate, spin, and maneuver in a variety of direction on multiple axes in orbit.

A vision is like water—you cannot conquer it by grabbing it. One has to flow in the direction of vision like a surfer finding his way to shore.

A man with a vision is not controlled or confined to his geographical location or residence. Someday he will not be sure where he will lay his head. Some of us have laid our heads at the same spot every night, yet our minds are in the deep gutter of distress elsewhere. Some individuals have cheated with people they have never met physically. Pedophiles, human traffickers, and cyberspace hackers have conquered many domains from the center of their living rooms. There are so many people who have invested in the real estate market and own properties in countries and states that they have never visited. Man's ability and potential is not trapped in his physical embodiment, unless his mind fails to activate his mental bridge. Man has been given the land, air, and sea as his domain; why not take it?

Let us become a movable bridge like the ants, like a mother carrying and moving with purpose in her womb. After the ants cross over to the other side, they do not stop to play. They transition into their role and function in their purpose.

If someone is counterproductive to your purpose, it's okay to recognize and accept when they have aborted the journey. Could it be that you are at your greatest when others keep moving?

Not everyone who shows up at your sickbed is there to wish you well.

The people who are closest to you in friendship and close association are sometimes far more detrimental than the individuals that you perceive to be distant and disconnected. The crowd came to celebrate Lazarus at his funeral but walked away at his resurrection. (Not everyone possesses the maturity to celebrate with you in your victory or smile at your glory.) Don't assume that they mean you bad. They are just at that stage of their maturity. When Moses came off Mount Sinai with his face radiating in divine revelation, many fearfully flee from his presence instead of embracing his elevation (Exodus 34:29–32). People are intimidated when you break away from the familiarity.

Know your purpose, and hold no one responsible and accountable for your state of happiness. Do good without attachment or in expectation of anything in return. Matthew 6 tells us that we should not do good deeds in order to be admired by others. Neither should we seek attention in public, but instead never let the left hand know what the right hand is doing. We should give our gifts in private, and our Heavenly Father will honor and bless us. Matthew 5:38–42 encourages us not to seek revenge but take pleasure in blessing our enemies by turning the other cheek, walking the extra mile, giving additional clothes even after being sued. If someone is in need, we should give, and do not turn away from those who need to borrow.

It is vitally important to recognize within yourself as being a carrier of blessings. The thermostat will always set the temperament of its existence. The thermostat will measure the influence of the outside entities and cause you to adjust to a state of survivability and adapt with flexibility. There is therefore no need to react out of character when others either enter or leave. You are there to serve your purpose and serve it well without conditions. Don't become a broken bridge by constantly watching the gratitude and temperament displayed by others. The one who says thank you may be less appreciative than the one you expected or anticipated to return. Martin Luther King Jr. implores us to be diligent in all that we do; whether we are called to be a street sweeper, do so like Michelangelo would paint or even as Beethoven would compose his music or Shakespeare wrote poetry.

There were ten lepers who were miraculously healed. One returned to show his appreciation and was made whole. Jesus did not react as though being aborted or treated with great ingratitude by the other nine individuals. He proved to the leper who returned that He (Jesus) was able to make him complete and greater. We should take on this pattern of thought and treat situations and circumstances with the same approach. The people who failed to return with gratitude forfeit their own blessings. I do not need to retaliate, cut off the source, or become vindictive in the process. I should also have or develop the maturity to understand that people are just as equally important in the success and advancement of life.

People who have entered our life have the leverage of freedom to leave, just as much as we do not possess the authority to enslave or keep them. I am also guilty within the scope of my personal limitations and tunnel vision. We at times dwell too much in the realm of desire to possess, yet we despise relational restraints. We develop anger and bitterness over our inability to control while lacking the discipline to even self-guide.

Have you ever driven with a passenger who is not a driver yet dictates the temperament of the driver at every speed, turn, and route? They are a human GPS that sees around the corner, because at every congestion, you are being told that you shouldn't have taken that route. Such a mindset evolves into evasiveness at the presence of encountering obstacles and challenges. We are never conditioned or developed the discipline to embrace the challenges of life as an object lesson and great learning tool. This is why many individuals rather get comfortable in executing a task in a more complex and difficult way, because it's familiar and does not require much thinking and analyzing. We develop anxiety and temper tantrum, like a child breaking his pencil because mentally he couldn't figure out the math problem. Instead, he would rather carry a heavy box of books to the office for the teacher than apply logic to solve a math problem while sitting comfortably. The mind initiates its own obstruction and causes you to stand still looking at the wall, failing to realize there is a door just blending with the same color as the wall. When he figures it out, he smiles at his naivety and comforts himself by asking how come he failed to notice and how simple it was to open the door like the Red Sea. Some of us are still living in regrets. It is even worse when others do not have elements in mind to regret, because they are still oblivious in the rut and fail to process thoughts of recognition to realize the possibilities of greatness.

There was a television series with the world's dumbest criminal, which showed a robber who tried to escape by pushing the door. He then waited until the cops arrived and surrendered, only to realize that he should have pulled the door open instead of pushing it. We laugh at this missing element and failure to execute the required thoughts for freedom. He was caged by his own mental immobility. How many of us contain information like puzzles trying to find their proper order of sequence and arrangement? We look at the ants going around in what is perceived to be confusing motion, not realizing that their productivity is digging and building a colony right underneath the house that is about to collapse with humanity. We then depart because the value has been depreciated by the ants' kingdom that decided they will make progress in a "unified now," while we slumber and sleep.

Truth or Science Fiction

We marvel at science fiction movies and believe that one day movies like *Star Trek* and *The Jetsons* animation will unravel before our eyes like the revolutionary breakthrough of three-dimensional printers. Science fiction movies are becoming more practical and manifest into nonfiction as man walks into knowledge and truth. The famous singer Bob Dylan in his song said, "You may be the devil or you may be the Lord, but you're gonna have to serve somebody." The indisputable reality of death can leave the mind in a state of despondence like watching a sci-fi film, distorting the mind to differentiate reality. Death is for sure and has an appointment date with every man who has entered this world through a miraculous portal. Some people have concluded that we have entered this dimension by evolving. Yet our fear and emotion reveal our true desire for love, companionship, and eternal life. Death is like when God told Moses to get up because I am about to send you to a place that you have never been (Genesis 12). Moses agreed by choice, but death will one day be our chauffeur. Below is an illustration through a story that depicts the journey of one of two destinations and the bridge that is likely to take us there. Do you believe it is science fiction that may one day baffle the mind and prove otherwise?

There was a certain rich man who was clothed in purple and fine linen and fared sumptuously every day. But there was a certain beggar named Lazarus, full of sores, who was laid at his gate, desiring to be fed with the crumbs which fell from the rich man's table. Moreover the dogs came and licked his sores. So *it was that the beggar died*, and *was carried* by the angels to Abraham's bosom. The rich man also died and *was buried*. And being in torments in Hades, he lifted up his eyes and saw Abraham afar off, and Lazarus in his bosom.

Then he cried and said, "Father Abraham, have mercy on me, and send Lazarus that he may dip the tip of his finger in water and cool my tongue; for I am tormented in this flame." *But Abraham said, "Son, remember that in your lifetime you received your good things, and likewise Lazarus evil things; but now he is comforted and you are tormented. And besides all this, between us and you there is a great gulf fixed, so that those who want to pass from here to you cannot, nor can those from there pass to us."*

Then he said, "I beg you therefore, father, that you would send him to my father's house, for I have five brothers, that he may testify to them, lest they also come to this place of torment." Abraham said to him, "They have Moses and the prophets; let them hear them." And he said, "No, father Abraham; but if one goes to them from the dead, they will repent." But he said to him, *"If they do not hear Moses and the prophets, neither will they be persuaded though one rise from the dead."* (Luke 16:19–31 NKJV; emphasis added)

The Great Chasm

There is a great chasm and dimension that occur at the point of physical death. Every second in hospitals across the globe, we witness the miraculous portal entry to the earth's domain by humanity through the birth process. This is definite and cannot be challenged as we physically observe and experience this process in the delivery room. The "opposite" process, which is death, results in a different exit plan and portal. Nobody has ever made a telephone call to say that "I have arrived safely. I will see you when you die and get here soon." Interestingly, there is a great gulf between two destinations that neither the rich man nor Lazarus is able to cross, even with a heart of compassion. Quite ironically is the impossibility to cross this gap, but easier and possible to be resurrected from "rest" or return from the dead to warn others who are alive if they were willing to listen. The poor man who lived a righteous life was carried through a portal through a certain dimension by angels. The rich man, on the other hand, was buried and had a view of the poor man resting in the bosom of Abraham in a state of comfort and tranquility, while he was consciously in a state of torment. Who was the chauffeur responsible for transporting the rich man to the realm of "burial" destination? Now your mind may be entering sci-fi mode. Who gave the key necessary to unlock and access this path of travel? Is there a special protection for the ones who are walking through this dimension unimpacted? Is there a correlation with the "three Hebrew boys in the fiery furnace" who were not burned yet others outside the furnace destroyed by the heat *(Daniel 3)*? What kind of bridge and through what portal or dimension was this man Lazarus transported? How long did it take, or did they even travel within the medium of time? Is this why demons are said to transcend or seek legalized entry to the earth's portal domain, by physically possessing the human or some physical body? They then seek to separate the human spirit through physical death, sending us back to a resting or burial place. This tactical operation is like revoking our license to purposefully remain in the earthly domain. The Quran as well as the Holy Bible spoke of Jesus's (Isa) Immaculate Conception (portal entry) who took on flesh (human body) that granted direct access in human form to the earthly domain.

How many crimes and accidents do we see resulted in instant separation of life from the physical body? This body will decay and return to the broken-down state that many constitute to evolve or have originated. Will man pretend as though life and consciousness are just energy dissipated? Is this why we desire to one day reunite? Is it logical for man to attempt to create means and ways of time travel yet reject the possibility of the supernatural dimension? Can man naturalize and neutralize the supernatural yet accept the reality when it's proven in his natural ability and discovery to be possible? Is this man assuming the role of lordship and despising the Master? Why is it easier to return from the dead than to get a bridge to cross over from Hades? The only bridge to take us across to safety into eternity is accessible from the portal point of earth. Will you cross the bridge like an ant to the other side or panic according to the world's affair and circumstances? If there is such a bridge to take us to a place that we have never been, yet sure and destined to go, wouldn't it be of a poignant interest to find such a bridge? Let's see a report of someone who narrowly escaped and made it to the bridge. He developed the swift thinking like an ant.

> One of the criminals hanging beside him scoffed, "So you're the Messiah, are you? Prove it by saving yourself—and us, too, while you're at it!"

But the other criminal protested, "Don't you fear God even when you have been sentenced to die? We deserve to die for our crimes, but this man hasn't done anything wrong." Then he said, "Jesus, remember me when you come into your Kingdom."

And Jesus replied, "I assure you, today you will be with me in paradise." (Luke 23:39–43 NLT)

Recently in the news, there was a man on death row who was exonerated within seconds of walking to the death chamber for execution, not because he was innocent but because the family forgave him of his crime after reading a letter of apology, then made a legal petition, which was approved. He was ecstatic to know that he survived. As the thief on the cross was facing a death penalty and uttered those words of request and believed within his heart and mind, this became the passport to his portal entry point into a place where many will one day be admitted. Since every man was born in a sinful state and is in need of a safe entry and portal access, what are the required acknowledgment, needs, and conditions of the heart to reach this final destination?

Many individuals claim not to know how to communicate with their Father our Creator. But knowing that God is closer than a friend who already knows our thoughts and needs should give us enough thrills to allow our heart to speak with Him sincerely and express our every need. We should never allow the omniscience (all-knowing) of God to hinder us from expressing our concerns. This is no different from a child, self, or spouse yearning and being empowered by words and expression of love, even when we already know that we are being loved. The man who was seconds from being electrocuted spoke from his heart and believed. Whenever we hurt someone, our conviction and conscience propel us to apologize and change. We can take this same effort and initiative to cross the bridge into eternity by developing this daily walk and talk with God. He will guide us with His Word as we diligently read and absorb it. The only bridge to take us across to safety into eternity is accessible from the portal point of earth. Anyone can access this bridge with our heart, mouth, faith, and the power to believe and accept. Below is provided a few avenues and transitory key points in aid of such process.

> In the same way, there is more joy in heaven over one lost sinner who repents and returns to God than over ninety-nine others who are righteous and haven't strayed away! (Luke 15:7 NLT)

> But if we confess our sins to him, he is faithful and just to forgive us our sins and to cleanse us from all wickedness. (1 John 1:9 NLT)

> People who conceal their sins will not prosper, but if they confess and turn from them, they will receive mercy. (Proverbs 28:13 NLT)

> Jesus said to him, "I am the way, and the truth, and the life. No one comes to the Father except through me." (John 14:6 ESV)

> For there is one God, and there is one mediator between God and men, the man Christ Jesus. (1 Timothy 2:5 ESV)

> He is the propitiation for our sins, and not for ours only but also for the sins of the whole world. (1 John 2:2 ESV)

> And there is salvation in no one else, for there is no other name under heaven given among men by which we must be saved. (Acts 4:12 ESV)

Other scriptural references:

Acts 3:19; Matthew 3:8; 2 Chronicles 30:9; 2 Peter 3:9; Matthew 9:13; Matthew 4:17; James 4:8; Joel 2:13; Revelation 3:19; Ezekiel 18:32; Acts 17:30; Mark 1:15; Luke 5:32; Zechariah 1:3; Acts 2:38; Luke 15:10; Proverbs 1:23; Luke 17:3–4; Ezekiel 22:30; Luke 1:17; 1 Peter 4:12; 1 Peter 3:18

Understanding Self, Others, and Purpose

Individuals with the personality of ants can be misunderstood. Ants are focused and are goal oriented. Ants are always on the move and in search of new opportunities. If you do not share the same oriented goals of the ants, you can become distraught and utterly disappointed. You can develop victimized feelings of rejection or being underappreciated.

If boundaries are not established in advance, relationships can become like an ant living with a tree. The ant constantly looks for warmth and comfort in the trunk of the tree. The ant absorbs and enjoys the comfort, the warmth, and the feeling of belonging. On the other hand, the ant cannot truly reciprocate, give back, or rejuvenate that which it has absorbed and sucked out of the tree. On the other-hand, the tree requires nutrient and desires a photosynthesis relationship, due to admiring of the ants' self drive, yet compromise, overly compensate and neglects itself. The tree is fearful to let the ant feel as though it is not appreciated, so it runs the risk of jeopardizing the relationship while losing its fervor. If the tree doesn't fully understand itself, the tree will overextend beyond its limit in order to solicit attention from the ant.

The ant, which is a go-getter, will eventually lose interest; and the tree, on the other hand, becomes confused and develops self-guilt by wondering how the tree reached that stage. The ant, which might not be fully selfish, has blind spots and tunnel vision. The ant will start to pursue new goals and develop the interest and propensity toward another tree.

So many relationships have been overlooked because we prioritize agenda, while emotional needs become malnourished. The ant will become insensitive and not realize the extent of its action and the role it played in depleting the tree. The relationship is now in a turbulent mode of separation; the ant keeps going, while the tree is standing dry and still, trying to bounce back from a dying vine in bewilderment.

If your relationship is at this place, wipe your tears. Don't hold on to what is seasonal. As a tree that stands in the countenance of God, you have got to draw strength from Psalm 1:3 KJV:

> And he shall be like a tree planted by the rivers of water, that bringeth forth his fruit in his season; his leaf also shall not wither; and whatsoever he doeth shall prosper.

A tree faces various storms in a lifetime. There are times when we are giving shade and comfort to a lot of people who are toxic and not vital to our mental state of being. When the storms of life appear, a tree can never get up, run, or change its location. As a tree, I might be encountering some storms, I might be bending for a while in my deep struggles, but I will springboard and bounce back faster than I was bent. A tree has to realize that I am built for this reason and season. A tree has to recognize that I have the mental fortitude and the physical resiliency.

God wants to propel you to your destiny but first has to reveal to you that once you have stopped giving shade and support, the people that you think were with you permanently will disappear faster than you can imagine, or even without explanation.

> But he himself went a day's journey into the wilderness, and came and sat down under a broom tree. And he prayed that he might die, and said, "It is enough! Now, LORD, take my life, for I *am* no better than my fathers!"
>
> Then as he lay and slept under a broom tree, suddenly an angel touched him, and said to him, "Arise *and* eat."
> (1 Kings 19:4–5 NKJV)

Elijah the Prophet fled after he was threatened by Jezebel. According to verse 4, Elijah came and sat down underneath the broom (juniper) tree. Elijah became suicidal and wished to die. Elijah became perplexed, felt like his work was of no value, lost his confidence, and thought to himself that life is not worth living. He received food, in which he ate and found strength for his forty days' journey after being asked, "What are you doing here, Elijah?" (v. 9).

Mental health crisis has become a major epidemic throughout the world. Anxiety, lack of sleep, stress, and depression can cloud our mind to the point in which everything in life is perceived as a major storm. You will become like a sheep falling behind the herd and become vulnerable to the wolves of life's circumstances. Our mind is one of the greatest weapons to fight against the fierce wars of life. We have to remain engaged and find newness and meaning to life every moment of the way. We have to stimulate and refresh our outlook by appreciating the people around us every day. It may take just a smile and one intentional compliment each day. We can reserve and refrain from negative comments even if we believe we have a point and should be heard.

> "For I know the plans I have for you," declares the
> LORD, "plans to prosper you and not to harm you, plans
> to give you hope and a future. (Jeremiah 29:11 NIV)

When you reach the end of self and make God your total and ultimate source and solution, your life then evolves with great meaning. You strive with purpose, and the tree will benefit others fruitfully.

The broom tree was supplying shade and comfort to someone who has given up on life. Elijah was becoming comfortable and stagnant and overextended his stay. It took divine revelation for Elijah to comprehend that he is not the only surviving prophet, and he cannot overextend his stay and depend on the tree. Elijah couldn't blame the tree for not providing adequate shelter or support.

Many individuals in life function as a tree and are providing support to those who constantly miss the divine revelation and have normalized a dysfunctional and toxic relationship. People are holding the tree obligated to its purpose and develop a false sense of expectation and entitlement.

If you function as a tree and enjoy the company of someone (ant) sitting in your presence with total dependency, you may enjoy the ultimate submission. But wait until your season changes, your leaves fall off, then you will discover that you too have some seasonal friends. As a tree, if you are self-focused, you may not realize that someone is suicidal right at your feet. Even when that person walks away, you may turn the mirror on yourself like many mothers and fathers who constantly wonder and dwell in self-guilt pondering where they went wrong. It's incumbent upon us to understand ourselves and constantly test the pulse of others around.

Letting go can be difficult; but we do not want to enable, stabilize, or cripple the growth potential of people in our lives.

As a tree, we may have to pass on the baton and cheer others on like birds scattering seeds, who will excel to heights and avenues that we are not destined to go. The will of God will not multiply us to venture in every dimension imaginable! Let us guard our hearts, celebrate, and enjoy the success of others. Someone has led us along a path of blessings and success as much as others around us are being blessed. This is why Jesus had to ask Peter, "What is to you if I choose to do whatever I want with John, my disciple?"

Tyler Perry encourages us to understand ourselves with a great analogy of the "leaf, branch, and root people" in our lives:

> I have this tree analogy when I think of people in my life, be it friends, family, acquaintances, employees, co-workers, whomever . . . They are all placed inside what I call my tree test. It goes like this:
>
> LEAF PEOPLE
> Some people come into your life and they are like leaves on a tree. They are only there for a season. You can't depend on them or count on them because they are

weak and only there to give you shade. Like leaves, they are there to take what they need and as soon as it gets cold or a wind blows in your life they are gone. You can't be angry at them, it's just who they are.

BRANCH PEOPLE

There are some people who come into your life and they are like branches on a tree. They are stronger than leaves, but you have to be careful with them. They will stick around through most seasons, but if you go through a storm or two in your life it's possible that you could lose them. Most times they break away when it's tough. Although they are stronger than leaves, you have to test them out before you run out there and put all your weight on them. In most cases they can't handle too much weight. But again, you can't be mad with them, it's just who they are.

ROOT PEOPLE

If you can find some people in your life who are like the roots of a tree then you have found something special. Like the roots of a tree, they are hard to find because they are not trying to be seen. Their only job is to hold you up and help you live a strong and healthy life. If you thrive, they are happy. They stay low key and don't let the world know that they are there. And if you go through an awful storm they will hold you up. Their job is to hold you up, come what may, and to nourish you, feed you and water you.

Just as a tree has many limbs and many leaves, there are few roots. Look at your own life. How many leaves, branches and roots do you have? What are you in other people's lives?

Bizarre Moments in History

Sometimes we have drifted so far to the point where God has to communicate to us by giving others a divine revelation to get our attention. Peter became convinced in his heart by believing the deception of his mind. The rooster had to remind Peter that his heart is incapable, and his mind is limited to construct a bridge in a realm that he is unable to enter.

> Then he began to call down curses, and he swore to them, "I don't know the man!"
>
> Immediately a rooster crowed. Then Peter remembered the word Jesus had spoken: "Before the rooster crows, you will disown me three times." And he went outside and wept bitterly. (Matthew 26:74–75 NIV)

How many of us are living a lie by self-deception, constantly inflating our own self-hope while the foundation is rotting away? *Do we take care of our physical health, mental health, spiritual well-being, and family members, healing their pain and frustration, refraining from being a burden?* Or do we conclude it will get better while no change has been made?

There was a king of Moab known as Balak. Fear and rage entered his heart to the point in which he sent for Balaam to destroy the Israelites and place a curse upon their life. Balaam attempted the task but was faced with major opposition by a great phenomenon when God made a donkey speak in order to get his attention.

> When the donkey saw the angel of the LORD, it lay down under Balaam, and he was angry and beat it with his staff. Then the LORD opened the donkey's mouth, and it said to Balaam, "What have I done to you to make you beat me these three times?"

Balaam answered the donkey, "You have made a fool of me! If only I had a sword in my hand, I would kill you right now."

The donkey said to Balaam, "Am I not your own donkey, which you have always ridden, to this day? Have I been in the habit of doing this to you?"

"No," he said.

Then the LORD opened Balaam's eyes, and he saw the angel of the LORD standing in the road with his sword drawn. So he bowed low and fell facedown. (Numbers 22:27–31 NIV)

What elements is God using to get our attention today? Whatever it might be, it is for a reason that is greatly beneficial to our well-being. It may not be a strange rooster, donkey, or inanimate object; but there are signs and caution postings in our lives that warrant our immediate attention. Will we continue speeding down the express road of life, or will we look up at the exit signs and service centers? Many questions are being asked, and our minds are so distracted to the point where we lack the accurate interpretation. Our mental capacity will search internally for reasons and answers, but great is the one who relies externally and solely on the wisdom of God.

When Jesus came into the coasts of Caesarea Philippi, he asked his disciples, saying, Whom do men say that I the Son of man am?

And they said, Some say that thou art John the Baptist: some, Elias; and others, Jeremias, or one of the prophets.

He saith unto them, But whom say ye that I am?

And Simon Peter answered and said, Thou art the Christ, the Son of the living God.

And Jesus answered and said unto him, Blessed art thou, Simon Barjona: for flesh and blood hath not revealed it unto thee, but my Father which is in heaven. (Matthew 16:13–17 KJV)

Many pieces of advice will come our way, but what are the divine will and the wisdom of God imploring us to do?

As one reflects upon the historical events, it is undoubtedly the systematic operation and mindset of ants. Ants know the time, signs, seasons, and changes in weather conditions. Ants constantly store up necessities, build infrastructures, and respond strategically as warranted. *Could it be possible that the Lord has embedded in the mind of ants not only designed intelligence, but also divine revelation? It's amazing that the magicians and "wise" men couldn't interpret the dream.* But a man known as Joseph who relies on God is able to discern beyond mere intuition. God communicates with animals as depicted in Noah and the ark, Balaam's donkey, the raven that fed Elijah, and the rooster that crowed at Peter's denial, among many other circumstances. Is it at all possible that God constantly communicates with the animal kingdom and therefore implores us to learn from them? We need to plant the Word of God in our hearts so that in storm season, we will be anchored. Man is like a tree planted by the rivers of water; the dry season and carnal nature will not be able to war, deplete, or devour the connection and foundation of the roots. Famine may be on the surface of the land, but your root is anchored in the storehouse of the Holy Spirit.

This, my friend, starts with oneself. Let us make it our point of interest to intentionally love, cherish, and appreciate another. Call someone you have not spoken with for a while. Tell someone you love and appreciate him/her. Tell someone you are truly sorry for the hurt and pain you have caused. Be different—be a better you!

CHAPTER 10
EAGLES' TENACITY AND
PERSEVERANCE
(Power of Vision)

It is hard to determine who is more insane: the man in his right
mind who sees things that do not exist or the man out of his mind
who lacks the ability to comprehend the scope of literal reality.

—M. Reid

The Eagles' Preparation: Tornado (Removing the Layer)

The Eagles' Equipping: 9/11 ("Molting" State)

The Eagles' Response: "Is There a Pilot on This Plane?"

This chapter is filled with my personal life story and experiences.
If anyone is in leadership, dating, or married or desires to pursue a
relationship, I would strongly encourage that you keep this chapter
close to your heart. The introduction focuses on the personality of the
physical eagle. The chapter then transitions into a series of personal
life stories that parallel the journey that everyone will one day likely
encounter. Every reader has the built-in potential to soar beyond bounds
like an eagle.

Humanity is oftentimes compared and contrasted with the eagle. It is therefore vital that we understand the qualities and traits of the eagles. Nothing in life of great quality comes easy or is just given to us. Our success is usually one more step or application of self after a failure or discouragement. The eagle usually has one partner for a lifetime. The eagle usually produces an average of two eggs for that life span. When you have a limited option with entrusted treasure and legacy, your choices, scope, and perspective of life should be handled delicately and wisely.

Eagles are an interesting phenomenon and creation. An eagle is symbolic of bravery, heroic act, someone well rounded and holistic. Eagles have great success stories in life and soar to heights that the majority may not attain in a lifetime. There is a great book that transformed my perspective of life, *Think and Grow Rich*. In this book, a renowned journalist and author by the name of Napoleon Hill attempted to interview Carnegie Hall on his success story. But instead, Hill received something more profitable. He was given a task and funded to interview five hundred men of great wealth, who started out with nothing except thoughts and ideas with organized plans. These successful men shared their experiences and how they acquired such wealth and magnitude of heightened success. Some of these men were inclusive of John D. Rockefeller, Thomas A. Edison, Charles M. Schwab, Henry Ford, and F. W. Woolworth, among many others. As I began to delve into this book, I noticed that there were many failures before that one breakthrough of discovery leading to success. It is interesting to note that Thomas A. Edison attempted over one thousand times before the light bulb was successful and eventually revolutionized the world with electricity. How about if he had given up and refused to persevere?

The Eagles' Preparation: Tornado (Removing the Layer)

How did the eagle develop such discipline and attitude for success? At birth, the eagle is born in a nest that has been designed with three layers. The top layer is very soft and comfortable to keep the eaglet safe and secure. The next layer below is a bit harder than the top, to prevent becoming comfortable and stagnant. The last layer has sharp objects, thorns, and thistles that are meant to cause the eagle to become very uneasy, desiring to exit the nest with enough discomfort to get ready for survival and become independent. The mother or father eagle would then push the young eaglet out of the nest so that it can learn to fly and develop strength in its wings and the skills to maneuver.

It was a Sunday night in Texas, North America. Many individuals were watching the football game in the comfort of their homes and confinements. The city has been equipped and prepared with sirens in case of emergencies. Individuals started watching the news broadcasts of impending tornado and imminent threats to life. To many people's surprise, the tornado was just a few minutes away, traveling rapidly and making erratic motions with the possibility of heading in any unknown direction. It didn't matter how comfortable people were in their "nest"; everyone had to scramble, flapping their "wings" and wondering if God will come to their rescue. As individuals gave their testimonies, reflecting on their state of panic, they explained that they were only at the mercy of God.

Such is the life of the eaglet, being pushed into panic, going through a tornado phase. The father eagle would then fly below and catch and assist the eaglet in its frantic state against gravitational force. Before long, the eaglet is sharpening its flying skills for self-independence. It's very obvious that this family is stable, has a plan and vision for the eaglets, invests training, spends quality time, and executes diligence strategically in unity.

Eagles do not associate with other birds. Our circle of association will have a direct impact on our progress in life. The infamous Bruce Lee was trained by Ip (Yip) Man. Bruce Lee, in his writings, explains that his master did not train or spar with his students. The reason for this is that it would impact his flow of perfectionism. The master has recognized that any simple repetitious act can formulate habits that impact our standards for excellence. Many people in life will criticize you for setting aside, sacrificing, and investing time in self that could have been used in associating with others. Bruce Lee was one of the only students who had been given the awesome privilege of practicing with his sensei (master).

Many individuals want to glorify in the success and glamour but are unwilling to partake in the steps of the process and travel the journey.

Eagles will invest in the developmental stages of life in order to soar and dwell in higher heights later in life. Some individuals stop after three years in college, not realizing that another two or three years would have placed them on a platform of success in the top 20 percent of society. Now they begin to struggle and compete with the majority of competitors at the base level, as opposed to the large volume of available career positions unoccupied and waiting to be filled at the top.

During times of severe storms, the ordinary birds fly away south to dry areas. Some people will run away from relationship storms, flee educational goals, refute self-development, negate health and physical conditions, and abuse friendships and trust. They have never been taught to embrace the tornado circumstances as fire drill preparations for life. These individuals are more willing to pursue fights, conflicts, and verbal arguments with more strength, severity, and perseverance than the very essentials in life. Quite ironically, eagles fly into the storm winds. Eagles have prepared thoroughly for the circumstances of life. They will maintain stability even after the storm has passed. Like an airplane that flies into the direction of the wind to create lift underneath its wings, the eagle flies head-on into the direction of the strong wind and spreads its wings. Before long, the wind elevates the eagle above the storm clouds. The very entities, obstacles, and challenges from which many other birds have fled, the eagle approached as its opportunities. When many birds find themselves flapping their wings all day and becoming tired, eagles soar and glide in search of prey. Eagles hunt from the air. Having a heightened view will give greater self-confidence to observe, calculate, and differentiate the temporal from longer-lasting challenges. As eagles glide high in the sky, they have a great peripheral vision and view of life's available resources. They can see fish in the sea and river, as well as animals running on the land. Eagles can assess dangers, do not have to react, can exercise timing to execute decisions with precision, and will at most times have guaranteed success.

Too often in life, we are found without a plan. We do not have any short-term and long-term goals. Without hesitation, an individual should be able to list his plans for the next five, ten, and fifteen years. Life does not happen by chance; it takes deliberate planning. If we constantly fail to dream and explore new horizons in this rapidly changing world, the nonessential things of life will preoccupy and fill our time capacity.

> Then the LORD answered me and said: "Write the vision And make *it* plain on tablets, That he may run who reads it." (Habakkuk 2:2 NKJV)

A very interesting book, *The Seven Habits of Highly Effective People*, challenges us to write down our goals, get pictures, and put them in places that will constantly remind us and trigger the zeal and passion to pursue these goals. We should not remain comfortable in living life by chance and attribute such as living by faith. Faith is being able to see the world like our forefather Abraham, whom God told to look upon the stars, which is a reflection of his blessings. In the book of Genesis 12, Abraham saw his future beyond his life span. Yet at times, we cannot see next week. We have to dream big and refuse to approach life with fear. God specializes in the things that man discounts as the impossible.

"It always seems impossible until it's done!" is a famous quote by Nelson Mandela.

We limit the realm of faith by doubting the greatness of God. In Luke 1:20, Zechariah became muted/dumb and lost his voice because he doubted the message that God had sent to him. We have been conditioned to accept failures. We are comfortable, because failing is easy and sure, which causes us to be fearful to venture into the unknown of discomfort and uncertainties.

In life, based on our culture, experiences, or the negative distribution of news, many people react to the sounds and stigmas of the storms. We run away from job recessions, inflations, stock market, and housing instability. On the other hand, the eagle sets the standards and is aware that it has the potential and ability to adapt and adjust to the changes of life. The eagle knows that storms will always come and contain opportunities, but no storms last forever.

The Eagles' Equipping: 9/11 Molting State

There is just something about the puzzle pieces of life. Initially they look chaotic but then seemingly fall into place occasionally with unexpected help and blessings along the way. During the unfortunate circumstances of the collapse of the World Trade Center, 9/11, many individuals lived to tell their testimonies about the simplistic yet most profound encounter in their lives. After all, living to tell the story is indeed a major blessing. This will let any atheist tell you about the goodness of God. Testimonies included individuals missing the bus because they had to change shoes, purchased Band-Aid for blister, and purchased cough drops after feeling sick. Apparent delays were pieces of puzzles coming together as they were grateful for God safeguarding their lives. The apparent insignificant and irritating oppositions of life can be the most essential. The shepherd boy David did not understand that taking care of sheep was God's way of fostering his heart with humility to eventually lead people as a king. The forgotten shepherd boy didn't realize that fighting off lions and bears would make him become a great warrior to destroy Goliath. The simplistic things in life are often filled with profound life lessons. In all the things that we do, we should embrace and execute as worship unto God. Very soon the eaglets start to glide and maneuver throughout the sky and appreciate the journey after looking back to reflect on the many things that didn't make sense at the time. It reminds me of teaching my son and daughter to rollerblade and ride the bicycle. Initially, there was a lot of resistant to the different techniques and length of time needed to invest into quality training. Now I am the one holding my heart and asking them to slow down! Nothing is insignificant!

Molting State

Eagles, when in preparation for new seasons of greatness, accomplishments, and changes, will go on the back side of the mountain and shed their feathers. They will stay away from all vulnerable, dangerous, and potential detrimental situations. Men and women should be aware of their low seasons in life.

The eagle during its lifetime goes through what is known as the molting state. The eagle, after flying, soaring, hunting, and taking care of the eaglets, in different weather conditions and challenges, accumulates dust, dirt, and oil within its wings and feathers. This causes the eagle to become slow, tired, and lethargic. The eagle then hides out on the back of the mountain. The eagle defeathers itself. The eagle feels unloved, lonely, vulnerable, and unattractive. But in its waiting, the eagle knows there will be a shift, the eagle knows there will be acceleration, and the eagle knows that it will regrow its feathers to soar out of its challenges and rise to victory. But boundaries have to be set and have to be followed. Patience is practical and active waiting, so time has to be approached realistically.

I can recall going through my military training; being away from my wife and children was a major challenge. I immediately set boundaries. I did not drink and refused to even start drinking. If anyone ordered alcoholic beverage, pineapple and orange juice was my option. When others were planning for designated driver, I decided to remain in my sober and conscious mind. When others were on the verge of Article 15 (Reprimand), suspension, and almost losing their job, I was thinking we knew the potential dangers before we walked to the edge of the cliff. When others were wondering if they contracted sexually transmitted disease, wondered if they got impregnated, I made a conscious decision not to engage in any conversation that would stimulate the emotion of self or others. If others of the opposite gender were getting a bit close, I told myself that I am equally responsible to either attract, lure, or allow others to enter my circle or get too close to be emotionally attached. I refused for anyone to conclude that they were being misled. I refused to enjoy the notion or gratification of being liked or being chased after. I saw women as my sister, my wife, and my mother and treated them as such. I told myself that someday that will be someone's wife, mother, or in-law. I did not want to be part of their history of being used and abused or have an encounter that will cause a woman to lie, deceive, or cover up her history of the negative and irreversible past to her future family.

I told myself that true character is doing what is right even when I am the only person standing. I live, believe, and know that the Holy Spirit is omnipresent and knows my thoughts even before the actions are activated or before my potential is developed.

Would not God find this out? For He knows the secrets of the heart. (Psalm 44:21 NIV)

As for you, my son Solomon, know the God of your father, and serve Him with a loyal heart and with a willing mind; for the LORD searches all hearts and understands all the intent of the thoughts. If you seek Him, He will be found by you; but if you forsake Him, He will cast you off forever. (1 Chronicles 28:9 NKJV)

I told myself that every action is preceded by a thought, and it's impossible to define such actions as a mistake when it is consciously executed. It may be influenced, but boundaries established are like erecting levees to stand against the storm. These values I held dearly, and they were my anchor throughout my journey. I fasted on a weekly basis. I was surprised to find out not many individuals understood the benefits of fasting, much less to fast. Fasting is that eagle's molting state; it defeats the carnal nature and brings the spirit man into sensitivity to the voice of God. My entire being and body remained under subjection to God. I refused to think about intimacy knowing that my wife was several states away. I soon realized how powerful I can become in defeating the carnal motives by not allowing thoughts to activate my emotion. A man needs to be well balanced by understanding when he is being mentally burned out and vulnerable.

Grooming and disciplining our children is equipping them through the molting state as they produce feathers. The eagle has one partner for a lifetime. The eagle is a protector that remains aware, informed, and involved, ensuring that there is no room for being absent and allowing the snake to eat its eggs. How many fathers and mothers are absent and blame circumstances for choices made by their children? Many parents too often react consequentially to their children, as opposed to implementing and setting guidelines that will impart and formulate good growth and discipline. Children will always encounter issues that you pray and hope they will not experience. The Word of God tells us that folly is found in the heart of a child. But it's vital that as parents, we train them to spread their wings and rise above the negative effects. Almost every parent will remember and identify with doing the same nonsense that a child does. Imperfection lets you put a smile on your face and say, "Yep, that was once me." It gives us a heart of compassion and causes our grace to be sufficient. Eaglets are searching for guidance and direction. If there are no boundaries and expectations laid, then poor choices and exploration will be erected as the new norm and standard. The eaglet will sleep away its potential in the nest. Later in life, demands when being improperly developed will be misunderstood as excessive unrealistic expectations. Children will be quick to tell you that you are never there, so you are not qualified to give your input, after the choices were already made. This is why a parent who is absent sometimes feels defeated in administering discipline. If we are not careful, we compromise our parental role and try to be more of a friend. In the long run, discipline is like a seed planted; the child will grow to appreciate its benefits.

As a society, we have to protect our future generation of children in every race, age, culture, and background, from the unfortunate odds of life and from being exploited. There are no parents who feel comfortable with their teenage daughters getting pregnant. Physically, mentally, and emotionally, there is a great physiological imbalance in the developmental stage of a teen. The laws and school rules that are implemented will never be the ultimate solution. Introducing contraceptives into the school system will alarm any parents who see their children in possession of any issued entity. Abortion is a measure executed after the result of the actions that lead to unwanted pregnancy. This shows that there is a flaw in the decision-making and the choices that lead to pregnancy. There ought to be more emphasis on making wiser choices that will not lead to actions that can no longer rectify or undo the results of the situation.

There is an author known as Luke, who made reference in the first chapter of his writing about two cousins who were divinely connected while in their mother's womb.

> As soon as the sound of your greeting reached my ears,
> the baby in my womb leaped for joy. (Luke 1:44 NIV)

There was a divine connection between two unborn boys who their mothers recognized will revolutionize the world. How much value and potential have we recognized in our children? How often do we water that plant into greatness?

> I planted the seed in your hearts, and Apollos watered
> it, but it was God who made it grow. It's not important
> who does the planting, or who does the watering.
> What's important is that God makes the seed grow. (1
> Corinthians 3:6–7 NLT)

Do we constantly try to grow and motivate our children by highlighting the negative? Do we ask questions like "How come you failed?" "You can do better," "Your brother and sister did well," "I expect better"? All these comments have been equated to telling the child that you have failed or fell below standard. Let us reassure our children that they are not defined by their grades, but it's just a reflection of needed areas of adjustments. If we stop dreaming and fail to see the greatness and vast opportunities of life, we will convey the same contagious sense of hopelessness to our children. Parents should be actively engaged; deliberately put plans on calendar; join support groups; go on dates; and bring children to museums, parks, educational seminars, Broadway shows, and educational plays. Children should be encouraged to get involved in sports and arts and learn to play musical instruments.

We need to protect the greatness of our children. The eagle believes in the eaglet before the egg is produced. It is very obvious and evident by the preparation of the nest. We ought to treat our children as precious kings and queens entrusted to us, not when they become a president but now! As we continue to delve into the story of the unborn boys, it reveals another author by the name of Matthew who articulated in his writing the plot made by a king known as Herod to kill a generation of young boys, in order to find one main baby who leaped for joy while in the mother's womb. There was a prophetic word that this newborn baby would one day become king. This enraged Herod who thought that he would eventually become substituted.

> Herod was furious when he realized that the wise men
> had outwitted him. He sent soldiers to kill all the boys
> in and around Bethlehem who were two years old and
> under, based on the wise men's report of the star's first
> appearance. (Matthew 2:16 NLT)

The potential of an individual is recognized before he/she enters the world. The mother and father come into an agreement and create a child with irreversible life. The parents are well aware of the greatness and potential of this great creation even before a physical birth (Jeremiah 1:5; Jeremiah 29:11; Ephesians 1:4–5). It is vital and important for a parent to protect the child morally, spiritually, emotionally, and physically and nurture that child to self-actualization. Eagles guard their eggs in hot and cold blizzard conditions. Mary and Elizabeth recognized that they were each carrying in their womb an extraordinary child, destined for a purpose.

The challenges that our children face are the burden of their capacity filled with greatness and that the enemy has recognized the impact they will make.

It's imperative that the child reaches heightened awareness of the greatness that he/she possesses. If the eagles were not trained to recognize their greatness, they would soon discover that the precious egg that they failed to protect may not be presented another opportunity. Getting upset may be too late. (Genesis 27: Esau gave away his birthright and then became angry and rebelled against his family and God when he discovered his poor choices and the consequences of his foolish action.)

My wife and I were conversing about the different radio and television talk hosts whose spouses were recently involved in marital affairs and infidelity. The radio talk hosts were strong critics of issues concerning other couples and media propaganda. It must be rather challenging to be a victim of issues that you are an advocate against.

As I begin to reflect, it is important to let it resonate that the eagle is a bird that sheds its feathers to rejuvenate itself. Upon shedding its feathers, the eagle reaches a state of vulnerability and is prone to be attacked and exploited. The eagle therefore hides on the back side of the mountain, away from dangers, interaction, or yielding to unwarranted circumstances. It is in this time and season that the eagle feels rejected; the eagle feels alone; the eagle feels demystified; and the eagle feels stripped of its beauty, power, and strength. The eagle, seeing other eagles soaring high, feels as though others soaring cannot relate to its present circumstance.

Many individuals who are in a relationship can relate to instances in which one party believes that the other spouse is clueless or insensitive or just cannot relate to the depth or intensity of hurts and painful experiences. This can be mentally calculated by the one who is hurting, to develop thoughts and feelings of rejection, and perception of a disconnection. It is vital that the person who is hurting recognizes this as being a state of great vulnerability.

(The comparison syndrome, in which one constantly compares and judges his/her relationship by the standards and accomplishments of others, can trigger and create unrealistic expectations and demands on the other.)

If someone walks in and offers some solution, relief, fulfillment, or satisfaction to the hurting person who has the desire to be understood or the quest for emotional connection, it can be like giving a cup of water to a person in the hot desert. The hurting individual will develop the inclination to yield to the source of satisfaction and can mistakenly equate satisfaction to loving the source while the supply exists. Many subordinates are naturally attracted to their leadership and influence, because it guarantees a series of growth process, belonging, value, and significance. How many are willing to admit that not everything that the inner man desires is worth pursuing? Self-sacrifice can be of great value, while accomplishments can be detrimental and grave demise.

> The leech has two daughters—Give *and* Give! There are three *things that* are never satisfied, Four never say, "Enough!": The grave, The barren womb, The earth *that* is not satisfied with water—And the fire never says, "Enough!" (Proverbs 30:15–16 NKJV)

As a child growing up, my close relatives would tell me, "If a stranger offers you food, do not accept it." The devil knows how to entice you with the desires of your heart.

> When you sit down to eat with a ruler, Consider carefully what *is* before you; And put a knife to your throat If you *are* a man given to appetite. (Proverbs 23:1–2 NKJV)

Don't Leave the Mountain or the
Nest Until You Grow Feathers

> But they that wait upon the LORD shall renew their strength; they shall mount up with wings as eagles; they shall run, and not be weary; and they shall walk, and not faint. (Isaiah 40:31 KJV)

We should know our limits and not cross the path of unwarranted grounds and solicited circumstances. An eagle's eggs left unattended are vulnerable as an eaglet leaving the nest without parental guidance. It is no match for a conniving snake. The adult eagle should not leave the mountainside until it grows feathers. As strong as the memory of its strength may be, such eagle will be like Sampson searching for its strength only to recognize that it is gone. A dangerous man will study what a woman desires and facilitate her likes by flourishing her with enticing gifts in order to win her heart.

A dangerous man knows what a woman likes to hear, and fills the void of her lack. A woman will desire certain things and entity, not because she desires good gifts, but because she suffers from low self-esteem. A woman will have intense cravings and desires because of her history of abuse, neglect, and low self-worth, regardless of her beauty. A woman will attempt to hide behind her beauty and wear a facade to escape her undeniable reality of psychological consuming thoughts and struggles. A man who lacks wisdom will believe that he is doing a good deed by facilitating the need of such woman.

My grandmother always imparts knowledge by telling me not to feed strange animals. Very soon I realized that the animals, whether cats or dogs, would not leave my doorsteps. The animals are inclined to remain where the source and supply of the desires rest. A man who lacks wisdom will begin to cry when he cannot understand how he poured out everything that he possesses to this woman, but she left for another source. It is simple! The physical desire for food will always exist; it is the source and measurement for survival. Otherwise, lack of hunger or no appetite results in starvation and death.

The emotional desire of a woman is a desire of importance and survival. When one aspect is filled, another is discovered or activated. It creates an illusion of growth and expansion. If such woman lacks wisdom and possesses a judgmental approach, she will feel the need to graduate from her current relationship. Her educational accolades, knowledge, increased salary, and dignified and glorified position of power will cause her to despise the simplicity of her husband. She will be embarrassed if her husband does not fit into her new circle of power and cannot articulate the code language of her circle of influence. She will now feel tempted to treat him as though he is outdated and irrelevant to her current status. Even in the midst of lovemaking, she feels as though she is devaluing herself by allowing a man of low status to explore her body.

While preaching one Sunday afternoon, I gave the congregation a scenario in a paradoxical form, because the room was filled with many children.

I explained how there are many relationships in which husbands and wives are in conflict, and the wife uses her body as a weapon by denying him access. This could be intentional or even by emotional isolation. I used parental guidance—"PG-13"—and gave the scenario by explaining in the form of a story. I conveyed that a husband is like a delivery truck driver who at times works late hours up until midnight. He knows and is well aware that the supermarket occasionally closes by 8:00 p.m. (implying that the wife may be asleep before he reaches home). All of a sudden, the truck driver starts to see these twenty-four-hour convenience stores that appear to always be accessible. This is in reference to temptation, emerging distractions inclusive of text and telephone conversations. The milk that is available at the convenience stores is usually close to their expiration as opposed to the supermarket that has fresh products, referring to the sanctity and honoring of your vows. You know there exists a major problem when such product becomes enticing to consume. Many truck drivers will still stop to deliver products, pick up returned goods, or make a quick purchase to satisfy hunger. If any man lacks wisdom, he is encouraged to ask. Man naturally possesses desire. It takes the power of God to exercise wisdom and self-control over carnal desires, and to develop the strength to detach from earthly possessions.

A man who lacks discipline can easily justify his poor sense of decisions by using his wife's low enthusiasm, lack of sex, or not being engaged in the moment. Sexual encounter is mental engagement, interest, enthusiasm, and emotional and spiritual connectivity. Delayed response and lack of interest can render a conclusion of devastated state of rejection. Attention given by others that seemingly fills this void can swiftly spiral into a love affair. Attention given by others in the form of hugs, kisses on the cheek, touch, handshake, smiles, or sacrificial hello(s) (going out of your way to greet) can offer validation, acceptance, and feelings of emotional understanding. A woman will offer her body for her own self-pleasure, and a man interprets it as love. A woman will offer her body as a weapon by sleeping with a man, because she wants to launch an attack against the wife due to dislike or jealousy. A woman can be a victim of abuse, neglect, and infidelity; and she gets satisfactory revenge by offering her body to another, even while being in a current relationship.

A woman will offer her body because in the process, it gives emotional connectivity, treat, and trade feelings of satisfaction and understanding. (A man/woman will and can subconsciously be jealous of your quality and standard of relationship or desirous of all the qualities and content that you have to offer. This man/woman will then launch an attack on you or even the thoughts of the person that you are involved with in a relationship. Sabotaging or accomplishing the feat of pushing someone off his/her pedestal can be satisfying to others. It's like a child removing the chair when another is about to sit and finding it hilarious as the whole class laughs!)

It is in this season that the eagle within recognizes your "human-ness" and vulnerability and protects itself and integrity by building boundaries on the back side of the mountain. Stay on the mountain, and avoid sexual conversations and innuendos, which can spark the emotional fire, desires, and thoughts that will incite arousal or plant divisive seeds.

Stay on the mountainside, because unknowingly your personality can be attractive and charming, unintentionally luring others into developing a like for you and conversely creating a gap between the one she has pledged her commitment.

The Eagles' Response: "Is There a Pilot on This Plane?"

This scenario is a true heroic story! "Does anyone know how to fly a plane?" Even though the same request was also depicted in a movie, this played out in a real-life situation. It was about thirty minutes into flight when a commercial 737 airline carrying over 150 passengers faced a major challenge. The flight attendant utilized the public address system to summon for a nurse, because there was a problem in the front of the plane. A few transmissions later, the flight attendant asked the ultimate question of whether there was a pilot on board, and if so, please indicate by ringing the call button. The pilot had suffered from a medical complication. One of the passengers on board was a US Air Force pilot traveling with his family. He responded to the cockpit, jumped into action, and assisted the copilot who had to assume control since the pilot was incapacitated.

Everyone at some point in life will be needed in the cockpit of the "plane" of his/her journey. Can the pilot jump out with a parachute and escape through the window of divorce leaving the family asleep on board, or will the pilot remain and fly the aircraft to safety? As a leader, you cannot afford to be asleep or distracted and miss the call button.

The eagle fights its battles in the air with great confidence. The eagle relies on the benefits of the higher dimension. The eagle has been trained and now recognizes the benefits of the preparation and equipping phases. The eagle sees the benefits of being pushed out of the nest, the molten stages, and being alone on the back side of the mountain. The eagle responds when summoned to the cockpit of life!

One of the common enemies of the eagle is the serpent. The serpent has very little strength when the eagle wrestles it in the air. The eagle belongs in a position of soaring and elevation. Too often, we put aside our values and greatness and step down to the common ground to wrestle with snakes. Before long, we are tangled up in situations that we have no business being involved. The snake does not have much evidence; but the eagle will shed some feathers because its presence, name, and recognition are always impressionable.

During my personal time of reflection, the Holy Spirit said

wherever your thoughts are mentally focused, your concentrated energy will be intensified.

Your mode of constant reflection will relive the moment of experience, even on the basis of assumptions or in the imaginative realm. Perception is reality! There are many individuals who are unable to differentiate lies, truth, facts, reality, or the imaginary. Unfortunately, all these factors can create the same wave of emotional turmoil, anxiety, and anger.

In a recent conversation with my wife, she shared that a friend reminded her of our time at a youth convention before we were married and how in love and attracted I was to her. It suddenly brought a rush and gush of refreshing feelings as it brought me back into the moments of such encounter. Eagles will never escape the pains of life!

As I conduct a mental survey and contrast, I can also confess that there were times in my life and early stages of marriage, I encountered challenges and pondered if I had married the right woman. Within the first year of our marriage, my wife and I had our son. I felt the attention that I truly desired from my newly beloved and beautiful wife dissipated and divided. As my wife faced the demands of fulfilling motherhood, spousal responsibilities, workforce, and a sense of guilt in not being able to occupy and fill the capacity of her husband's desire, we had to activate our faith. As a husband working long extenuating hours in a law enforcement organization, my faith and loyalty were now put to the test. My anger toward my wife was now intensified. People on the job were giving compliments and appreciation that I desired to hear from my wife. I learned really fast to disarm the effects of the compliments, even if they were genuine, before they were detonated and activated in my emotion. Wherever the attention of my wife was directed, it triggered my pain. If she was on the telephone laughing, I enjoyed the fact she had an outlet, but it's ironic that it triggered my pain. I began to slowly despise her attitude. I knew she was drained, exhausted, and tired, fulfilling her motherly duties. *But how about your husband?* my heart would ponder. Could my wife just articulate any justification for inflicting such inevitable pain? Would an apology be enough? I know it is obvious of her time being spent wisely. Even an apology would perhaps temporarily appease the pain. (I now identified as the victim.) I would probe myself, wondering if I got married too soon, or perhaps I was ill-prepared.

I wrestled with inner turmoil and pondered if this is manhood or a boy pretending to master the role of his obligation.

Why do others seem to be cruising comfortably on autopilot while I struggle to figure out the navigational instruments? Should I throw in the towel, quit at the start line, face public scrutiny, or suffer the infliction of pain and bruises to my ego? I guess I will have to fly my aircraft without looking back, like in times of war when pilots weren't sure if there will be enough fuel to return to base. I guess it's called a leap of faith!

During this time of crisis, elements of distraction would surface. There were many coworkers who would give compliments, ask if I am single, and make subtle comments like "You look like the faithful type" and "They don't make them like you anymore." As I maintained my integrity, thoughts of justification would confront my mental processing. I now had to challenge myself to grow and self-actualize. I had to remind myself that no storms last forever. I had to remind myself of the testimonies and life stories given by my church elders who had been married for over twenty years, twenty-five years, and forty-one years. I strongly stood by my wedding vows and declared that divorce will never be an option. I had to quickly come to maintain my soberness and admit that after a temporary satisfaction, I will also have the same desire and crave for a lifetime. So might as well I devote all that concentrated energy to my wife. I told myself that God is always in my presence, so there is no need to even try to hide from mortal men and women. I told myself, even though I grew up without an earthly father, that will never become the statistic or reality for my children. I would activate scriptures like "God will be my father when others forsake me." I would pray, "God, I know you will change this situation."

On my journey, I have discovered that in many culture, oftentimes we have not learned to face or embrace challenges. So we do not stand up or against our obstacles long enough to defeat them. We then go into flight mode and flee the condition. If we are not careful, we develop the propensity to fight the wrong and unnecessary war, against the wrong person, when the real fight should be teaming up as a couple and overcoming the forces and elements that oppose us.

How do we accomplish such? We need to strategize and establish healthy communication. If one reacts with anger, the other party does not have to respond in a similar fashion. How many compliments and acknowledgments do we give each other? Do we tell the person at the supermarket thank you but forget to tell our spouses thank you? Do we tell our children that we love them as they are going to sleep, and good morning I love you when they wake up? This will develop and establish an internal foundation of expectation and stability and a perception and perspective of the way and standard to be treated in this world. If we are not intentional, then dysfunction will set in and become the norm.

My wife and I have agreed that we will always communicate before going to sleep, any pertinent issues regardless of how we feel, even if this means to be discussed at another time. We have also agreed that we will always hold hands and pray a short prayer before either of us walks through the door. There are times when we may be upset with each other, but being intentional to willingly hold hands and pray with each other has rapidly eradicated some explosive anger. After I am finished praying, my wife would at times keep holding on to my hands to test my temperament. It would be inappropriate to pull away, especially after praying, so resolution to conflicts would become swift and effective. Ecclesiastes 4 tells us that two together is stronger. Let us team up together to conquer life and not be defeated with division. Let no one come in between, neither with self or opinions. Challenges will always come; but when we grow through them, we develop the strength, resiliency, and tenacity to persevere. Issues will always exist, so let us put on our fighting gloves and conquer and live a victorious life.

Not only will I just jump to the defense of my family when a robber or physical fight comes my way. I will fight for my family by loving my wife to the end, I will love my children unconditionally, and I will maintain my employment with integrity. There are so many poor choices in life that have gotten individuals terminated, incarcerated, and separated from their loved ones and family members. Recognizing such, I will therefore do and implore others to communicate, be present as a protector, use kind words, refuse to respond with anger, or be influenced by emotional turmoil.

The Eagles' Emotional Intelligence

While working with the Department of Transportation, I had written certain quotes and placed them on my desk next to my work computer. Every morning I sat down, I would read and regurgitate,

"My emotion will not dictate my response!"

This means that regardless of how you approached me, the choices of words that you used, body language, expression, or demeanor, I was intentional with the best of my ability to be led by God to search my heart and give me a positive response. Over the years, I have developed responsive strategies and have role-played many. I have seen other individuals and asked myself how I would have handled such situation. If you are sarcastic, I would put a smile on my face and respond in several ways such as the following:

1. I see that someone is a bit upset. I would genuinely ask/state, "If you would like to talk when you feel better, I am available."

2. I would say, "Thanks, God bless you too!" (even though their sarcasm had nothing to do with the content of my statement or response).

3. I would sometimes respond with a totally different topic like "Sure, he said he will be back in a few minutes." (I know that's not what the person had asked, but I was giving other information as a deterrent. The expression on their face will either lead them to believe that I did not hear the sarcasm the first time or cause them to retract, and then I observe if they are willing to take another chance with hurtful words.)

I also have to learn to overcome self and the comments of others. Many people will say that people are walking all over you and that they are taking advantage. But you have to know the depth and power of the God that you serve. Allow Him to truly fight your battles. Over the long run, your test of character and integrity will survive the short-term results of fights.

Dealing with self can be a difficult task. When we observe bad habits, we sometimes delay and reschedule positive change as opposed to making it positively instantaneous. We are more willing to fight the enemies that try to hurt our family. If a man or woman betrays our sons and daughters, we jump to their defense. But how about when I become the perpetrator with my negative words and actions? Do we want ourselves to be recognized as being guilty like the outside perpetrator? How about when our mind and thoughts recruit our body and soul to become the perpetrator of marital infidelity, affairs, and spousal abuse?

The person on the street should not try to hurt our family, but the one who holds the heart of the lover in his/her hands can squeeze the life to death then try to justify.

How many men and women are willing to fight and conquer self until self is defeated? Or is it okay for others just as much as it is allowable by us? Is it okay for us, the ones who are held at a higher standard?

One day while I was home, the way in which my wife responded caused me to realize that there was something bothering her. I have learned a long time ago to read between the lines, extract the essential, and set aside the sarcasm or filter out the nonessentials. As she was about to go to sleep, I asked her to be transparent and tell me exactly what's hurting or triggered her to answer in a way that obviously wasn't relevant to the nature of our conversation. She told me without hesitation what I had said out of anger several days ago. I totally thought we were past that hurdle and obstacle. Since then, I have made sure to consciously remember that the way I feel appeased after venting may not necessarily be the way another individual feels. I could have reminded her of the way in which she had addressed me that night. But the goal and objective is not to get equal or hurt each other. The goal is to outdo each other in doing great. So I embraced her and apologized and asked her to forgive me. She fell asleep in my arms and slept like a baby. She woke up with motivation and rejuvenated with a renewed mind. Kind words are medicine to the soul. You do not have to force others to apologize, because that still does not guarantee an authentic apology. I find that once you model and demonstrate your discipline, others automatically conform to such standard of exemplary role. Subsequently I expressed to my wife that if she is hurting, it is important that I know. Even if you believe that I already know or should know, even if it feels redundant, it is important that you express yourself to your offender, not others. I

259

expressed to my wife why I am always transparent with my hurts and pain. I want her to be aware, understand, know my vulnerabilities and weak moments, and also allow her to know that she is safe to be open and transparent as well. I also reassured her that I will not use her weak areas as a tool or weapon against her. The fight should never be among a circle of friendship. Conflicts will be inevitable, but it's important that we use them as opportunities.

Sometimes we are hurting severely, and the ones who may have triggered or inflicted the hurt are not aware. Sometimes the person who suffers the hurt may be hesitant to articulate his/her feelings of hurt and emotional pain. This hurting person oftentimes believes that expressing pain and emotional hurts will create an offense to the offender. The hurting person may also be hesitant to express himself/herself, believing that expression of hurt will create a perception of hypersensitivity or a weakling. A person who is hurting may be hesitant to express his/her hurts and pain, simply because he/she quite often causes similar pain in the lives of others. *So why bother to share my pain to experience healing, while I am equally guilty of inflicting similar pain and harm?* many people will rationalize. This hurting person may attempt to either put the pain behind him or push it in the realm of the past. Sometimes the hurting individual will give hints in an indirect attempt to strive for resolution. Some individuals who are hurting may speak about the hurt once, with sensitivity to avoid triggering further conflicts, and the expectation of instant healing, resolution, and reconciliation. Quite surprisingly, this hurting person will soon realize that speaking about the hurt once does not necessarily guarantee instantaneous healing or anticipated results.

I left a few pumpkin seeds in a container with water, thinking that I will roast the seeds at a later date. The seeds turned into several plants. So it is with the mind, which is like a garden; whatsoever thoughts we sow, the condition will inevitably grow and manifest itself. It is important that in seeking resolution, we do not constantly replay and meditate upon our thought, nor reflect upon our painful experiences and water the seeds of offenses. One healthy approach is to envision our experiences as a learning opportunity, whether joyous or challenging.

James 1 encourages us to count it a joy when we go through trials and challenges, because it makes us stronger.

Second, if it takes more than one conversation to express our hurts and pain, it is important that neither party attack the other but act as an aid and support to overcome these obstacles of hurt.

Third, if you find yourself to be hurting, and you also identify yourself to be an offender, it is important that you acknowledge to self and others that you are aware of your shortcomings and also the hurts that you have incurred. Be sincerely apologetic, allow yourself to develop the discipline for a positive change, and ensure that you receive your healing as well.

Fourth, it is unwise to compare yourself with others. There are things that others may do that do not affect you, but if you should execute the same action, it may trigger offense. Your weakness may be somebody's strength, and vice versa. Do not hinder your healing simply because occasionally you are an identical offender. Neither should we accuse the other of hypocrisy for causing the same hurt yet occasionally acting as the victim.

The scripture declares in Matthew 5:23–24 NLT, "So if you are presenting a sacrifice at the altar in the Temple and you suddenly remember that someone has something against you, leave your sacrifice there at the altar. Go and be reconciled to that person. Then come and offer your sacrifice to God."

It is even much more recommended if you are the one causing the hurt.

The Eagles' Interview

Many individuals who have the thoughts and intention to commit adultery often begin with self-propelling justification. I have spoken to many different individuals who begin their questions by asking, "How do you remain faithful?" or "How can you not cheat?" or "How do you have one girl for life? I just couldn't do it."

I respond to these men by asking, "If your wife should give you the same response or reasons for cheating, how would you feel?" The responses are unbelievable. These men fumed with self-contained anger as though it really happened. This exposed a deeper underlying struggle and issue. While these men were searching for justification to escape the guilt of their actions, they were consumed with fear of being victims. The stereotypical stigma of "What goes around comes around" and "Karma will get you" were lingering in the forefront of their minds. The reality is that the thoughts of a man become his window and outward perspective of life. His thought process and built-in perception become his self-created opponent. Whatever a man perceives and believes inevitably becomes his reality.

It is hard to determine who is more insane: the man in his right mind who sees things that do not exist or the man out of his mind who lacks the ability to comprehend the scope of literal reality.

My second approach usually probes to find out what was the nature of the conversation that led to such actions or infidelity. Some men respond that it just happened! I would then ask, "What if it was someone of the same gender? What would you have done?" These men would look at me like I was crazy. I was simply proving my point that everyone has a choice to exercise self-control and of the nature of the conversation to engage with someone.

My immediate follow-up question: "Why didn't you simply refrain from such action or walk away?"

The expected statistical response: "I couldn't help it!"

I would then ask, "What if she had refused? Would your urge be so strong where you would commit rape?"

The ethical response came out: "No!"

This means that action was consensual for both parties, regardless of who was more forceful.

My final statement: "Since you are married, why don't you wait until you reach home so that your wife can cool your fire?"

The reality of the situation is that many individuals have allowed their minds to reach a state of fantasy, curiosity, and lustful thoughts that solicit inappropriate desires, which if readily acted upon will lead to unwarranted and detrimental avenues. These thoughts of fantasy will not be fully satisfied genuinely by a spouse, since the concept is still lodged subconsciously in the cognitive of perpetuating activation. These thoughts and actions have to be put under discipline and subjection of the Holy Spirit. The world is already filled with media and sexually illicit graphics that insinuate and infiltrate the minds of the vulnerable. Lacking resistance or any mediation or filter is like an eagle flying distracted. Let us remain true!

About The Author

Marlon A. Reid, native born of Jamaica, West Indies, attended the Methodist Church. At age sixteen, he surrendered his life when he was invited to a Pentecostal revival in Mandeville, Manchester. He migrated to the United States in 1998, later enrolled in NYC College of Technology, graduated with a bachelor's degree in computer engineering and AAS in mechanical engineering, joined the United States Air Force, advanced his studies in leadership, and completed his AAS in avionic systems technology.

Sensing his passion and strong call of ministry over his life, he enrolled at Nyack–Alliance Theological Seminary, in pursuit of MPS concentrated in psychology and theology. Marlon serves faithfully in the field of law enforcement for eighteen years, inclusive of the NYC Police Department, Department of Transportation, and Correction Department, with humility, honored to supervise in the leadership position as captain.

He is the proud husband of his wife, Althea. They have two beautiful children: Seth and Gabriella. He is a preacher and mentor, who grants oversight to multiple churches within local organizations as district youth director.

INDEX

python, 67–68, 79, 86, 88, 95–96
python spirit, 86, 95

R

rape, 129, 131, 134–35, 262
    victim of, 48, 104, 133, 135, 194
Rebekah, 108
relationships, ix, xxi–xxii, 9, 11, 13–14,
    16–17, 20–21, 24, 34, 36, 38, 49,
    56–58, 60, 66, 72, 74, 80, 93, 95,
    98, 101, 112–14, 152–54, 158,
    160, 170, 181, 184–85, 188, 191,
    210–11, 229–30, 237, 248–49,
    251–52
    abusive, 24, 38
    out-of-wedlock, 20
    toxic, 104, 175, 231
rooster, 234–36
Ruth, 60–61

S

Samson, 31, 76, 114–16
Sarah, 107
Satan, 73, 185
self, 3–4, 11, 16, 22–23, 25–26, 34,
    38–40, 42–43, 45, 56–57, 59,
    61, 66, 68, 75, 77, 79–81, 86, 88,
    90, 92–94, 96, 116–17, 123, 145,
    148, 150, 154–57, 162, 181, 207,
    209–11, 227, 229, 231, 238–39,
    243, 257–59, 261
self-awareness, 111, 161, 168
self-confidence, 12, 86, 217
self-control, 21, 70, 73, 110–11, 167,
    182, 252
self-deception, 234
self-esteem, 23, 76, 80, 89–90, 98, 176,
    182, 250
self-value, xxi, 76
self-victimize, 161

serpent (*see also* snakes), xxi, 18, 66–69,
    71, 74, 76–79, 88, 90–91, 93, 95,
    98, 254
sexual immorality, 73
shame, 37, 96–97, 104, 137, 175–76, 193
Sharpe, Sam, 60
sheep, 40, 66, 77, 85–86, 103, 111, 113,
    117, 193, 231, 242
sickness, 20, 26–27, 200
Simon Peter, 235
sins, 28, 33, 94, 97, 99, 105, 132, 159,
    162, 169, 177, 182, 228
slavery, 10, 58, 60, 63, 99, 125
slaves, 55–56, 99
snakes, xxi, 65–67, 69, 71–72, 74, 76,
    78, 83, 92, 94, 132, 245, 254
    boa, xxi, 65–67, 79
    paradise, 67, 78–79, 82
    python, 67, 88
spiritual warfare, 97, 167, 169, 193
storms, xxiii, 48, 71, 86, 179, 203, 207,
    209–11, 230, 233, 240, 242,
    244, 256
stress, 9, 36–37, 87, 105, 219, 231
suicide, 6, 27, 77

T

threat, 67, 79, 123, 127, 130, 136, 138–
    39, 153, 165, 239
tornados, 200, 237, 239
tree, 2, 18–19, 66–67, 72, 75, 98, 133,
    188, 229–33, 236
    broom, 230–31
trust, xxiii, 9, 19, 21, 32, 34–35, 40, 55,
    59, 70, 74–75, 83, 131, 151–52,
    168, 215, 240

U

United States, 41, 43, 120, 128, 139–
    41, 265
Uriah, 70–71, 74